Y0-DYP-759

The Western University
on Trial

The Western University
on Trial

EDITED BY
JOHN W. CHAPMAN

Berkeley
Los Angeles
London

UNIVERSITY OF CALIFORNIA PRESS

University of California Press
Berkeley and Los Angeles, California
University of California Press, Ltd.
London, England
© 1983 by
The Regents of the University of California
Printed in the United States of America

1   2   3   4   5   6   7   8   9

Library of Congress Cataloging in Publication Data
Main entry under title:
The Western university on trial.
"Based on papers presented at the Third International
Conference of the International Council on the Future
of the University"—
Includes index.
1. Universities and colleges—Congresses.
2. University autonomy—Congresses.   3. Academic freedom
—Congresses.   I. Chapman, John William, 1923–
II. International Council on the Future of the Univer-
sity. International Conference (3rd : 1981 : Lisbon, Portugal)
LB2301.W44 1983   378'.1   82-20120
ISBN 0-520-04940-3

IN MEMORY OF CHARLES FRANKEL

CONTENTS

PREFACE

This book is based on papers presented at the Third International Conference of the International Council on the Future of the University (I.C.F.U.). The theme of the conference was "The Pursuit of Truth in a Changing World." For the site of the April 1981 meeting, the board of the council selected Lisbon to express the council's solidarity with scholars in the new Iberian democracies and to enable its members to become acquainted with conditions in Iberian universities.

The I.C.F.U. began as the International Committee on the University Emergency, established in 1970 in Norwich, England. The committee's founding statement on "The University Emergency" referred to: "the steady erosion of morale within the universities, the retreat from that ordered freedom that makes possible competition in ideas and cooperation in inquiry, and the steady draining away of commitment to the principle that the university must be a partisan of no creed or party and a critic of every creed and party." The committee then was concerned with the way in which, "Increasingly, from Berkeley to Berlin, political criteria are being used to evaluate academic performance." Wide acceptance of an adversary principle to organize university government was deplored. A leading purpose of the committee was "to strengthen the will to maintain professional standards of teaching and scholarship."

In October 1973, the committee held its first major international conference in Venice, and its theme was the future of the university. The papers then presented were published in *Universities in the Western World*, edited by Paul Seabury, the present chairman of the council. At that time we changed our name because it was clear that the Western university was faced not just with an emergency but rather with sustained assaults upon its integrity as an intellectual institution. These assaults are not only political in inspiration. They are grounded in moral and cultural sentiments profoundly inimical to academic values.

At the Venice meeting the primary purpose of the council was given definitive formulation by the late Charles Frankel, liberal philosopher and academic statesman of the first rank, to whose initiative we owe so very much and upon whose inspiration we continue to depend. Frankel wrote: "It is with this overarching objective in mind—the attainment of a new sense of shared purpose, the definition of the common principles of intellectual integrity and professional discipline around which the universities of the future ought to be built—that the I.C.F.U. was formed."[1] He then reaffirmed our supreme commitment to the truth and our obligation to conduct ourselves in accordance with that responsibility.

The I.C.F.U.'s second international conference was held in Toronto in the late summer of 1977. Here the topic was "Universities and Governments in Democratic States." The Toronto conference produced a new statement of purpose, designed to take account of how circumstances had changed since promulgation of the Norwich document: "Our main objective must be to discover how under changed circumstances universities can perform their major tasks of the discovery, advancement, and dissemination of learning, of the education of the young, and of contributing to the common good." As applied to the university, the principles of "democratization," "equalization," and "politicization" were denounced, while loyalty to the principles of "social justice" and "equal opportunity" was proclaimed. As the Toronto document concluded, "It should be evident that the attack on selection abandons standards, that the attack on merit rewards mediocrity, that the attack on excellence exalts inferiority, and that the attack on competence creates a world of incompetence."

After the Lisbon discussions once again the council clarified its concerns and refined its purposes. A statement by the council's board of trustees, dated 23 October 1981, pointed to problems and weaknesses that afflict higher education throughout the Western world. These include evaporation of opportunity for appointment of new scientists and scholars, grade inflation or equalization so prominent in the United States, vocationalism among students, and the disciplinary and departmental parochialism—indeed, the "feudalization" of knowledge—that has arisen. All this, the board held, is indicative of "a pervasive failure of nerve on the part of academics in the face of difficult times." The board called attention to present uncertainties about the proper relation between Western governments and universities, and the continuing controversy over the fundamental purposes of higher education. "The strengthening of the scholarly mission in the 1980s does not demand more funds for universities. . . . But it does demand rigourous selection of priorities, an understanding of the university's internal weaknesses and failures in morale, and a willingness to focus on broad educational objectives."

The university emergency brought on by political conflict and pressure may have subsided, but restoration of the Western university to a healthy condition may prove to be an even more exacting task. The fundamental and permanent purposes of the university—to pursue and teach the truth as best it can be had—remain at stake.

---

1. Charles Frankel, "Epilogue: Reflections on a Worn-out Model," in *Universities in the Western World*, ed. Paul Seabury, (New York: Free Press, 1975), p. 289.

Among other noteworthy activities, the council has published reports of its investigations of German, Swedish, and Italian universities, and it has sponsored a major study of the relations between governments and universities in western Europe and the United States.[2] The council has also over the last few years conducted a number of smaller-scale projects. With financial assistance from the Fritz Thyssen Foundation in West Germany, an academic ethics committee has been formed to develop a comparative report on the professional responsibilities of the teaching profession. An international meeting on the problem of federal regulation of universities in the United States was held in Washington, D.C., in the spring of 1981. In the fall of 1981, with the assistance of the Liberty Fund, the council held an international symposium on "University Autonomy and Academic Freedom in a Free Society" at the Harrison Conference Center, Glen Cove, New York. Through a newsletter edited by Nicholas Farnham, the council's executive director, members keep one another informed about academic matters throughout the Western world, Australia, and Japan.

The present volume, entitled *The Western University on Trial*, falls naturally into three parts. These are preceded by an introductory chapter, the purpose of which is not to summarize the contributions, although I do refer to some of them. Rather my aim is to present an independent statement on the purpose and design of the Western university, to offer a diagnosis of its trials and troubles, and to survey prescriptions that promise restoration of health and vitality. My analysis of the university's purpose and design is framed in terms of the concept of an academic constitution, the principles of which are extracted from both good practice and authoritative writings on

2. These four reports are:

German Universities Commission, *Report on German Universities* (New York: International Council on the Future of the University, 1978). The commission was composed of the following persons: Mattei Dogan, Director of Research, National Center of Scientific Research, Paris; Vittorio Frosini, Professor of Philosophy of Law, University of Rome; Olof Gustav Lidin, Professor of Oriental Languages, University of Copenhagen; David Martin, Professor of Sociology, London School of Economics; John Arthur Passmore, Professor of Philosophy, Australian National University (Chairman); and Paul Seabury, Professor of Government, University of California, Berkeley (Vice-Chairman).

Mogens N. Pedersen, Odense University, and Howard O. Hunter, School of Law, Emory University, Rapporteurs, *Recent Reforms in Swedish Higher Education* (Stockholm: Ratio, 1980).

Italian Universities Commission, *Report on Italian Universities* (New York: International Council on the Future of the University, 1982). The commission was composed of the following persons: Karl Dietrich Bracher, Professor of Political Science, University of Bonn; Mattei Dogan, Director of Research, National Center of Scientific Research, Paris; Louis Dupré, Professor of Religious Studies, Yale University; Jeanne Hersch, Professor of Philosophy, University of Geneva; Robert Hollander, Professor of European Literature, Princeton University; John A. Scott, Professor of Italian, University of Western Australia; and Edward Shils, Professor of Sociology, University of Chicago.

Hans Daalder, Professor of Political Science, University of Leiden, and Edward Shils, eds., *Bureaucrats, Politicians, and Universities: Europe and America* (Cambridge: Cambridge University Press, 1982).

the theory of the university. Although the university is an intellectual and not a political institution, it is not immune to the political dynamics at work in modern society. Indeed, as political sentiments for equalization and democratization gain ascendancy over the spirit of freedom, interests tend to be converted into rights, and the constitutional order of the university is subverted. For example, academic tenure comes to be conceived of as an earned right, not a status based on competitive excellence. In this perspective, the failure fully to constitutionalize our universities lies at the root of present discontents. This diagnosis implies its own remedy, difficult though that may be to administer.

Part I of this book offers a variety of essentially philosophical reflections on the purposes of the university and their effective institutionalization. All our authors agree that the distinctive purpose of the univeristy, taken as our paramount intellectual institution, can be nothing other than "intellectual progress," to use John Passmore's pithy expression. The Western university serves the freedom of the mind and so is anchored in our human nature. Our contributors also subscribe to the proposition that the modern sentiment of equality tends to hinder intellectual progress and to weaken respect for academic freedom and merit upon which progress depends. Throughout these essays we feel the presence of the ghosts of John Stuart Mill and Alexis de Tocqueville.

Intellectual progress depends on both the ardent and efficient pursuit of truth. Part II, which concerns policy more than philosophy, examines how research, both scientific and scholarly, is best organized, conducted, and financed, both within and without the university. The authors explore these topics from both disciplinary and national perspectives. They voice the worry that our research effort is insufficient in the face of contemporary problems and needs, and even more importantly, that investment in research at current levels and directions cannot sustain the intellectual momentum so characteristic of the West in recent centuries. A related concern is that the unity of teaching and research, a fundamental principle of Western higher education, may be under strain.

Part III confronts head on the problem of restoring and maintaining academic standards. Many feel that standards have declined in recent years, and the reasons for this are patently diverse, as our authors explain. They persuasively put forward cultural, political, financial, and organizational diagnoses along with implicit corrective recommendations. The very force and diversity of these analyses constitute measures of the depth of our plight.

The effort and expenditure required to present a volume like this are huge. On behalf of the council and its board, I wish to express our gratitude to the Calouste Gulbenkian Foundation for financial aid and the use of its splendid facilities in Lisbon. We are indebted for assistance also to the Exxon Foundation and the National Endowment for the Humanities. I wish to commend all our contributors for their devotion to the cause of the university. For very helpful consultations, I am grateful to Nicholas Farnham, Richard Flathman, George Armstrong Kelly, Paul Seabury, Edward Shils, and Peter Wiles. To my graduate assistant, Joseph Heim, my thanks go for both intellectual and clerical support.

J.W.C.
Pittsburgh, October 1982

Introduction:
The Western University
on Trial

JOHN W. CHAPMAN

Western universities have been on trial in one way or another for nearly twenty years. And it seems certain that trials will go on for some time to come. Both the moral and the intellectual integrity of the Western university are under fire, from within and from without, by those who would politicize, moralize, or deform an institution whose primary allegiance is to cognitive rationality, to disciplined search for truths. Many truths are bound to be offensive or unwelcome to some faith or conviction, to some material or cultural interests, or to ideologies resistant to rational criticism. And faculty members are reluctant to apply to one another academic criteria and standards that they know are valid and to which they are professionally committed. Given the sort of creatures that we are, perhaps it could not be otherwise.

THE EDUCATIONAL AND EXPRESSIVE REVOLUTIONS

The modern Western university, devoted to science and scholarship, is an achievement of a liberal civilization. That civilization is essentially procedural in its ways of thinking about nature and society. No other civilization—not the Chinese, Indian, or Islamic—invented an institution specialized for intellectual endeavor; this is unique to the West. Although it has Greek and medieval antecedents, the modern university is the culmination of an educational revolution that followed closely upon the Western

John W. Chapman is Professor of Political Science at the University of Pittsburgh.

political and economic revolutions. All these revolutions, as well as the earlier scientific revolution, have a common origin in the liberal unleashing of human rationality and individuality.

But we are not purely and thoroughly rational animals. Nor are we monistic, unitary beings. We are only imperfectly rational, and we are both individualistic and collectivistic in our sentiments and activities. Endless debate about human nature, and the different historical shapes that human personality has taken, should alert us to our fundamental contrariety.

Aristotle called us the political animal. The great German sociologist Max Weber held that we are deeply religious. And the American anthropologist Clifford Geertz defines us as cultural artifacts, inherently ideological and seekers of meaning in life. The late John Plamenatz of All Souls thought that our political experience reveals our ideological bent. Other Oxford political philosophers, Sir Isaiah Berlin and Professor Charles Taylor, speak of "expressivism" and point to an "expressivist revolution." This is understood as an essentially emotive and holistic revulsion—Romantic in inspiration—against the analytic, utilitarian rationalism of the Enlightenment. Liberal rationality and individuality have built societies that generate craving for communitarian warmth. Egalitarian cooperation tends to displace competitive differentiation as the human ideal. Taylor says that, "Deep expressivist dissatisfaction contributed to the success of Fascism, and underlies the revolt of many young people against the 'system' in contemporary countries."[1]

I suggest that from the record of our moral, political, and cultural experience one inference at least is clear and incontrovertible. Human beings are deeply ambivalent creatures, endowed with diverse and divergent needs, inclinations, and potentialities. We are pluralistic and "unfinished" in Geertz's diagnosis of our condition. And because we are, perhaps we had to become rational to gain some kind of balanced, integrated modicum of unity, some kind of personal and cultural stability, always precarious. Would it be too much to say that we are deeply Hegelian beings, doomed to a historical quest for moral and political equilibrium? Surely our essential and enduring ambivalence was captured by Charles Frankel when he said, "Man is the social animal that seeks privacy."[2]

In this psychological perspective the near coincidence of the educational and expressivist revolutions is no mere historical accident. This coincidence is the outcome of the tension between our individuated rationality and our desire for spiritual unity and moral significance. Indeed our contemporary predicament, including the trials of the Western university, is inherent in our ambiguous human nature.

1. Charles Taylor, *Hegel and Modern Society* (Cambridge: Cambridge University Press, 1979), p. 138.

2. Quoted by J. Roland Pennock, *Democratic Political Theory* (Princeton, N.J.: Princeton University Press, 1979), p. 508.

I offer these rather philosophical reflections to illuminate our situation. As the intellectual institution *par excellence*, the modern Western university is certain to face resistance from other and competing human tendencies. Still history shows that equally powerful is the human need to build and to secure an institution devoted to intellectual effort. For creatures constituted as we are, the only hope for a life worth living is to institutionalize a differentiated and balanced way of life in which all our intrinsic impulses have their appropriate places and avenues of expression. Human personality is multidimensional, difficult to equilibrate. So any truly human society must strive for equipoise of autonomous institutions and repel contamination of its intellectual institutions by extraneous impulse.

TRIAL AS TRIBULATION AND TEST

The trial of the Western university consists not only of present tribulations. The academic profession is on trial also in the sense that it is incumbent on our profession to put the university in order, to restore its intellectual integrity, and to hold fast to academic ideals and obligations. If we do not, the universities will face further and probably intensified public disapproval and political intervention, however unintelligent and damaging these attitudes and actions may be.

With reference to recent drastic cuts of university funding in Britain, Sir Peter Swinnerton-Dyer comments, "I think they reflect a belief that the university system needs to reform itself, and the only way it can be forced to reform itself is by financial pressure."[3] In western Europe, the United States, and Australia politicians exhibit a similar mood of hostility and suspicion. In the United States these feelings are directed in particular at the social sciences and the humanities, as shown in proposals to decrease severely their federal support and in the Reagan administration's apparent insensitivity to the long-term implications, both scientific and political, of its proposed measures.[4] The very cultural vitality of the United States—and of Britain, as David Martin discusses in chapter 13—may be at stake.

3. Sir Peter Swinnerton-Dyer, "Prospects for Higher Education," *London Review of Books* 3 (19 November–2 December 1981): 9. To underline the seriousness of the British situation, Sir Peter raises the specter of an act of parliament that would retrospectively abolish the practice of academic tenure.

4. On the condition of American social science, see Kenneth Prewitt and David L. Sills, "Federal Funding for the Social Sciences: Threats and Responses," *Items* 35 (September 1981): 33–47; and Kenneth Prewitt, "Annual Report of the President: 1980–81," *Annual Report: 1980–1981* (New York: Social Science Research Council, 1981), pp. 1–15. On the place of the humanities in American education and culture, see Report of the Commission on the Humanities, *The Humanities in American Life* (Berkeley: University of California Press, 1980). On the implications and consequences of federal policies, see two articles by Fred M. Hechinger in the *New York Times*: "Graduate Schools' Decline Leads to Wide Concern" (28 July 1981), and "Fulbright Grants Are in Danger" (17 November 1981). Consult also Robert Reinhold, "Research Fares Well, but Aid for Students Is Cut," *New York Times* (7 February 1982); Michael I. Sovern, "The Case for Keeping U.S. Aid to Colleges," *New York Times*

That Western publics and politicians should look askance at the universities is not unreasonable. Students once went on expressivist rampages, the outbreak of which was quite unexpected, and the causes of which remain mysterious to many.[5] In the United States and elsewhere, faculty became careless about the obligations that derive from academic ethos and citizenship.[6] In Europe governments imposed or tolerated "democratization" of universities, the consequences of which are examined by Peter Graf Kielmansegg (chapter 3) and Arend Lijphart (chapter 17); and in the United States the federal bureaucracy invaded the autonomy of universities to force application of nonintellectual criteria of appointment.[7] Moreover, university officers of administration failed to discharge their responsibility for the integrity of the appointive process. They did not insist that their faculties appoint only the best available persons according to the criterion of competitive merit. In consequence, a kind of localized nepotistic preferentialism became the operative appointment policy of many American universities.[8]

In the United States further deviations from professional discipline include the following: application of political criteria to candidates for appointment, especially to persons who have served their country in a political capacity[9] (although politicization of appointment has not by any means

Magazine (7 February 1982). Although federal budget cuts were not as large as earlier anticipated, according to Sovern investment in research and higher education is well below what is needed to sustain cultural vitality and ensure industrial survival.

5. Interpretations of the student rampages as essentially "expressive" phenomena are offered by: Talcott Parsons and Gerald M. Platt, *The American University* (Cambridge, Mass.: Harvard University Press, 1975); Edward Shils, "Plenitude and Scarcity: The Anatomy of an International Cultural Crisis," in *The Intellectuals and the Powers and Other Essays* (Chicago: University of Chicago Press, 1972), pp. 265–97; David Martin, "Mutations: Religio-Political Crisis and the Collapse of Puritanism and Humanism," in *Universities in the Western World*, ed. Paul Seabury (New York: Free Press, 1975), pp. 85–97; my "Personality and Privacy," in *Privacy: Nomos XIII*, ed. J. Roland Pennock and John W. Chapman (New York: Atherton Press, 1971), pp. 236–55; and my "The Liberal University and the Future of Liberalism," in *Say Not the Struggle: Essays in Honour of A. D. Gorwala*, 2nd ed., ed. H. M. Patel (Delhi: Oxford University Press, 1978), pp. 113–33.

6. On academic citizenship and ethos, see Edward Shils, "The Academic Ethos Under Strain," in Seabury, *Universities*, pp. 16–46, and Shils, "Academic Freedom and Academic Obligations with Some Thoughts on Permanent Tenure" (Paper presented at the I.C.F.U. Symposium on University Autonomy and Academic Freedom in a Free Society, Glen Cove, N.Y., 24 October 1981).

7. On European "democratization" see also German Universities Commission, *Report on German Universities* (New York: I.C.F.U., 1978), and Italian Universities Commission, *Report on Italian Universities* (New York: I.C.F.U., 1981). The American policy of affirmative action is analyzed by Edward Shils in "Government and Universities in the United States: The Eighth Jefferson Lecture in the Humanities," *Minerva* 17 (Spring 1979): 129–77. Consult also Roger A. Freeman, "Uncle Sam's Heavy Hand in Education," *National Review* (4 August 1978), p. 946 ff.; and John H. Bunzel, "Affirmative Action, Negative Results," *Encounter* (November 1979), pp. 43–51.

8. This appointive policy at the University of Pittsburgh is described in my "Tenure in the American University," *I.C.F.U. Newsletter* 6 (March 1979): 1–4.

9. See Sidney Hook, "The 'Radical' Tilt Against Academic Freedom," *Measure* no. 50

gone so far in the United States as it has in western Europe); faculty unionization, ostensibly for financial benefit and a greater share in university government, but in reality to legitimate defiance of the criterion of competitive merit; vast disequilibrium between supply and demand for academics, encouraged in part by the easy acquisition of tenured positions; toleration of deviation from academic morality in the form of political indoctrination and recruitment of students; grade inflation or equalization, which amounts to a refusal to perform the crucial professional duty of evaluation (in chapter 12 Allan Bloom explores the moral significance of this refusal); well-publicized instances of fraudulent scientific research; and willingness to cater to student demand for courses in academically dubious subjects.[10]

All this testifies to a disconcerting decline of professional morale and discipline. Small wonder then that politicians display contempt and the public loses confidence.

THE PRINCIPLE OF COMPETITIVE COLLABORATION

The Western academic world is a vast, unplanned and spontaneous order that operates on a principle of competitive collaboration in the advance of understanding.[11] This principle is an expression of the "instrumental activism" and "institutionalized individualism" that Talcott Parsons and Gerald Platt discern at the heart of Western liberal civilization.[12] In the case of the academic enterprise, its success depends upon commitments to intellectual objectivity and the criterion of competitive excellence. These are the professional commitments required to run the process of competitive collaboration, without which it slows and stalls. But fidelity to intellectual objectivity and achievement tends to weaken in an expressive and egalitarian age.[13] Respect for individual freedom and equal opportunity wanes as conceptions of liberal equality and social justice come to pervade the climate of opinion.

Paradoxically, in such an emotional climate private interests are let loose

(Spring 1980), pp. 1–2. (*Measure* is published by University Centers for Rational Alternatives, New York, N.Y.).

10. As Bernice Martin points out: "Women and ethnic minorities especially come to be treated as special ascriptive categories with their own world view, value system, and self-oriented subject matter. Women's studies, Black studies, and the like deny the possibility of objectivity, comparability, and equality in scholarship" ("The Mining of the Ivory Tower," in Seabury, *Universities*, p. 110).

11. For a superb analysis of the different kinds of knowledge, see Fritz Machlup, *Knowledge and Knowledge Production* (Princeton, N.J.: Princeton University Press, 1980).

12. Parsons and Platt, *American University*, pp. 42–43.

13. On objectivity, see Charles Frankel, "Intellectual Foundations of Liberalism," in *Seminar Reports: Liberalism and Liberal Education: Western Perspectives* 5 (Fall 1976): 3–11 (published by the Program of General Education in the Humanities, Columbia University); on competitive merit, Bryan Wilson, Introduction to *Education Equality and Society*, ed. Bryan Wilson (London: Allen & Unwin, 1975), pp. 11–38.

and tend to disintegrate professional discipline. The meritocratic university is redefined as a democratic association whose members are entitled to govern it as they see fit. But they share an interest in security of employment, which they convert into a right; academic tenure becomes an earned right. In this way, principles basic to the internal morality of the university, namely, equality of opportunity and fair evaluation, are discounted or discarded. Various forms of preferential appointment tend to displace appointment on the basis of competitive merit, a policy that runs directly contrary to the ethos of the Western university. As Edward Shils puts it: "The claims of ethnic or social origin, of political sympathy, of friendship and of mere seniority or presence and of patronage must be studiously expelled from all consideration when appointments and promotions are discussed and decided. This follows automatically from the commitment of universities to the ideal realm of understanding of the world, of man and his works. Anything less is treason."[14]

How did we arrive at this situation? What can be done about it? These are the questions I propose to answer. I begin by presenting the constitutional structure and morality of the Western university, particularly as they are displayed in its American variant. Then I shall attempt to explain why universities have drifted away from constitutionality, indeed why most academic institutions have failed to become fully constitutionalized. This diagnosis will lead us to an appraisal of remedial prescriptions.

CONSTITUTIONAL STRUCTURE AND MORALITY

My constitutional analysis has to do primarily with the American version of the Western university.[15] Fundamental principles of university autonomy and academic freedom are, of course, common to Western universities. These principles derive ultimately from freedom of the mind, as Raymond Polin eloquently argues in chapter 2. American and European universities differ mainly in matters of internal organization and appointive authority, and the differences are not all that great. In the United States, faculties propose candidates for appointment, and university officers rule on the proposal; in Europe this final authority is ministerial. Here I am not concerned with deviations by continental universities from academic constitutionality, namely, the democratization and politicization that began in Germany and spread to Denmark and the Netherlands.

The constitution of the American university is an interlocking structure of principles, practices, procedures, rights, responsibilities, and rather imprecisely specified obligations. Each and all of these derive their justifica-

14. Shils, "Government and Universities," p. 176.
15. Illuminating comparisons of American and western European universities are offered by Joseph Ben-David, *American Higher Education: Directions Old and New* (New York: McGraw-Hill, 1972). An unsurpassed statement of general constitutional principle is Robert M. MacIver's *Academic Freedom in Our Time* (New York: Columbia University Press, 1955).

tion from their contribution to the primary purpose of the university as an intellectual institution, intellectual progress. (We need not here consider the cognate purposes of the university, which include undergraduate education, professional training, and provision of various services to society and government, mainly by way of research and consultation.) The distinctive purpose of the Western university is to maximize the advance of understanding in the broadest sense, that is to say, to discover relations in both the natural and human realms of experience, as distinguished from the accumulation of uninterpreted data. Significant truth in the form of theory is the academic objective, as Nikolaus Lobkowicz points out (chapter 1), and the road to this objective is the use of reliable procedures of a systematic and scientific nature.

Institutionalized intellectual autonomy, understood as the right of the best qualified to define and to perform academic tasks without social or political interference, is the most fundamental of all constitutional principles. For without intellectual autonomy—freedom of the mind—there could be no institution that we would recognize as a university. The fundamental presumption is that intellectual may be distinguished from political activity. Even though intellectual work may and does have profound political consequences, it is not done for political purposes.

Next is the principle of political and philosophical neutrality. By political neutrality I mean that no genuine university as a corporate entity may adopt a partisan political position or take a stand on a political issue, even in the case of a deeply unpopular war. Of course, individual faculty members may do so as private persons and citizens. This is the external or political dimension of academic freedom. No academic may be rightfully penalized for exercising rights of citizenship. Still a decent regard for the obligations of academic citizenship is called for in political pronouncements.

Philosophical neutrality implies that no genuine university may espouse any particular philosophical or moral doctrine. In a practical way, intellectual, social, and political pluralism—characteristic of a liberal society—preclude philosophical partisanship. More fundamentally, philosophical conformity or uniformity are incompatible with freedom of inquiry. Again individuals may adopt and expound philosophies of life and ultimate reality as they best see fit, and do so in their academic capacity. Indeed much of social and political philosophy involves attempts to grasp and to define our cultural and political situation. Dispute and inconclusiveness are to be expected, as are the appropriate detachment and objectivity that the academic ethos demands, whatever the matter under consideration.

ACADEMIC FREEDOM AND TENURE
The principles of corporate autonomy and neutrality are the foundations on which are erected the institutional right to academic freedom and the institutionalized privilege of academic tenure, the specifically academic form of professional autonomy.

The right to academic freedom is a complex right. It is obviously not fundamental in the sense that natural, human, or constitutional rights are fundamental. Rather it is an institutionalized professional right, a right of office. But it is far more important than most institutionalized rights. For academic freedom partakes of a fundamental natural or human right insofar as it is "an aspect of equality of opportunity."[16] And equality of opportunity is simply an alternative formulation of the basic liberal natural right to freedom. In the liberal perspective the right to academic freedom is of supreme worth to those who desire to participate in the academic process of competitive collaboration.

This analysis of academic freedom accords with Robert M. MacIver's views. He identifies three dimensions of academic freedom: institutional, professional, and functional. Its functional dimension is the most significant. According to MacIver, the professional academic "is first and foremost engaged in the pursuit and communication of knowledge. This function is a community service, and its importance can hardly be overestimated. . . . It is a service to his country, a service to civilization, a service to mankind."[17]

An institutional right that derives from the fundamental purpose of the university, that partakes of the liberal equal right to freedom, and that also has utilitarian justification in John Stuart Mill's vision of man as a progressive being—this is a right of a very special kind. As such it cannot be confined to a claim to inquire and to teach in accordance with one's understanding of the truth, as many would define the right. This is but the core of the right. Nor can its acquisition be tainted by the extraneous considerations that Edward Shils so forcefully condemns. If ever a right depended for its acquisition upon demonstration of excellence—and to be excellent means to excel—it is the right to academic freedom. Hence intrinsic to the right is the practice of competitive appointment. That is to say, both institutional purpose and individual right are embedded in the concept and practice of academic freedom.

While academic freedom is certainly a right, the status of academic tenure is less clear. Academic tenure—permanent appointment, or appointment without limit of time—is defended as an essential protection of academic freedom and the guarantee of independence of judgment. In the latter respect, the case for tenure is similar to the use of life appointment to sustain an independent judiciary, a practice for which Alexander Hamilton argued. Still many regard academic tenure as a privilege—important and beneficial, but still something less exalted than a right. But MacIver refers to the scholar's "right to a status adequate to his responsibility and consonant with the high service that he renders to society and to civilization."[18] Tenured appointment is also a recognition of competitive excellence and a prize for which competition is as intense as it can be.

16. Parsons and Platt, *American University*, p. 154.
17. MacIver, *Academic Freedom*, p. 10.
18. *Academic Freedom*, p. 238.

Yet another view is offered by Parsons and Platt, that "the tenure system is based on commitment, competence, and performance."[19] Their reference to performance may carry something more than a hint of qualification. As is the case with academic appointment and freedom, tenure should be obtained only on application of the criterion of competitive merit. But unlike the right to academic freedom, academic tenure must be sustained; it confers a special obligation to perform as a trusted professional. Confirmation of the promise of accomplishment, not equality of opportunity, is crucial. From this angle, tenure appears more a privilege than a right. For it has always been understood that tenure could be revoked for adequate cause, whereas the right to academic freedom may be infringed but not revoked. No doubt, the notion of adequate cause has received a moral interpretation; in the American university, intellectual deficiency in and of itself has not been considered actionable. Still, no status that smacks of aristocratic privilege can be sustained without performance of the function that it is designed to secure. Academic tenure is not a form of secure employment of the kind that obtains in a civil service. Both the expectations and obligations attending tenured appointment are greater than those accompanying bureaucratic employment.

In any event, the practice of academic tenure, whether viewed as a right or a privilege, has yet to be improved on as the best way to institutionalize professional autonomy and to evoke dedication to academic ideals. This is the case even though any freedom may be misused, or any privilege abused. Academic freedom is betrayed when academic appointments are made on other than academic grounds. Academic tenure is abused when it is seized for the sake of personal security at the expense of individual rights and university purpose. Some misuse of both freedom and tenure is to be expected and is tolerable. But massive misappointment is unacceptable, fatal for a fiduciary profession.

THE PROCEDURES OF ACADEMIC APPOINTMENT

Much of what I have said about the principles of competitive collaboration, university autonomy, and neutrality; about academic freedom and tenure; and about the imperative of competitive appointment is universally applicable to Western universities. I turn now to consideration of American appointive procedures and their rationale. Here we find a division of authority between faculty and administration, the aim of which is reliably to discover, appoint, promote, and tenure the objectivity best-qualified persons. Appointive procedures have their justification as the most effective ways in which to achieve this purpose. Appointment is at the very heart of the academic constitution.

The late Arthur W. Macmahon of Columbia University, a distinguished professor of American politics and administration, offered a classic formula-

19. Parsons and Platt, *American University*, p. 377.

tion and justification of appointive procedures in a statement prepared for his university. In appointments to tenured positions, the Columbia procedures provide for review of departmental nominations by ad hoc committees. According to Macmahon, "The membership and the procedures followed by the ad hoc committee are of crucial importance to the University. The President of the University or a senior officer of administration should be a member of every ad hoc committee." Macmahon then affirmed that: "It should be the concern of the ad hoc committee to ascertain whether the department has made an adequate canvass of persons who should be considered for the post for which the nomination is made, and whether the individual recommended may reasonably be said to be the best person obtainable for the proposed work at the proposed level of appointment in the light of all relevant considerations."[20]

In addition to the classic prescriptions of Macmahon, documents, faculty handbooks, and committee reports from a number of universities serve to confirm the reality of the American academic constitution.[21] All, in one terminology or another, proclaim the supremacy of the criterion of competitive merit in both tenured and untenured appointments. For example, according to the rules of the Massachusetts Institute of Technology, "Each appointment or reappointment to the staff should be based unequivocally on the reasonable belief that the appointee is the best candidate under the terms of the appointment." Of special interest is Harvard's precaution against the policy of "nepotistic preferentialism," that is, the appointment of persons already members of a faculty to tenured positions on the ground that they meet local academic standards. Harvard says that: "It is vital that the department's case not only document the excellences of the nominee but also state explicitly why this candidate was recommended over other names closely considered. Although always necessary, this comparative aspect of a department's case assumes particular importance when the recommendation is for a promotion from within."

So too is the University of Chicago on its guard against localism. With reference to an assistant professor who is being considered for reappointment or promotion, Chicago prescribes that, "At this point, he should be considered as if it were a new appointment." And Stanford University also seeks formally to protect equality of opportunity against nepotistic pressures: "If the recommended candidate is not the first choice, explain why

20. Arthur W. Macmahon, *The Educational Future of Columbia University* (New York: Columbia University, 1957), p. 38. Charles Frankel assisted Macmahon in the preparation of this document. For a more recent and equally authoritative analysis and justification of appointive practices, see Richard A. Lester, *Antibias Regulation of Universities: Faculty Problems and Their Solutions* (New York: McGraw-Hill, 1974).

21. Among others, I have examined the regulations of the following: University of California, Berkeley (1969), Harvard University (1971), the University of Chicago (1972), Massachusetts Institute of Technology (1972), Princeton University (1972), Stanford University (1972 and 1975), and Yale University (1972).

higher choices are not being put forward. If the candidate is already a member of the Stanford faculty, explain why he is recommended over other individuals in his field."[22]

These are the essentials of the process of academic appointment as set forth in the constitution of the American university. Notice that the process is designed to take advantage of departmental expertise. The convention that affords departments the right to take the initiative in recommending candidates for appointment is founded on their special competence in the academic disciplines. The presumption is that the department is better able than any other body to identify the best prospect among the candidates for appointment. Departmental expertise and initiative entail departmental obligation to perform faithfully and scrupulously this crucial function in the appointive process. Failure to discharge this responsibility and consequent deterioration of a department warrant its suspension, a measure for which American university officers of administration have the authority.

Departmental organization and the corresponding departmental prerogative to nominate for appointment—along with the creation of the graduate school—are the distinctively American innovations in the Western university. But the departmental right to propose does not imply the right to dispose; departmental autonomy is not absolute although much respected. The final authority to appoint is rightfully, and should be effectively, vested in administrative officers, for they have a right to veto departmental recommendations. Theirs is the responsibility for the integrity of the appointive process.

UNCONSTITUTIONALIZED INCENTIVES

It is appropriate, indeed imperative, to reaffirm constantly the obligations assumed by university faculty, obligations that I summarize by reference to academic constitutional morality, the crux of which is devotion to the academic constitution. As Parsons and Platt remark, "The tenured member is expected to fulfill high standards of fiduciary responsibility and is trusted to do so."[23] But danger of corruption on the part of both faculty and administration is ever present. Departments and whole universities do deteriorate. The academic profession itself may fall into the grip of nepotistic preferentialism. Evidently devotion and trust are not enough; they cannot stand against unconstitutionalized incentives. Here, economic analysis helps to explain the dynamics of academic decline.

Economists regard human action as governed by individual incentives. Some incentives depend importantly on their institutional context. In

22. This paragraph and the preceding one draw upon my "Tenure in the American University."
23. Parsons and Platt, *American University*, p. 131. Note also their point that "Tenure-collegiality is essential to the fiduciary character of the academic role. Tenure is a symbol of membership in the type of collegial collectivity organized about the implementation of fiduciary responsibilities" (p. 367).

certain situations, a classic example of which is the medieval commons, action on individual incentives produces externalities that are to the detriment of all. In the case of the commons these incentives lead to overworking and overgrazing the land, the tragedy of the commons. For the economist, the solution to the problem of harmful externalities is to internalize them, that is, bring home to individuals the costs of their activity. Internalization is the point of private property; it forces people to conserve and to husband, rather than competitively to squander, their resources.

Now apply this type of analysis to the situation of the American academic profession. In particular, consider the incentives that operate in an unconstitutionalized system of higher education. And remember that for imperfectly rational creatures a constitution is essentially a method of binding oneself against behavior that one will later regret. No rhetoric of constitutional morality can prevent these incentives from generating immensely harmful externalities in the form of damage to the university as an intellectual community, to its students, and to society. Unless they can be induced to internalize these externalities, faculty will abandon academic freedom and so release one another from exposure to the criterion of competitive appointment. And they will grant themselves jobs for life at the expense of the coming generation of scholars and scientists. This is the tragedy of the academic commons. For if each member feels that even if he remains faithful to the constitutional ethos, others will not, and therefore he best act to his own advantage, in effect all agree to dilute academic standards and the appointive process, whatever the external costs. Unconstrained by constitutional structure and undeterred by constitutional morality, incentives that work to destroy professional integrity and discipline take hold of people.

The dynamics of academic decline produce a kind of collusion that need not necessarily be open, as in the organized drive to unionize a university. Rather destructive agreement, arising from the incentives at work in an unconstitutionalized university, may well take the form of an implicit mutual understanding to live and let live, to exploit the university by turning it into a kind of club, permanent membership in which is assured to those on the waiting list—the "tenure track," as it is known in the United States—so long as they meet the local standards of appointment. In consequence, the resources of the academic system, namely, tenured posts, are gobbled up without stint.

Of course, to speak of a tenure track is to display a thoroughly illegitimate attitude toward the appointive process as prescribed by the academic constitution. But this attitude prevails, as a mere glance at American university advertisements illustrates. Indeed the concept of a tenure track institutionalizes the unconstitutional policy of nepotistic preferentialism.

In my observation, the American bureaucratic policy of affirmative action has been applied to relax the criterion of competitive merit for women and minorities; this practice legitimizes and consolidates unfortunate attitudes and incentives. After all, people ask themselves why they should expose themselves to the criterion of merit when others, their competitors, are evading it. Of course, this means that the policy of affirmative action finally tends to militate against those whom it is supposed to favor. It is less easy than many imagine to circumvent the dictates of equal opportunity and individualized justice.

This application of economic thinking to the university reveals why departments and faculties cannot be expected to adhere to the academic constitution and to fulfill their obligations on a voluntary basis. It is not only a matter of corruption. It is, more realistically, a matter of the personal and well-nigh universal incentives that naturally develop in situations lacking appropriate constraints. In the university, as in the polity and the economy, the problem is to devise constraints that bring individual rationality in line with collective rationality. For the university, the academic constitution provides the solution to this problem. To constitutionalize individual incentives is the appropriate response to academic decline. In the university both moral and intellectual integrity depend on their effective presence. Trust itself requires institutionalization.

ADMINISTRATIVE CONSTITUTIONAL RESPONSIBILITIES

Professional obligations to the university as an intellectual institution are too weak and too diffuse, and too apt to be overridden, to provide effective incentives without authoritative support and sanction. Earlier we noticed that the American academic constitution divides authority over appointments between faculty and administrators. Final appointive authority is allocated to the officers of administration. But administrators' responsibility goes beyond that for individual appointments. Their paramount responsibility is for both the procedural and substantive integrity of the appointive process itself. For the discharge of this responsibility, administrative authority is wholly sufficient according to the American academic constitution. Legally speaking, American university presidents are Hobbesian sovereigns, to whom their faculties stand in an advisory relation. Unfortunately, the majority of American university administrators probably do not so interpret their authority and responsibility. They tend to become politicized in the sense that they are overly responsive to faculty attitudes and pressure; academic leadership tends to dissolve into negotiation; no one speaks for the academic constitution, and few have the moral authority that would be required to impose constitutionality on their faculties. But this is simply to admit that the great majority of American institutions of higher education are either unconstitutionalized or partially so. They neither appoint competitively nor adhere to high absolute standards for appointment. They are neither governments of law nor governments of men who take their responsibilities seriously.

In this light we can better understand why a show of administrative authority may be attacked by faculty as despotic tyranny. Many American faculty members ask for greater departmental autonomy and call for a greater share in so-called governance of their universities. All this reflects a persistent will to invade the constitutional authority and responsibility of the administrators.

In the United States the notion of university governance is bruited about with a view to increasing faculty participation in it. But in reality no such governance exists, for universities do not take corporate decisions, or do so only very rarely. If all the members of a university perform their constitutional duty, there is nothing much else left to do, and what remains to be done is best left to executive initiative. If the administrative officers are negligent or stupid, then the proper line of action is to get rid of them, not to usurp their authority and compromise their responsibility. The notion of governance as applied to universities is essentially an ideological weapon used by faculty against administrators to deform the academic constitution. I know of no American faculty that has called upon its administration to discharge its responsibility for the integrity of the appointive process or that has united against administrative officers for having failed to do so.

In these times faculty emphasis upon collegiality has also become ideologically colored. To be sure, the university is a stratified collegial association. However, the collegial aspect of its nature does not transform the university into a participatory democracy. Nor does collegiality absolve faculty and administrators of their differentiated and complementary duties. Collegiality has become a kind of code word for academic egalitarianism. And academic egalitarianism is not merely another expressivist phenomenon; it too functions to delegitimize responsible academic leadership.[24]

ACADEMIC TENURE IN THE UNITED STATES

According to a report of the National Science Foundation on tenure practices in science and engineering departments in all American universities and four-year colleges with tenure systems, the proportion of total faculty tenured in the academic year 1978-79 was 67 percent.[25] The physical

24. For an egalitarian conception of the theory of the university, see Amy Gutmann, "Is Freedom Academic?: The Relative Autonomy of Universities in a Liberal Democracy," in *Liberal Democracy: Nomos XXV*, ed. J. Roland Pennock and John W. Chapman (New York: New York University Press, 1983). Compare the following: George Armstrong Kelly, *The Trammeled University* (Cambridge, Mass.: Schenkman, 1974); Howard O. Hunter, "Universities and the Needs of Local and Regional Communities," *Minerva* 18 (Winter 1980): 624–43; and Derek Bok, *Social Responsibilities of the Modern University* (Cambridge, Mass.: Harvard University Press, 1982).

25. The statistics on tenure in this section are from three sources: National Science Foundation, "Tenure Practices in Universities and 4-Year Colleges Affect Faculty Turnover," in *Science Resource Studies: Highlights*, NSF 81–300 (Washington, D.C.: National Science Foundation, 1981); Frank J. Atelsek and Irene L. Gomberg, *Tenure Practices at Four-Year Colleges and Universities*, Higher Education Panel Report, no. 48 (Washington, D.C.: American Council on Education, 1980); and *Academe: Bulletin of the American Association of University Professors* 66 (September 1980).

sciences had the highest proportion tenured (76 percent), the social sciences the lowest (63 percent). In the physical sciences an additional 20 percent were in tenure-track positions, that is, appointments that make one eligible for consideration for tenure according to mainly local academic standards. In the social sciences, 30 percent of the faculty held tenure-track positions. Further, in American private universities in the physical sciences 74 percent were tenured, and in the social sciences, 59 percent. The corresponding figures for public universities are 78 and 68 percent. Of science and engineering faculty who did not have tenure at the beginning of the 1978–79 academic year, over 75 percent were in the tenure track. Finally the American Council on Education reports that 69 percent of the humanities faculty in all institutions were tenured, with another 24 percent in tenure-track positions.

Consider now the tenure decisions in the academic year 1978–79. Of persons considered for tenure in the physial sciences in private universities 97 percent were approved, and the rest were eligible for reconsideration; in the social sciences, 76 percent were granted tenure. The corresponding figures for public universities were 74 and 56 percent.

For all institutions, fewer than 1 percent of all faculty were involuntarily released without formal consideration for tenure, including those who resigned because of anticipated failure to receive tenure. Evidently once appointed a person was practically certain to be reappointed and considered for tenure, and the vast majority would be so considered on a noncompetitive basis. Failure to get tenure and involuntary separation together contributed about 2 percent of turnover of full-time faculty in American institutions of higher education.

The National Science Foundation discovered that American academic administrators expected the tenure-approval rate to rise in the future, especially in the social sciences. "The social sciences tend to have greater proportions of young doctorate faculty than do the physical sciences and engineering fields. Thus, it is likely that more of the senior faculty in the latter fields would have already served their probationary period and been granted tenure." [26] The concept of probationary period, as is tenure track, is offensive to the American academic constitution.

Look now at tenure data compiled by the American Association of University Professors. Among a selection of public universities, the following percentages of their faculty are tenured: California Institute of Technology, 78.6; University of California at Berkeley, 80.2; University of Colorado at Boulder, 81.0; Indiana State University, 77.2; University of Kansas, 78.3; University of Massachusetts at Amherst, 76.7; Michigan State University, 77.1; University of Minnesota at Minneapolis, 71.8; Kent State University of Ohio, 80.1; Ohio University, 79.4; and the University of Wisconsin at Madison, 79.3. According to my computation, the average

26. Atelsek and Gomberg, *Tenure Practices*, p. 4.

percentage tenured of fifteen more or less representative state institutions is 79.3.

Compare the above proportions with the percentages of faculty tenured in American private universities: Stanford University, 75.1; Yale University, 52.5; University of Chicago, 67.0; Johns Hopkins University, 51.8; Harvard University, 55.1; Princeton University, 61.0; Columbia University, 56.1; Cornell University, 72.3; and Brown University, 79.0.

Finally notice what may well be the most heavily overtenured academic institutions in the United States, the state colleges of Pennsylvania. The top five of these colleges, of which there are about a dozen, average out at 91.6 percent tenured, with one at 95.1 percent.

In the early seventies the American Association of University Professors established a commission to investigate and to recommend on tenured appointment in American higher education. The commission reports that, "Most institutions—94 percent—place no limit on the proportion of their faculty who may be tenured." The commission then asserts: "*In the commission's nearly unanimous judgment, it will probably be dangerous for most institutions if tenured faculty constitute more than one half to two thirds of the total full-time faculty during the decade ahead.*" [27] The American academic profession ignored this responsible recommendation. Indeed, essentially unconstitutionalized universities were bound to ignore it, given the nature of the incentives to which they were vulnerable.

These statistics on American tenure policy depict serious institutional and professional default. Clearly the rate of tenuring, especially in the physical sciences, is too high. Still, with a few exceptions, the great constitutionalized universities have behaved in a responsible manner. They have kept proportions of faculty tenured at reasonable levels, and they have appointed competitively. But the vast majority of American institutions of higher education are unconstitutionalized. They recognize no upper limit on the percentage of faculty tenured, and they appoint from their tenure tracks, that is, they give preference to their own people. They do not insist that candidates for permanent appointment stand in national competition and so accept an internal restriction on the application of strictly intellectual criteria. [28]

CONSEQUENCES OF AMERICAN TENURE POLICY

The flooding of American higher education with people who have not been exposed to the criterion of competitive excellence cannot but have unfortunate consequences. The academic profession was warned in a timely manner about the implications of its tenure policies. In 1977 Chancellor Richard C.

27. American Association of University Professors, *Faculty Tenure* (San Francisco: Jossey-Bass, 1973), pp. 6 and 50.

28. A number of chapters in this volume deal with the situation elsewhere. At the 1981 I.C.F.U. symposium on "University Autonomy and Academic Freedom," Professor Thomas Nipperdey of the University of Munich reported on the state of affairs in West German universities today. He remarked that tenure is often granted after three years of appointment

Atkinson of the University of California at San Diego, then acting director of the National Science Foundation, pointed to: "A substantial increase in the proportion of tenured faculty members: by 1974 tenured professors accounted for an overall average of 70 percent in the sciences and engineering, with physics professors at 78 percent and professors in chemical engineering at a high of 81 percent."[29] On another occasion, Dr. Atkinson said that "these trends threaten to lock out younger Ph.D.'s from tenured faculty positions. In some disciplines, it is not an exaggeration to fear that we may lose an entire generation of bright, young minds."[30] Not many spoke out as did Atkinson, and the blockage of appointees that he decried has come to pass. Today concern is often expressed about the future capacity of American scientists to compete for Nobel prizes.

As for the humanities in American universities, a salvage program of sorts is now under way. The Andrew W. Mellon Foundation has pledged some $24 million for investment in a graduate fellowship program for humanities students.[31] The objective of the Mellon program is to save for the humanities exceptionally able young persons who would otherwise turn, or be turned, away from an academic career.

The consequences of American tenure policy involve not only damage to the university insofar as its capacity to perform as an intellectual institution is impaired. Fundamental rights are infringed also. Aspirants to an academic career have a right to be considered on their academic qualifications alone, without facing exclusionary criteria. Students have a right to the best education they can get and use. Failure to provide this constitutes a further denial of equality of opportunity. And society has a right to expect from the academic profession disciplined and trustworthy behavior. All these rights have been overridden. It may also be that the national security of the United States is endangered insofar as that depends on the pace of technological advance.

FURTHER DIAGNOSTIC REFLECTIONS

With the exception of the leading institutions, both the way in which and the extent to which tenure is granted in American universities are indefensi-

---

and that there is great pressure to grant it. Apparently in Britain many institutions award tenure on the basis of a three-year probationary period, and David Martin's statistics (chapter 13) show a clear decline in the quality of academic appointments, especially in the polytechnics. In contrast, at the 1981 I.C.F.U. symposium Professor John Passmore said that the Australian National University limits tenured posts to 50 percent and requires all candidates for these posts to stand in national competition.

29. Richard C. Atkinson, "The Threat to Scientific Research," *The Chronicle of Higher Education* (28 March 1977).

30. Atkinson, "University Research and Graduate Education" (Remarks to the Annual Meeting of the Western Association of Graduate Schools, Albuquerque, N.M., 7 March 1977).

31. Fred M. Hechinger, "What Must Be Done to Save The Humanities?" *New York Times* (26 January 1982).

ble. The American academic profession is disintegrating into a collection of defensive guilds, each with its own "track" to tenured security. It is no wonder that American academics indulge in grade equalization. If they refuse to grade themselves, how can they be expected to grade their students? Sheer consistency of attitude dictates that no one should be rigorously appraised.

How and why did this essentially pathological condition come about? The short answer, of course, lies in the failure fully to constitutionalize the universities. After all, the point of the academic constitution is to enforce competition and so constrain people against opportunistic and self-indulgent action. In this respect the university is like any other human institution in that it is composed of rules and procedures to ensure compliance with those rules and is backed by an ethos whose strength determines the health of the institution. But why the failure to constitutionalize? This question provokes further reflection.

In the liberal philosophy of life, equality is wedded to freedom in that its very meaning derives from freedom. Hence the basic liberal right is the equal right to freedom, to equality of opportunity. Any institution like the Western university, the success of whose mission depends on enforcement of equality of opportunity and respect for individual merit, will be profoundly implicated in the eclipse of the liberal philosophy of life. When equality becomes detached from and opposed to freedom, as it has in our time, cultural and institutional transformations will inevitably follow.

From a cultural standpoint the expressivist attitude toward life, to which I called attention earlier, tends to emphasize unity at the expense of individuality. And unity is a feeling that is inherently localistic and so easily translates into frozen pluralism as each institution withdraws into itself. Then we get both academic guildism and reactive assertions of group rights, a kind of vicious dialectic. Moreover, the expressivist temper tends to detach equality from freedom and so gives rise to egalitarianism. That is to say, expressivism weakens respect for both individual rights and individual accomplishment; striving for excellence is castigated as a manifestation of elitism. And, as we have seen, expressivism works to legitimate attitudes and incentives that are fatal to academic constitutional morality. In a cultural perspective, therefore, the rise of romantic expressivism—tantamount to the demise of the liberal philosophy of life—helps to explain our institutional decline.

In an economic perspective also, the Western university displays responsiveness to deep trends in Western civilizations. For some time now people have been turning away from economic freedom and reliance on the market to politics to advance their interests. This politicization of life is approved by many political philosophers of liberal egalitarian or Marxist persuasion.[32] In the Western university politicization takes a number of forms.

32. The following are exemplary statements of these trends of thought: Amy Gutmann, *Liberal Equality* (Cambridge: Cambridge University Press, 1980); C. B. MacPherson, *The*

First is the introduction of the *Gruppenprinzip* into the universities of West Germany and its adoption elsewhere on the continent.[33] Second is the application of political ideology to academic appointments, the continued practice of which would put an end to the Western university. And third, there is the distinctively American form of politicization in which faculty exert pressure on one another and on administrative officers for mutual protection. Moreover, American academics seem increasingly willing to forsake their obligation to truth in order to proselytize their students and colleagues. For example, economic theorems appear to be no longer valid or mistaken, but rather radical or traditional. The ideal of intellectual objectivity is driven out by demands for ideological balance. All these trends reflect repugnance for an open society. It seems that power is what really counts in both the economy and the academy.

From a purely political viewpoint, the American university has been taken over by a Madisonian faction that is using its power to subvert the academic institution, to defy important rights, and to harm the public good. This experience should remind us that a fundamental purpose of constitutionalism is precisely to prevent domination by a faction, especially a majority faction. In the unconstitutionalized universities of the United States effective control has passed to the faculty, which is only to say that American academic administrators have not enforced the rules.

Reflection on the pathology of the Western university from these complementary perspectives—cultural, philosophical, economic, and political—reinforces one's appreciation of just how serious our condition is. We are in a cultural and institutional crisis, not just a passing state of disorientation. Academic integrity in hiring, grading, and teaching may be vanishing in the wake of opportunistic behavior the causes of which are both deep and manifold. And administrative authority is dormant or deficient. In such circumstances institutional degeneration is inevitable. We live with the vicissitudes of our own ambivalence.

CONSTITUTIONALIZATION

Restoration of academic health depends, first of all, on revival of morale, on arousal of self-respect, and creation of a climate of opinion intolerant of mutual indulgence. But this in turn depends on putting a stop to diffidence and opportunism. People require assurance that their fellows will stick to the rules of the game, otherwise mutual uncertainty generates preemptive and protective action. Long ago Thomas Hobbes explained the dynamics of rulelessness.[34] Respect for academic freedom, for equal academic oppor-

Life and Times of Liberal Democracy (Oxford: Oxford University Press, 1977); and Roberto Mangabeira Unger, *Knowledge & Politics* (New York: Free Press, 1975). I appraise these trends in "Justice, Freedom, and Property," in *Property: Nomos XXII*, ed. J. Roland Pennock and John W. Chapman (New York: New York University Press, 1980), pp. 289–324.

33. These developments are analyzed and appraised in German Universities Commission, *Report on German Universities*.

34. For a more recent analysis of the characterological and motivational consequences of

tunity, cannot survive in a Hobbesian "state of nature." The university is not immune to the political dynamics on the understanding and control of which we have built our free societies. To think otherwise is both fatuous and arrogant.

I suggest, therefore, that constitutionalization of the Western university should now become the prime objective of the academic profession. This is the prescription to which my analysis of our condition clearly points. As a secondary and contributing objective, rectification of damage already done to the university, and to society at large, is very much in order. In particular, we need to deal with deformations of the appointive process and the consequent abuse of academic tenure.

RENEWABLE CONTRACTS

One prescription that deserves serious consideration is to replace academic tenure with renewable contracts of, say, seven or ten years.[35] Review of performance at specified intervals would, of course, make it possible to remove unproductive people, provided a will to do so exists, and at the present time this is problematical. There would be pressure to keep faculty members on so long as their work was satisfactory, all things considered. But conformity to "satisfactory" as a standard perpetuates nepotism and guildism. Moreover, to base the academic profession on bureaucratic contracts of employment would seriously depreciate its status. A hiatus between status and function would thereby be created. And could the profession, so depreciated and denigrated, continue to attract able men and women, who in any case will seek independence, however it is to be had? Professional autonomy is the only real alternative to financial independence, and an academic career offers the latter only to a few. Finally, abolition of academic tenure would be tantamount to admission that universities cannot be trusted to discharge their responsibility for intellectual objectivity and progress. The case for academic autonomy in all its forms would be clouded. The trial of the Western university would conclude with a confession of guilt.

In my opinion, these considerations warrant rejection of the prescription of renewable contracts. Those who do not agree may wish to imagine the incentives that periodic mutual appraisal would arouse. Intellectual and moral independence could be even harder to come by, as people sought refuge in cliques. And Hobbesian diffidence would strike at universities as intellectual communities.

---

statelessness, see Richard A. Posner, *The Economics of Justice* (Cambridge, Mass.: Harvard University Press, 1981), part II. For the harm that unconstrained, opportunistic action does to both economic and intellectual progress, see Douglass C. North, *Structure and Change in Economic History* (New York: W. W. Norton, 1981).

35. Use of ten-year renewable contracts has been suggested by Robert Orr, Dean of the Graduate School of the London School of Economics. See his letter and my reply in *I.C.F.U. Newsletter* 6 (August 1979).

EARLY RETIREMENT WITH OPTIONAL RETENTION

A proposal for early retirement combined with optional retention of productive persons is put forward by Sir Peter Swinnerton-Dyer. His plan is designed to cope with conditions in the British universities. But presumably it could have a wider utility. According to Sir Peter: "If tenure is to continue at all, it needs to be combined with a substantially lower retiring age. A university could continue to employ, on either a whole-time or a part-time basis, those who had reached retiring age but were still active and vigorous: but it would no longer have to continue to employ those who were not."[36] This policy might very well help universities through the current difficult period of few available tenured positions. It would certainly demand administrative integrity of a high order. But like the Mellon Foundation's plan to strengthen the humanities, Swinnterton-Dyer's prescription would not cure the American disease of academic protectionism. Only open competition for a limited number of tenured appointments can do that.

INDEFINITE TENURE

Professor Edward Shils of the University of Chicago suggests that the practice of academic tenure should be revised. He would convert "permanent" into "indefinite" tenure. According to Shils, permanent tenure does indeed protect academic freedom, but it "also protects the individual against the sanction of discontinuance of his appointment for insufficient conscientiousness in teaching, indolence, dishonesty and incompetence in research and severe deficiency or subversion of the performance of the obligations of academic citizenship." Therefore, he recommends that the practice be revised, but not completely discarded. Instead of permanent appointment universities would confer presumptive permanence of tenure, that is, continuing appointment would be conditional on meeting a reasonable standard of achievement. This conditionality is the difference between permanent and indefinite tenure. Shils insists, of course, that "Reviews of presumptive permanent, or qualified permanent, tenure would be explicitly restricted to considerations of the academic's achievements in the fulfilment of the obligations in teaching, research and academic citizenship."[37]

No doubt Shils's concept of indefinite tenure could be used to dispense with persons who do not live up to expectations. Still the proviso must be: given that both administrations and faculties have the will to do so. This may well be the case in our leading universities, but they are the least likely to have to deal with defaulters. Determination to enforce standards of performance is unlikely to be present in institutions where both faculty and administration are corrupt. Indeed it might be easier to get tenure-tracked universities to constitutionalize than to deal with specific cases of academic

36. Swinnterton-Dyer, "Prospects for Higher Education," p. 10.
37. Shils, "Academic Freedom and Academic Obligations," pp. 29, 49–50.

failure. Another question is whether revokable tenure would encourage or discourage more rigorous appraisal of candidates. People might be tempted by the thought that, after all, the decision to grant tenure is not final.

But the real inadequacy of indefinite tenure is that it alleviates only some symptoms of our sickness. The American academic system is infected with both irrelevant criteria of appointment and excessive tenuring. Restoration of health depends, above all, on limiting tenured appointments and opening them all to competition. There is no alternative to constitutionalization.

THE WESTERN UNIVERSITY ON TRIAL

Universities in the Western world are on trial today mainly because they have failed to protect professional merit against political ambition or personal security. In part, the explanation of this failure is cultural. Much about the modern temperament is illiberal. And the attractions of power and political ideology also weaken respect for intellectual objectivity and individual rights.[38] From defective conceptions of human individuality and social justice a destructive will to politicize all of life arises.[39] But to blur the line between political and academic activity is fatal to the case for university autonomy. The very idea of the university depends on maintenance of this distinction.

The rest of the explanation as to what went wrong is structural and situational. Unconstitutionalized universities are prone to invasion by unprofessional criteria; they tend to turn into clubs or guilds with waiting lists;[40] and they find it difficult to resist importunate demands for permanent membership. In the absence of constitutional constraint, attitudes and incentives are generated that debilitate both intellectual integrity and professional morality.

The fate of academic freedom epitomizes our condition. Academic freedom is a complex of rights that derive from both the mission of the uni-

38. See Guenter Lewy, "Academic Ethics and the Radical Left," *Policy Review* 19 (Winter 1982): 29–42.

39. The consequences of politicizing the economy are explored by Lester C. Thurow, *The Zero-Sum Society: Distribution and the Possibilities for Economic Change* (New York: Basic Books, 1980); Dan Usher, *The Political Prerequisite to Democracy* (Oxford: Basil Blackwell, 1981), and Mancur Olson, *The Rise and Decline of Nations: Economic Growth, Stagflation, and Social Rigidities* (New Haven: Yale University Press, 1982).

40. The American concept of the tenure track implies that at the end of a probationary period a person must be either promoted or let go. To avoid this decision, some institutions have introduced the status of tenurable, which is awarded to persons deemed good enough to keep, who are then appointed until an opening appears in the tenured ranks. This protective innovation has been denounced by the American Association of University Professors as follows: "Assuming they have fully earned an entitlement to tenure, there can be no justification for continuing them in a less favorable and more vulnerable status than their tenured colleagues" (quoted by Richard P. Chait and Andrew T. Ford, "Beyond Traditional Tenure: Extended Probationary Periods and Suspension of 'Up-or-Out' Rule," *Change* 14 [July–August 1982]: 53). Recent changes in the regulations of the University of Pittsburgh permit removal of a person from the tenure track either temporarily or permanently.

versity and the liberal philosophy of life. Academic freedom as applied to the university implies a claim to institutional autonomy. In its departmental guise academic freedom confers initiative in appointments, the aim of which is to foster selection on the basis of professional merit. For individuals academic freedom means not only freedom to think, teach, and write. It is the academic application of a fundamental principle of justice, namely, equality of opportunity, the right to advance through intellectual merit without let or hindrance by inappropriate tests. This is the fundamental right that the Western university has failed scrupulously to protect. Here academic administrators are deeply implicated for they have constitutional responsibility for the integrity of the appointive process.

In the Western university, because it is an intellectual and not a political or a moral institution, a single objective reigns, namely, intellectual progress. In consequence, more so than in any other human institution, individual rights to liberty and justice should mesh smoothly with social welfare and progress. No conflict arises between individual excellence and social utility. On the contrary, academic injustice damages not only individuals but also society. Both liberal and academic justice dictate resurrection of the individual's right to academic freedom. Only then will the trial of the Western university be over and its future secure.

PART I

The Idea of
The University

1

Man,
Pursuit of Truth,
and the University

NIKOLAUS LOBKOWICZ

What has happened to instigate a meeting of more than a hundred scholars
from all over the world who are concerned about the future of the university? Most of us would be inclined to answer somewhat as follows. In the
late 1960s, a student movement, spurred on by the media and a few
influential philosophers of a utopian bent, became worldwide and developed an ideology that combined a number of ideas hitherto foreign to the
academic world. This ideology was taken up by politicians, who had little
understanding of the situation, and by junior faculty, who sensed an opportunity for more rapid promotion. They began to press for change, and
irresolute legislators, wavering ministers, and weak university presidents
gave in to preposterous demands. In consequence, we all work in universities deformed by silly ideas proclaimed by obstinate ideologists, universities that have lost their standards to the shibboleth of the age, equality.
Instead of studying and teaching, both students and professors have, to a
large extent, become politicians. Instead of upholding academic standards,
universities try to become small democracies or instruments for the democratization of society. Organizational and political questions preoccupy us.

What we must now do, therefore, is really very simple. We must return
to our old standards and ideals. We must fight the "spirit of the age" in the
name of the university, one of the oldest institutions of the West.

Nikolaus Lobkowicz is Professor of Philosophy and President, University of Munich.

This prescription applies to universities throughout the West, although each nation's schools naturally require somewhat different remedies. In fact, the accuracy of this prescription is so obvious that even some of the most passionate democratizers would subscribe to it. In Germany only a few rigid radicals continue to argue that the so-called university reform of the 1960s and 1970s yielded beneficial results. I suspect that more and more educators everywhere are reaching similar conclusions. Therefore, rather than reiterate what all of us know, I wish to probe deeper. We must more clearly articulate the causes of our disease in order to specify a cure.

TRANSFORMATION OF VALUES

First, let me suggest that it is much too easy to say that everything that happened was caused by the wave of ideological thinking. Certainly, the ideas that came to the fore in the course of the student "revolution" were essentially Marxist, and we can even identify the most influential ideologists. Moreover the upheaval in the academic world took place almost simultaneously with basic political changes, so much so that it is difficult to separate cause from effect. Yet ideology explains very little of what goes on in the world. After all, it is by no means evident why any ideology, including Marxism, should suddenly acquire enormous resonance. It is even less clear why ideology should influence academic institutions. Many ideologies have had no influence whatsoever on the academic world. Why and how did we become vulnerable to the ideological disease?

My first hypothesis or claim is that we live in a time of radical change, and my second thought is that we should be very surprised indeed if this did not affect the universities first. This turmoil is mainly caused by technological advance, but its essence is spiritual. Our societies no longer seem able to transmit their values to the new generation. Why is this the case? Ronald Inglehart, noting the prosperity and peace that have prevailed in the West since World War II, claims that people who lived through the depression and the war cannot convey their moral outlook to children who have experienced neither.[1] There is something to this, but I think that the forces that work to transform our values are much more profound and enduring than most of us realize.

Consider the following circumstances as fundamental causes of value transformation. The peasantry has virtually disappeared, and this was the social class most active in the transmitting of values and traditions. The large traditional family is no longer; in Germany, couples have 1.4 children. Modern transportation and the mass media, especially television, force upon us a world in which a primitive past confronts a utopian future and in which terrifying butchery coexists with human hope and decency. The present is much too discordant and polyphonic; there is no harmonious cultural melody to encourage personal integration; we are deeply disinte-

1. See Ronald Inglehart, *The Silent Revolution* (Princeton, N.J.: Princeton University Press, 1977).

grated, in this respect comparable to the people of the early modern baroque era. And empirical science penetrates and permeates the most private and intimate corners of our lives; hence everything becomes hypothetical and provisional; with virtually nothing unquestioned, the sense of stability and permanence evaporates. It is patent, whatever the reasons, that it has become infinitely more difficult than it was in the past for parents to hand down their moral outlook to their children. We live in an age of spiritual distress and psychocultural dissolution.

VULNERABILITY OF YOUTH

In this situation it is not surprising that the young look for and succumb to simplistic ideologies that minister to their unease and confusion, and that identify an enemy. So it is even less surprising that the worldwide uncertainty about values erupted at the universities. After all, among other things universities are just overly large crowds of young people, separated from their families and thus especially prone to deep collective insecurities and receptive to anything novel. Moreover, universities are intellectual institutions in which the newest theories and ideas, many of which are untested and unreliable, are propounded and considered. The transformation of values is encouraged by intellectuals, so-called, and they cluster in the universities.

Some might say that such commonplaces are irrelevant to our present situation. The so-called student revolution is in the past, and the overwhelming majority of students are now no longer in conflict with their parents, teachers, or society at large. Students and younger faculty are becoming traditionalists, quietly returning to the central and tested values of our culture. In Munich, we have had for several years now a return to what Germans call *Innerlichkeit*, that is, "inwardness": to a new interest in poetry and music, to inoffensive aesthetic experience. There is even a revival of genuine religiosity, and interest in anything that smacks of everyday politics has declined.

However, for two reasons I incline to skepticism about these developments. The first is that, as Inglehart correctly points out, the value revolution is mainly a silent one. Undue attention to the more dramatic events easily distracts us from recognizing that revolutionary upheavals are only surface manifestations of deeper forces. Moreover, absence of open conflict may mean only that everyone has worked out a tactic to settle disputes quietly. Adults concerned with education have become more tolerant, indeed downright permissive. The young have become more resigned and pragmatic in their outlook; they know that one cannot change everything all at once; there is the "long march through the institutions."

DEFORMATION AND POLITICIZATION

Second, whether or not the value revolution continues, it has already profoundly transformed our universities. To be sure, the extent of this transformation varies from country to country. In some, legislation incorporated the demands of the radicals; in others, such as the United States, where universities are not organized and directed by the state, the damage may be less severe or more ephemeral. Still, in spite of national differences, all our universities display common deformations. All have become much more vulnerable to political influence, whether from within or without. Our universities have become highly sensitive seismographs that register even the slightest change in the political atmosphere. This politicization is largely attributable to our universities' having come to understand themselves as democratic institutions. In some countries, students and junior faculty, either directly or through their political associations, have an important say in vital policies. They have seats in university senates, department councils, and appointive committees. Even trade unions take part in running universities. In other countries, students and assistants have relatively little influence, and democratization finds expression in the universities' responsiveness to government policy, which impairs university autonomy. In fact, the idea that the university ought to be democratic has led everywhere to a significant decline in autonomy. Governments, parties, and politicians wield influence in the university that was unheard of twenty years ago. Yet this loss of autonomy, resulting from the insistence that the university accommodate political trends and ideologies—this politicization of the Western university—would not be a truly serious matter were it not accompanied by even more radical forces working from within. Just twenty years ago, the university was quite immune to intellectual fads and ideological thinking. Today each and every trendy vogue claims to be a scientific or scholarly breakthrough and as such demands academic recognition. Everyone willing to refuse new and likely spurious "disciplines" is now called an impossible reactionary, an enemy of democracy and the people, even a fascist. Consequently, what Hannah Arendt called "nonexistent" subjects burgeon like mushrooms! Since no one has the time to become competent about the exotic excrescences, universities are increasingly populated by incompetent people "teaching" subjects whose academic standing is, to say the least, in serious doubt. The students, who sense the growing uncertainty about academic standards, respond by doing, as little work as possible and then perversely, and yet not without justification, complain that we do not offer them the stimulating regimen they need to mature.

It is, of course, difficult to show in every case that the crumbling of academic standards is clearly related to either the value revolution or politicization. One suspects that as a disease progresses, one or another organ will cease to function even though not directly afflicted. Some standards yield to ideological onslaught; others disintegrate for the simple reason that not only, to quote Dionysius Areopagita, the *bonum* but also the corruption is *diffusivum sui*.

THE IDEA OF THE UNIVERSITY

So far I have contended, first, that university deformation is not due primarily to ideological infiltration, rather to a deep and often silent transformation of morals; and second, that one would expect the value crisis to first emerge at our institutions of higher learning. My third, and I think, most significant point is that the crisis of the Western university, our institutional deformation, arises mainly from our failure to ask and answer the question, What is the university good for? If those who now complain will look back a bit, they will see that we have been living for quite some time with a scandalously obscure notion of what the university is and is good for. It is imperative that we articulate the idea of the university and its relation to human nature and society.

Looking back at his revolution, Lenin is reported to have said that to make a revolution it is not enough to want power; the ruling class must be sufficiently resigned to its fate to give up. Lenin's dictum helps us understand why the universities were so quickly overcome by the "spirit of the age." According to Lenin, the ruling class quits, not because they see no personal advantage in fighting on, but rather because their only reason to hold out is class interest—and they are ashamed, as it were, to fight for this alone. When students, junior faculty, some allegedly progressive senior faculty, and politicians began to agitate for change, university presidents and traditional faculty caved in because their only defense was that their lives would be disrupted and made less comfortable by such change. Armed with this motive alone, they could not resist the revolutionary enthusiasm.

I contend, therefore, that the future of the Western university depends decisively upon our articulation and propagation of an "idea of the university" that is valid and compelling. The notion of an "idea of the university" I borrow from John Henry Newman's famous lectures, delivered in 1854 when he was the founding rector of Dublin. The university as Newman and we understand it has been in the pillory for the last decade. That understanding of the university must be reestablished and legitimated in the eyes of our contemporaries. The traditionalist argument that the university's antiquity justifies its continuation will no longer do. To be sure, people of wisdom believe that an institution's venerable age and long, hallowed tradition oblige their support.

But most of our contemporaries value only immediate utility; our climate of opinion is devoid of wisdom. Thus a better reception is accorded the argument that a nation's wealth and well-being depend on a plethora of well-trained scientists and professionals. In Germany, for example, one hears routine warnings against the "Japanese threat," that is, the danger that Japanese products will swamp world markets, reducing the rest of us to penury. This prophecy is by no means as cogent and persuasive as it first seems, for Japanese productivity is rooted in the superb morale of Japanese workers, not in the quality of their universities. Further, this essentially utilitarian consideration does little to validate the mission of the university as a total institution. Most of the subjects taught in universities have slight if any immediate bearing on economic efficiency. And the subjects that do have direct impact on productivity—engineering, agronomy, forestry, dietetics, economics, and business administration—could be taught, and maybe better, at specialized professional schools rather than at the university.

PURSUIT OF TRUTH

These reflections force us to think about what elements or principles define the nature of the university. The only persuasive answer, it seems to me, is that universities are schools whose faculty not only transmits but also, most importantly, increases knowledge in the broadest sense. In other words, the fundamental and distinctive mission of the Western university is the pursuit of truth. University teachers cannot be other than creative scientists and scholars. Clearly, this special mission provides at least a partial justification for the university. For Western society, at least in contrast with Islamic society, must have an institution devoted to both research and teaching, to fundamental discoveries and their swift dissemination which sustain the dynamism of an advanced industrial society. And it is natural and appropriate, indeed most advantageous, to have professional schools associated with the core university faculties. This is an especially appropriate arrangement for those professions the practice and advance of which depend on an appreciation of scientific and disciplinary research. It would, of course, be possible to have two sets of institutions, one for research, and the other for professional training. But the conduct of research and professional training in the same institution facilitates the implementation of discoveries. In this respect, the Western university compares very favorably with its Soviet Russian counterpart, in which research and training are systematically separated between the Academy of Sciences and the ordinary so-called universities.

Still the university is something more than a collection of professional schools in which instruction is based on, or at least intimately related to, fundamental research. After all, good professional schools could perform their own research. What distinguishes universities from professional schools is that they are comprehensive institutions, that is, they combine and offer a great range of subjects widely different in nature. The classical university encompassed theology, the liberal arts, law, and medicine. Documents from the late Middle Ages treat these disciplines as a unity. So understood, theology serves the spiritual goal of mankind, the liberal arts prepare for theological investigation; and law and medicine both serve the social and bodily needs of man. Today, of course, no such simple scheme can be used to validate the university curriculum. Still we do have a criterion by which to decide which subjects should be taught, and which should not be taught. The university should offer only those subjects that require their professors to pursue the truth.

Moreover, the multiplicity of subjects taught confers an enormous benefit. It permits the university to combine professional training and cultural enlightenment. The basic reason that the same institution should offer sciences, both natural and social, and humanities, is that we have no need of scientists who are technocratic barbarians, nor do we need humanists who have no appreciation of the significance of science.

AN INTELLECTUAL AND MORAL COMMUNITY

Finally, we must recognize that the Western university is an intellectual and moral community. If we are to formulate and defend an "idea of the university," we must emphasize this aspect of the institution. After all, much of the recent discontent and turmoil have to do with the university's communal character. This is transparent in the strategies once used by students and assistants: class disruptions, teach-ins, sit-ins, strikes, demonstrations, threats, and public insults. But even the dispute over academic standards has to do with the university as a community. No doubt, some thoroughly competent professors do not give a damn about incompetent colleagues. Fortunately, most of us do care, for we are concerned about the future and the fate of the university as an intellectual and moral community. We strive to maintain its ethos even though we may not have very definite conceptions about the nature of the university.

It is difficult to specify the kind of community a university should be, especially if we wish to be realistic. Many of our universities are preposterously big, fragmented into units scattered throughout our cities. Both faculty and students tend to be self-centered, as so many people are in our time. If a university has a real campus and four to six thousand students an experience of community can be naturally come by. My own university, Munich, has over forty thousand, living all over the town in rented rooms that often are little more than dreary holes, useful only for sleeping. In these circumstances an experience of community is all but impossible. If faculty and students have no sense of institutional unity and solidarity, the university may well be a fine factory for professional training, but it has nothing in common with either the *universitas professorum et scholarium* or the *universitas literarum*. Recall that in Latin *universitas* meant originally—in the Bologna of the late eleventh and early twelfth centuries—the same as the later concept of *nationes*, namely, a community of scholars and students who ate, prayed, and studied together. This was so much so the case that *universitas* was originally most commonly used in the plural, *universitates*.

HUMAN ACTIVITIES

Now I wish to submit an interpretation of "university community" that may seem rather philosophical and abstract, yet I think it best expresses the institution's very essence. My interpretation is based on a tripartite distinction developed by Aristotle. In several places in his works he asks, What is the most fundamental division of human activity? His conclusion is that man is first a creature who makes things, for example, ships, houses, and river embankments. This is *poiesis*, making or producing, the activity by which men procure the *necessitates vitae*, the necessities of life. Second, man is a being who acts. He plays the flute, conducts politics, behaves as a moral being; this is *praxis*. *Praxis* differs from *poiesis*, which has its outcome in a work (ship, house, or dam), in that it finds completion in being done well. A person engaged in political, moral, or economic activity finds fulfillment not in a product, but rather in the perfect doing of the activity itself. As a moral and political animal, man never really finishes anything; yet he can achieve completion at any and every moment of his life, simply by doing well whatever he is up to, and ultimately by being a good man, that is, by being good at being a man. Third and finally, man thinks and theorizes. He may theorize as a "maker" and he does so as a "doer." But there remains a realm of thought whose purpose is not to get what one needs or to act well, rather just to know. This is a third distinctive activity, *theoria*. The Greeks considered this man's highest form of activity, as explained in the final chapter of Aristotle's *Nichomachean Ethics*. Among other things, it is the human activity most concerned with the divine, for the ultimate object of contemplation is God and his reflection in the universe. It is the activation of man's highest capacity, the *nous*. And in thinking man is most fully free.

If we look at our world from the Aristotelian point of view our activity may be categorized as follows. There is the universe of technology, production, and commerce; of social and political action; of cultural activity, including the pursuit of truth. Aristotle does not distinguish between religious contemplation and science. This distinction comes with Neoplatonism. The university, as originally conceived, is the only human association in which men come together solely for the purpose of knowing. Some come as teachers and make *theoria* their profession; others come to learn. But all are united by a single purpose, the pursuit of truth for its own sake. Of course, students attend a university for professional training, and professors make their living by teaching. Yet their one common purpose is devotion to truth, which is the defining characteristic of the university. Truth may be provisional or definitive, deep or superficial. Yet if the university is not informed by the conviction that there is truth worth pursuing for its own sake, that can be taught and learned, that is objective, then it is not a true university. For a true university is a form of institutionalized theory and objectivity. This quality defines the university and confers upon it dignity and autonomy, even sovereignty.

INSTITUTIONALIZED THEORY

This definition of the university as "institutionalized theory" is rather grand, to be sure. Most of what is taught at the university is mundane. To a religious person, above all to a Christian, *theoria* in the sense of science and scholarship is by no means man's highest form of activity. Our universities teach more courses that concern "making" and "doing" than *theoria* in its ultimate sense. Still the ultimate nature of the university as a community is as a band of truth-seekers. Its unique aim is the pursuit of truth, manifold but finally unitary, about the universe and our place in it.

This search for truth gives us our standards of achievement, our genuinely academic standards. This unending search justifies our very rituals and ethos, without which a university cannot survive. And this commitment to objectivity is the precise target of the current attack on the university. Those against whom we defend the university feel that it should be in business and politics, that it should be some kind of a democracy, governed by trade unions and industrial management, and that it should be concerned with society as a totality. We cannot and do not deny that universities operate in a democratic society. Faculty may belong to unions and political parties, or they may serve as consultants to government and business. Still we must insist that the university be informed and governed by the spirit of truth, the search for which requires a high degree of independence and autonomy. It requires tranquility and detachment that must arise from within and cannot be enforced. The academic morality of our standards issues from the very nature of the university. Insistence on these standards of performance is not arbitrary tyranny, rather fidelity to our institutional ethos.

It seems to me imperative that we make explicit and public an "idea of the university" that is worth fighting for, and this can only be the concept of the university as institutionalized truth-seeking. But this is not enough. For our opponents argue that the truth we seek as scientists and scholars is far from divine, and so its pursuit cannot and should not be an end in itself. Certainly, it need not be an end in itself; thinking and theorizing serve to enhance and dignify practice, *praxis*. Curiously the Marxists and other ideologists do not understand "practice" as moral action but as *poiesis*, that is, making. They hold that the intrinsic purpose of seeking the truth, and hence of the university, is "production," both industrial and political. They want to "produce" peace, justice, and paradise on earth.

We must not reject this vision out of hand. In fact, defenders of the university often risk overstating their case by speaking of the university and its pursuit of truth in quasi-religious terms. Not only for Marxists, but also for Christians is there profundity in the assertion that the discovery of secular truth, and even philosophical and religious truths, is not man's supreme goal. Since we cannot justify the university as "institutionalized theory" that embodies the ultimate destination of man, we often fall back on another line of defense. We ask to be allowed our corner of tradition; we are curious men, and curiosity is legitimate. This plea is not unreasonable, but is ultimately implausible, above all to the current generation. It is as unpersuasive as the proposition that we need universities with high standards to maintain Western prosperity. Most of the arguments put forward in defense of the university are such half-truths: that it is a sanctuary for the curious, is devoted to truth-seeking, prepares young people for life, and so on.

PHILOSOPHICAL ANTHROPOLOGY

These reflections suggest that we need deeper and stronger foundations for the "idea of the university." Indeed, we need something like a philosophical anthropology to build on. As is the case with much contemporary debate, the debate on the university is really a controversy over human nature, what man is and could be, his nature and destiny. In reality, the dispute about the university is a sign of a much more serious crisis. We no longer have a common understanding of ourselves, of man. Until we create a persuasive philosophical anthropology, we cannot hope to secure the future of the Western university.

Let me illustrate my meaning with a reference to recent German experience. The expression *Leistung* is usually translated as "achievement," but the word connotes athletic performance. It was incorporated into managerial ideology to denote hard and effective work on the part of all employees. When Herbert Marcuse spoke against the *Leistungsgesellschaft*, the achieving society, he had in mind the "all-out" nature of the effort demanded by our industrial ethos. Many sought to defend against Marcuse's criticism by saying, quite rightly, that without strenuous effort productivity would fall, maybe drastically. But then the debate took a problematic turn. Feeling that high school and university students were not asked to do their best, government ministers and professors began to call for *Leistung* in the schools. As a result, our students, mostly cooperative and diligent, are now confronted with an ideology that makes them feel desperate. They are constantly urged *etwas zu leisten, Leistung vorzuweisen*, to achieve something, to make big achievements. Now the students, and not only they, begin to ask, Why should we make this tremendous effort? Why should we slave to pass exams? Is this the meaning of life? Do we want to participate in a society that demands constant achievement for its own sake?

We can ask much the same questions. We advocate high academic standards. Why? Are high standards valuable only because they are high? Are we in danger of raising standards and scholarly criteria to the point of falsity or absurdity? Are we not hiding our own insecurity behind demands that we could never meet?

I cannot answer these questions, nor can I solve the problem that is at their root. But I pose them because they point to the need for an anthropological foundation for our conception of the university, its spirit and criteria of accomplishment. I am inclined to think that the notion of *Leistung* is not applicable to academic institutions. What we expect from ourselves and from our students is not record-breaking performances, that we all be Sebastian Coes or Karpovs. What we want and can rightfully expect is high-quality effort, to do what we do as well as we can. Instead of talking about *Leistung*, about standards imposed, so to speak, from the outside, we should begin again to cultivate the idea that human activities have their own inner moralities, their own immanent standards. Nothing man does sloppily can bring him *eudaimonia*, meaningful happiness. In thinking about human nature, I have been deeply influenced by St. Ignatius, the founder of the Society of Jesus, who said that everything, even the lowliest activities, ought to be done for the glory of God and with authentic intensity. And by Monsignore Escriva, the founder of Opus Dei, who refers to the Christian's duty to sanctify his daily work: "Above all, do it as well, as perfectly as you can."

THE ETHOS OF AN INTELLECTUAL INSTITUTION

We live in crisis, a crisis of the university that has spread through the Western world. We rightfully speak of a crisis of *the* university. From the inception of the crisis, the university has responded to the ideology that it ought to serve society. For a decade we have contended that "society" so conceived is nothing but a superstition, and to try to serve that pseudo-entity only leads to the politicization of the university, indeed to its ideologization. The university serves society best by being itself, a place of tranquil, disciplined, and objective thinking, the best preparation for any profession, and the only way truth can be had.

Yet we may still be in danger of overstating our case. We are accused of living in an ivory tower, of systematically neglecting the problems that bedevil mankind. This accusation is false, thoroughly ridiculous. The engineer, lawyer, sociologist, or historian who teaches at a university does nothing but work on human problems. The university cannot serve mankind, however, by becoming a political weapon, only by adhering to its inner morality. The university is above all an intellectual institution, inherently devoted to theory, science, and scholarship. Its justification is neither the mere satisfaction of human curiosity nor service to society. The university does not exist for its own sake; as an educational institution it is not an end in itself. But it is not society, taken as an abstract entity, that the university serves. Rather it is mankind and, above all, the young people.

ILLUMINATION

My message is that the university springs from our human nature, from our moral psychology. Perhaps we should again use the language of virtues, even purely intellectual virtues. Many of the coats of arms of our older universities have an inscription about wisdom, the supreme intellectual virtue, perhaps the greatest of all virtues. Yet it is now very difficult to speak about wisdom in the university, for modern science is not wisdom, rather mostly operational knowledge. But if we do not establish a sapiential dimension of academic life, if we do not seek truth that is embedded in wisdom, if we do not seek "illumination," as the Oxford motto has it, we shall fail. We may have efficient training schools, devoted to excellence, but the true university is not a technocratic institution, any more than it is a political institution. The central virtue of the university, seen in the light of wisdom, is thoughtfulness, pensiveness, the recognition that truth is al-

ways more complex and elusive than we are tempted to believe. And by
"we," I mean scientists and scholars. A meditative posture is not a euphemism for toying with ideas, engaging in moral and intellectual relativism,
or trifling about the human condition. It is the disciplined reflection on our
nature and condition, and it alone will enable us to restore and preserve the
Western university.

2

Freedom of Mind
and University Autonomy

RAYMOND POLIN

I am convinced that any individual worthy of the academic vocation considers the autonomy of the university an essential condition of its existence. For the university is *par excellence* the place where people gather who are devoted to the life and the freedom of the mind. The activities of the mind, from whence spring every culture, are imagination, invention, creation, analysis, and synthesis. These require the absence of any external authority or constraint. In a word, and philosophers will understand me, mind is freedom. Universities are associations created to cultivate the activities of mind, that is to say, the activities of freedom. Their mission is the pursuit of truth through freedom, the free work of the mind.

We must add that any culture lives through innovation as well as by tradition. By culture I mean *Bildung*, that which constitutes a forming of minds to consciousness, to freedom, and to method. The very word *education* implies that to be educated is to be not only directed and guided, but also driven out of a condition of insufficiency and minority into adulthood. Educated people are self-conscious, masters of themselves, autonomous, capable of accomplishing their purposes with a disciplined liberty.

Autonomy of the university is intrinsic to our understanding of education. It is necessary for fertile teaching, effective research, and creative invention.

Raymond Polin is Professor of Philosophy at the University of Paris, the Sorbonne.

SPHERES OF AUTONOMY

The spheres of university autonomy derive directly from the very nature of the cultural and scientific activity that is the heart of an educational institution. It is an absolute necessity that those who galvanize the university must enjoy complete freedom to follow their inspiration and fulfill their vocation. They must be permitted freedom of intellectual initiative, without any restraints imposed by individuals or institutions. Intellectual work transcends any political structure or dogma. From a political standpoint, intellectual effort is essentially anarchic.

Appointment to the university must depend on high intellectual merit. Our academic standards must be severe. But once a person has demonstrated talent, his personal rhythm of research and creation must be respected and must remain beyond any form of control. To be sure, respect for academic freedom involves risks; not all professors live up to their promise. But these risks must be taken for the good of the educational mission.

In the university everything depends on people and on their abilities. Consequently, the university's decisive autonomy lies in its choice of people, in its appointive process. To maintain the intellectual caliber of the university, a uniform and fair system of collegial appointment should be established. That is the only way to ensure equality of opportunity to individuals and to sustain the morale of those engaged in cooperative research.

A university must also have autonomy in such pedagogical matters as the selection of students, the grading of their examinations, and the setting of the level and nature of study. Each university should be free to express its own will and to determine its academic objectives. Some will choose to become elite institutions. Others will be specialized. Still others will opt for open admissions and become mass universities. Some institutions will cater only to undergraduates, for we need colleges as well as universities. All these are legitimate forms of educational enterprise, because all meet important needs.

Last but not least, I point to financial autonomy, which is certainly the key to all the other freedoms. Unfortunately it does not depend on the will of the faculty. Today even private universities rely heavily on governments for financial sustenance.

LIMITS AND OBSTACLES TO AUTONOMY

Academic autonomy has meaning only in its relation to a certain situation, according to certain conditions, and as opposed to specific threatening constraints. In a sense, autonomy is never granted or established once and for all; it must be continually won and protected.

A university, as a spiritual entity, is both a means to and an expression of a culture organized in the form of a state. A university is a privileged locus of cultural creation, interpretation, transmission, and diffusion. The cultural autonomy of a university is essentially relative to its cultural surroundings. It consists in the capacity to maintain a certain distance and a certain independence from the passing fads, fashions, and the more vulgar manifestations of its surrounding culture. This independence is essential to preserve its capacity for critical reflection and appraisal. The academic ethos calls for an attitude of detachment. Moreover, a university has a duty to culture at its highest level. The task of the university is not merely to preserve and transmit culture but also to enrich, create, and renovate. Indeed, part of the task of the university is to guide the evolution of culture.

The same is true of the university's relation to its social environment. The university cannot escape from its society, for that provides its material and financial support. Rather, the university has to meet various needs of its society: the provision of scientific and technological advances, the education of people who will manage its component institutions, and the training of people for the various professions. So far as possible, the selection and education of students should be performed in consonance with the structure of vocational opportunity afforded by society.

It would be absurd to try to ignore these cultural, scientific, and social requisites. They must be met, and they need not deform the university or deflect it from its central purposes. For a university shows its autonomy by its choice and level of specialization, by the quality of its academic accomplishments, and by the competence and dedication of the elites that it produces. It is especially incumbent upon the university to preserve a large domain for disinterested studies of a cultural nature. Highly personal research and originality are necessary ingredients in a genuine university.

Any university worthy of its name has to resist cultural, ideological, and political pressures that would bend it to requirements irrelevant to the life of the mind and loyalty to truth. A host of pressure groups try constantly, from both without and within, to subordinate the university to secular powers and movements. Such lobbyists seek to subvert academic ideals and corrupt the university, and their methods include propaganda, dogma, indoctrination, and cultural, even physical, terrorism. In response, the academic community must exercise autonomy in the shape of intellectual virtue, what Aristotle would have called dianoetic virtue, which requires us always to aim for the truth, respect the freedom of others, and remain lucid about our personal values. The will for autonomy takes the form of a will for intellectual honesty and loyalty to truth. Without this, there can be no salvation for the university.

And we cannot overlook a final kind of constraint, a very specious one, that comes from within the university: the hardening of tradition. Many universities are venerable and prestigious institutions whose history and traditions represent an immense and honored achievement. But prestige and memory may sometimes conceal anachronistic research and dead subjects, shield intellectual laziness and spiritual lethargy, or allow the vain to continue to live on past success. In these cases, autonomy requires the revival of intellectual freedom and the reaffirmation of the creative mind. The life of the mind is the spirit of freedom rooted in just appreciation of tradition.

WISE AND FOOLISH UNIVERSITIES

Like individuals, institutions may use their autonomy for good or for ill. There have always been both excellent and mediocre universities, but in the 1960s we learned that there are also foolish universities, those which, lacking firmness of aim and discipline, became fascinated by ideologies and were seduced by an instinctive tendency toward anarchy. Their faculty welcomed any kind of cultural "revolution." Urged on by students, caught up in delirium and sometimes aided by passive or stupefied governments, these academics spread and scattered everywhere their anticultural and antisocial notions. They betrayed the academic ethos and politicized the university.

That we have good and poor universities is normal and not dangerous. Every society needs several levels of culture and different types of elites. Open competition usually establishes hierarchies well understood by the public, and allocates, according to their competitive merit, faculty and students to educational institutions. But this new phenomenon, the foolishness injected into cultural institutions, and even into universities of the highest traditional quality, generates all sorts of moral and cultural disorder. Open competition now fails to order and stabilize the system of higher education. In consequence, the state is called upon to intervene in our foolish and often bewildering universities.

THE STATE AND UNIVERSITY AUTONOMY

The task of maintaining the integrity of our universities raises the issues of state intervention and state universities. Of course, and for good reason, we are here dismissing educational institutions that belong to totalitarian regimes, for they are called universities only by way of courtesy. We are concerned with the liberal university as it has become established in free societies.

For two centuries now, state universities have existed in France. Some American professors teaching in private universities may mistakenly assume that French professors lack academic freedom. But the cost of modern universities is so high that very few can afford to be private, as some are in the United States, and live on their own income. And no university is so wealthy as to be able to refuse government research contracts. The problem of the autonomy of universities in their relation to the state is a universal one.

The danger I imagine we fear most is not likely to be realized in liberal democratic states—that is, the danger of political or ideological pressure in education and instruction, in the direction of research, or in the selection of faculty and students. Before 1968 French universities were free from any political or ideological orientation. Our state universities were truly independent from the state.

However, the influence of the state on universities is certainly increasing, inasmuch as the state intervenes in the organization of society and the management of the economy. The modern tendency is for the state to administer more and more the life of the nation. The mission of the universities—their educational obligations and scientific research—becomes increasingly important to governments, which therefore create more precise and detailed plans for education. Such extensive social planning cannot but entail the intervention of the government in the life of the universities. Systematic planning by managers who are not humanists tends to neglect the cultural mission of the university and to emphasize sheer output rather than quality. Should this planning continue or expand, the sciences and their technological applications will become more and more privileged at the expense of the humanities.

As the state's centralized planning becomes more extensive, the university's self-government and self-management progressively decline in independence. For example, the granting of degrees and the determination of the requirements for each degree have always been the prerogatives of each university, an important symbol of pedagogical autonomy. But in countries like France, the national government, now responsible for the universities, has added to the traditional degrees—the *baccalaureat*, *licence*, and *doctorat*—a national "guarantee," that is to say, a value independent of the university that grants the degree. This system has been adopted despite the near impossibility of imposing on all universities a national and uniform standard for the merits of candidates. In reality, this guarantee prevents any real competition between the universities, and it operates to mask the efforts of the best and the weaknesses of the worst. This nationalization of degrees is one of the principal obstacles to the pedagogical autonomy of our state universities.

Finally, the state has appropriated to itself the recruitment of teachers, who become civil servants, rather than leaving this matter to the faculty and administration of the universities. Again the state requires a "guarantee" and so establishes a system of selection under its own control, such as a national committee of experts organized under ministerial direction. But, as we have already argued, a university loses its personality and integrity when its faculty does not determine its own composition. The school then ceases to be a university and becomes a bureaucracy. At the very least, even if university management requires administration by specialists, the options, the decisions—in a word, the politics of the university—should depend solely upon the faculty.

REASONABLE AUTONOMY OF STATE UNIVERSITIES

We have discussed the necessity for university autonomy, the current threats to it, and the dangers of its abuse. We now must consider what constitutes a reasonable degree of autonomy.

Private or public, a university performs a public service. As an institution, it has public consequences of all sorts and so must inevitably be accorded a public status. The state, and especially the liberal democratic state, which is an enterprise managed by intellectuals, is thoroughly justified when it both looks after the university and exercises ultimate control over it. In a modern society, the relations between government and the universities are both necessary and important. The only question is, How are these relations to be organized and institutionalized?

The general principle is that laws and rules are necessary to prevent dangerous excesses and abuses of either foolish or unrealistic autonomy. However, within this legal framework, university management and recruitment should be left to university personnel. Moreover, the government should establish and provide for permanent competition among the universities. Such competition would be the best stimulus for both efficiency and progress.

General grants should be given to the universities so that each can make an autonomous allocation of its funds according to its distinctive goals.

Minimal requirements could be imposed on all universities that wish their degrees to be recognized by the state. However, above and beyond these minimal requirements, each university should be left free to determine the level of its standards.

The state could organize a preliminary selection of potential candidates for any post in the different ranks of the faculty. Again, each university should be left free to elect, at each rank, its own members. Otherwise, bereft of all responsibility and all capacity for autonomous direction and orientation, the university will become a machine, devoid of initiative, reflection, invention, and identity. Then, one would no longer refer to Harvard, Oxford, or the Sorbonne. Rather one would say "University 75.451" or "University 44.347"!

We must be persuaded that neither laws nor rules will transform universities into creative institutions, into fruitful and fertile centers of science and culture. Laws can have only a negative effect, preventing abuses, blocking foolish fantasies, and avoiding the worst.

People are all that matter in the university; their abilities, morals, and conduct are decisive. In a healthy university, individuals' loyalty to academic ideals and the academic ethos expresses a way of life whose substance is the intense vocational application of diverse talents. Such loyalty implies the will for an even greater perfection, by which I mean respect for truth, for freedom, and for academic merit. Laws do not make universities. Intellectual virtue—that is, academic excellence—does, for the university is an essentially intellectual institution.

To summarize, the university as well as culture lives in liberty, by liberty, and through the activities of the human mind. A reasonable autonomy is the *sine qua non* of university health and the academic calling.

3

The University
and Democracy

PETER GRAF KIELMANSEGG

Thinking about the autonomy of the university tends to proceed on two assumptions that are rarely questioned. First: the autonomy of institutions devoted to research and teaching is highly desirable and should be defended if threatened. Second: autonomous universities constitute an essential element of democracy, that is, university autonomy does not merely fit reasonably well into the constitutional framework of democracy, but rather university autonomy is an integral feature of democracy because it is a way of institutionalizing freedom of research and teaching. Both these assumptions must be scrutinized in the light of recent experience and present trends in Western societies. Thus we may identify more precisely some of the important problems that the university faces in a democratic environment.

ACADEMIC FREEDOM AND INSTITUTIONAL AUTONOMY

Our understanding of university autonomy will not be advanced unless we take account of the distinctive concerns of the individual scholar, the institution of which he is a member, and the scientific community. These distinctions are appropriate, because freedom of the individual scholar, self-government of the university, and autonomy of the scientific community— of science as such—are very different things indeed. We need to analyze, on the one hand, the relations between individual freedom and institutional

Peter Graf Kielmansegg is Professor of Political Science at the University of Cologne.

government, and on the other, the relations between individual freedom, institutional government, and the autonomy of the scientific community. Is university self-government conducive to freedom for the individual? How is autonomy of the scientific community related to individual freedom and institutional governance? These questions cannot be adequately addressed so long as *autonomy* is used in a vague and global manner to encompass the concerns of the individuals, institutions, and science itself.

The right of the scholar to pursue the truth as he sees fit and to teach the truth is the prime objective. From this follows two propositions. Institutional self-government is to be understood and justified as a means to this end. And the scientific community must have operational autonomy if society is to respect either individual academic freedom or institutional self-determination as an effective way to secure this right. Both of these propositions demand further comment.

The first proposition about means and end requires us to examine the effect of institutional self-government on individual freedom, especially when the question is raised as to the legitimacy of autonomous universities. Historical experience reveals that a surprising variety of institutional arrangements are in fact compatible with a high level of academic freedom. It is probably the case that without a certain minimum of self-government by the university there will be no freedom of research and teaching for its members. But beyond this minimum, informal rules of conduct and the attitudes of the people involved seem to be more important than formal regulations for the manner in which governments treat universities. For example, the scholar in the classical German university, with its rather limited autonomy, certainly enjoyed no less freedom than Anglo-Saxon scholars who worked in institutions that were truly self-governing. However, history also shows that threats to academic freedom may very well arise in academic systems that permit a high degree of institutional self-governance. In this connection recent German experience is somewhat ambiguous.

Clearly, the German tradition of a government-dominated system of higher education was one of the causes of the disastrous developments of the late 1960s and early 1970s. Since higher education was a service provided and financed by the state, parliamentary majorities felt free to, and in fact did, turn the universities upside down. This is what the *Zeitgeist*, or climate of opinion, seemed to demand. Moreover, most European democracies with government-controlled university systems overreacted to the so-called student rebellions. In countries with a strong tradition of academic autonomy, the universities were largely left to themselves to cope with the challenge. And by and large the universities did better than the politicians and the bureaucrats, simply because they were less willing to embrace the follies of the day. Our experience would seem to dictate the conclusion that institutional autonomy is likely to weaken the impact of social trends and moods on the universities. And this is highly desirable.

DEMOCRATIZATION OF THE UNIVERSITY

In Germany during the first phase of "reform," legislation worked to enhance self-government in the universities. The hope was that once the universities were converted into democratic commonwealths, they could be left to themselves. Just the opposite, of course, turned out to be the case. In the so-called reformed university academic freedom was, at least temporarily, much more severely threatened from within than it had ever been from without, aside from the time of the National Socialist dictatorship. Institutional self-determination was a facade behind which countless serious and sometimes even brutal infringements of academic freedom took place. Indeed, it was the legal basis for these invasions. This experience provides, in my opinion, clear evidence that a university organized as a representative democracy, that is, as a constellation of competing and warring groups, is quite unlikely to transmute institutional self-government into individual freedom of research and teaching, even under more favorable circumstances than existed in Germany during the seventies.

Now Germany has entered a third phase, in which again government interference is regarded as the greatest danger to the university. Somewhat surprisingly this view is shared by both the more progressive and the more traditional universities. Among the many causes of this convergence of opinion, I think it cannot be denied that "democratization" is one. For it gravely damaged the capacity of the universities to conduct their own affairs.

THE SCIENTIFIC COMMUNITY

I turn now to the autonomy of the scientific community. *Autonomy* is often used as though it were merely synonymous with *freedom*. This is, of course, mistaken. To be autonomous means to be subject to a law, a self-imposed law. This is exactly what I have in mind when I speak of the autonomy of science.

Science cannot operate in anarchy. We require criteria that distinguish science from other methods of seeking the truth; standards of logic and evidence are the rules upon which the claim of science to produce objective and reliable knowledge is based. Scientists act as self-directed legislators in defining, applying, and enforcing their community's standards and rules. The scientific community also has the task of evaluating performances and conferring professional esteem and reputation. The claim to academic freedom would perhaps not be unfounded were there no scientific community that performs these functions. But the freedom of individuals would be precarious. For the right to academic freedom depends on the objectivity and integrity of science and scholarship, which cannot be sustained without some system of autonomous supervision. Without mutual supervision based on shared criteria, science, as we understand it, would itself come into question. Western science is a fundamentally collective enterprise.

But this is only one side of the coin. To be sure, the freedom accorded individuals to pursue truth needs to be supervised and validated by an autonomous and international body of scientists. Still this legitimate oversight and validation can also hinder individual freedom and the advance of knowledge. For science can degenerate into rigid orthodoxy that defends the conventional wisdom. Indeed, as the history of science shows, a degenerate "science" may become actively hostile to creative effort.

SCIENCE AS POLITICS

Let me illuminate aspects of the delicate relation between the autonomy of the scientific community and the academic freedom of the individual with light derived from recent events in Germany. From what I have already said, it follows that the scientific community cannot operate without a fundamental consensus of scientists on the constituent principles of science. During the last decade this consensus was seriously challenged—indeed, partially destroyed—in some fields by the contention that science is and should be an essentially political activity. This notion is, of course, the accepted doctrine of the New Left, whose ideology expounds that the supreme value of science is not truth, but rather the political objective usually referred to as "emancipation." Many who adhere to a political definition of science deny that truth, as the paramount objective toward which genuine science is directed, really can be had. For them it is not a matter of displacing truth with politics; they simply deny the existence of such a thing as truth.

Nevertheless, I believe that the New Left thinkers of this persuasion have displaced cognitive objectives with political ones. No doubt, a good deal of highly sophisticated argument could be devoted to this issue. But in the final analysis, science cannot be both a political strategy and a strategy of truth. This is evident from the apparent impossibility of embracing the political idea of science without dogmatizing about how to achieve the desired political goals. Politicized inquiry lacks that crucial openness to evidence and experience that characterizes genuine science.

This notion of science as a political strategy leads inevitably to the concept of the university as an organization that can and should be used to transform society, a thesis that in turn requires a complete redefinition of the role of the teacher or the academic examiner, a position of strategic importance. The university at Bremen, among others, was—and to a considerable extent still is—an exemplar of this conception. I will not detail how this metamorphosis was put into practice. Suffice it to say, at certain institutions teaching degenerated into political instruction and indoctrination, and examination standards collapsed.

Let us now return to the proposition from which I began, namely, that the scientific community cannot function without basic consensus. Without agreement on the foundations of science, the mutual and supportive relations among individual freedom, institutional self-government, and the autonomy of the community of scholars must and will crumble. Further, the ethos of truth is the only basis for consensus in the realm of science and scholarship. When loyalty to a political program overrides this ethos, consensus will evaporate, no matter what the content of that program. As scientists and scholars we must not allow anyone to ignore recent German experience in this matter.

DEMOCRACY AND ACADEMIC FREEDOM

I turn now to the second of the two assumptions on my agenda. I wish to determine whether it is really as self-evident as most people usually think. Does there exist a natural and undisturbed harmony between democracy, as a political system and social reality, and the ideal that teaching and research should be free? Or are there possible tensions, perhaps even collisions, between democracy and academic freedom?

We are all very well aware of the fundamental interdependence of freedom and truth. The totalitarian systems of our century have proven that to abolish freedom requires the control of thought. In this sense academic freedom is a necessary ingredient of democracy. And constitutional democracy probably offers a better guarantee than any other political system that academic freedom will be respected and valued.

But interdependence does not exclude friction. One argument—of some importance in contemporary debate in Germany—is that as society provides more money to universities, and at the same time becomes more dependent on the professional skills taught at universities, it should demand more influence over their conduct. Indeed, it is natural to think this way, and the demand is thoroughly legitimate. Hence the public has recently become concerned with university curriculums and overall academic efficiency.

As the institution that provides professional training at the highest level, the university is bound to be exposed to external influence. The claim that universities should have an exclusive right to determine what kinds of knowledge and what professional skills are required by society and the economy simply does not make good sense. In these matters the university cannot stand aloof from society and pursue its intellectual tasks without regard for social needs. That the university is an intellectual institution does not sanction its divorce from society.

We reach a similar conclusion about academic efficiency. University systems that are based on competition, that are in a sense market systems, have always had to accept some kind of external appraisal of their efficiency. This can be a galvanizing stimulus. Other systems are well advised to develop and to learn to live with standards of efficient performance. With so much money involved, anything less would be preposterous. Of course, conflicts arise when governments insist on applying criteria of efficiency, and governments may be both insensitive and clumsy in their application of these criteria. Witness the situation in Britain today, among others. Still I doubt whether the real interests and needs of the parties involved are genuinely incompatible. Institutional efficiency and intellectual vitality go together.

However, the case is different in at least two issues of the highest importance. Here principles essential to each side, the university and democratic society, clash. The first such issue concerns equality.

EQUALITY OF OPPORTUNITY AND EGALITARIANISM

Institutions that educate, the school and the university, have always been avenues of social mobility. They work to counter inherited structures of inequality based on ascription rather than merit and achievement. In this manner educational institutions are, and have for a long time been, important forces in the secular trend toward greater equality. But these engines of mobility also produce new inequalities, those based on performance, and— what is more—they legitimize this new inequality. Today the function of allocating access to scarce positions and goods, accomplished in traditional societies by the established social hierarchy, is assumed by the educational system. In advanced industrial societies the educational system has an almost monopolistic power over life chances. In consequence, enormous pressure is brought to bear on the system to promote more people to the highest educational status available. The greater the importance attached to formally recognized educational achievement, the greater that pressure is.

Thus the educational system in a democratic society cannot but become the stage for a fundamental conflict of values. On the one hand, the trend toward equality has not been halted by the withering of traditional structures of inequality. Rather the drive for equalization turns to new targets, that is, to the new forms of inequality based on achievement. The new demand is for equal chances for everyone to have access to the positional goods, which are by definition scarce. So equality of opportunity gives way to egalitarianism. On the other hand, the educational system cannot function as an educational system without selection and discrimination, without grading and ranking. Only a selective and competitive system can be both fair to the individual and efficient as a system. It cannot advance everyone to the top, not even a majority. The university stands right at the heart of this conflict of values, and hence its autonomy comes into question. I believe the university must stanch egalitarian pressures and defend with courage and firmness its duty to evaluate. Justice to individuals and academic integrity here coincide.

THE MOMENTUM OF KNOWLEDGE

The second contentious issue is whether the advance of knowledge can and should be in some sense guided and controlled. Members of the high-technology societies display a deep and growing resentment against the very momentum of the advance of knowledge. People feel that we are producing knowledge and new capacities at a speed that renders us unable to cope with their consequences. They fear we are not able even to identify such consequences before they exert irreparable damage. This is indeed an alarming state of affairs. For, as we know, our very survival may be at stake. Many also feel that the public has no say about the directions in which research is moving, because the growth of knowledge and development of new technologies are both autonomous and self-perpetuating processes. In a word, we have become afraid of our own genius and inventiveness. All this applies, of course, primarily to the natural sciences, but to the social sciences as well, for they change our view of and our relations to ourselves.

A REAL DILEMMA

If my analysis is correct, the demand will soon arise for some form of social control over science's autonomous and self-perpetuating processes. But, no one has thus far discovered how to exert control without seriously hampering the potential of science on which we all depend. It is even possible that any attempt to control intellectual progress could mortally wound science and the free pursuit of the truth.

Dilemma is often used in a rather vague way, but here we have an authentic dilemma. Again the university is at center stage, and its autonomy begins to seem of dubious value. The capacity of the international scientific community for responsible autonomy, that is, for rational self-government, may well be our only hope. Given the international anarchy in which we live, that hope may not be worth very much. In the years ahead the relations between the university and democracy are very likely to become even more strained than they are today.

4

Quality and Equality
Reconsidered

GERD ROELLECKE

John Gardner's famous question has moved the world: "Can we be equal and excellent too?" His question expresses the tension between the promise of a better life for everyone, especially through more education, and the fact that some live in the sunshine while others are in the shadows. This disparity, we are told, so incensed students at Berkeley and elsewhere that they rose in revolt on behalf of the weak and downtrodden. Today, almost twenty years later, we see that the tension between equality and quality has shaken the world but not improved it. The reason is certainly not that the rebellious have been bribed with jobs and offices. Rather, the question was wrongly put, relating the possibility of both equality and excellence to us all. But who does Gardner's "we" represent? Does "we" refer to all persons considered as moral agents? Then we are already equal and excellent too, simply by virtue of being autonomous. Or does "we" denote society with its myriad distinctions? Then we are equal before the law, but moral and intellectual excellence is our private affair. Or does the "we" signify both the rational individual and society? Then our question cannot be answered according to the rules of logic, for the law of the excluded middle posits that something cannot be both itself and something different.

Thus we must reconsider the relation between quality and equality. Let us leave the well-worn paths of debate about educational policy and assume a somewhat wider perspective. In the first part of my analysis, I want to

Gerd Roellecke is Professor of Public Law and Philosophy of Law at the University of Mannheim.

discuss the origins of the problem of quality. I shall then explain why the relation between excellence and equality has become a political issue. Finally, I shall suggest how to ease, if not entirely resolve, this fundamental tension.

HUMAN EQUALITY AND INEQUALITY

Let us consider first the origin of the problem of distinction and human excellence. If we examine the thinking of antiquity about the relation between quality and equality, we are surprised to discover that down to the middle of the eighteenth century human inequality presents no problem. The real problem concerned equality. As Aristotle reasons: "Thus justice would appear to consist in equality; and this is indeed the case. But this is not true for all, but only for those who are in themselves equal. For it may also be said that inequality is just, and so it is; but again, this is not true of all, but only of those who are not in themselves equal." Regarding political participation, as we know, Aristotle resolves the issue by way of the virtue of justice. The just person has a sense of proportion; he avoids extremes. Thus even virtue becomes a matter of allocation, though Aristotle joins to this the demand that unequal social status be inwardly accepted. Aristotle could not assert otherwise, because no other argument could explain the differentiation of the Greek world into democracies, aristocracies, and monarchies, each with its distinctive justification. But this very diversity made it impossible for his stipulation to be met. The demands society made on individuals were so very different that to accept them necessitated the sacrifice of personal integrity. Political diversity implied personal disintegration.

Early Christians rejected Aristotle's solution to the problem of human inequality through the fusion of virtue and social status. Certainly Christianity has not eradicated inequalities, but it offers a more generous interpretation of the human predicament: in the kingdom of heaven all are equal before God, even as in this vale of tears they are unequal. Therefore human yearning should be directed toward the heavenly kingdom; here and now, suffering, poverty, and injustice mark the pilgrimage to eternal peace. This vision enables people to endure with dignity the worldly order of inequality, by inwardly detaching themselves from it. In this perspective, worldly distinction is not to be gloried in, for it may easily foment sin in the shape of vanity and its counterpart, envy.

For fifteen hundred years, this Christian interpretation of the tension between human moral equality and natural inequality enabled people to cope with social reality in a rational and cooperative manner. Only in this context can one appreciate the Reformation, which brought heavenly equality down to earth in the form of the community of Christians in the priesthood of all believers. Two consequences result from this novel idea. The first is that work in this world becomes meaningful and significant, a "calling." Since the city of God begins in the community of the Christian church, so to speak, it is worth reforming this world on the divine model. Of course, God calls to salvation whomever he wills. "We are called," Calvin wrote, "not in accordance with our virtues but according to God's election and grace." But divine election is not hidden from us; we can see whom the Lord has called by viewing the success bestowed on their work.

Protestantism is not a return to Aristotle. For success in work is related not to the perfecting of an established natural order, but to God's grace, on the one hand, and to the equality of all Christians, on the other. Thus success is detached from the preestablished natural or divine order of guilds, estates, and classes, and society is open to functional differentiation. Worldly success is bestowed by God on the individual as his personal quality or excellence. Salvation through distinction is possible for all, if only they have faith.

But faith began to decline, for the second consequence of the Reformation was a hypertrophy of the idea of God that inevitably led to secularization. Once heavenly equality descended to this world, human equality once more became open to scrutiny, and the inequalities in the Christian church failed to meet the heavenly criterion. Now worldly inequality was not merely the prelude to eternal equality in heaven, and social disparities could actually be blamed on God. This was more than the idea of God could sustain, even though Protestant theology tried to attribute inequality to inexplicable grace.

With the dissolution of the natural and divine orders, and with the fading of God's grace, the quandry reversed. Whereas up to this time the issue was the equality of the unequal, now the scandal is the inequality of equals. If all men are ultimately equal, where does social inequality come from? asks Jean-Jacques Rousseau. Excluding attempts to save the natural or the divine order on the grounds of heredity, race, or class as regressive, Rousseau ponders two answers, one indebted to the Reformation, the other to Augustine.

The first, quasi-Protestant, answer is given in the Declaration of the Rights of Man and the Citizen of August 1789: "Men are born free and with equal rights, and they remain so. Social differences can therefore be based only on the common well-being," according to Article One. Like the true Christian, man as citizen is equal and free. But the grace of God is superseded by the common good, contributions to which justify inequalities. This ethical formula does more than take account of the secularization of the world. First, economic success is seen to take its significance from particular functions. The common good is an exceedingly abstract concept, but it does preclude a class justification for inequality. The person who is good at what he does is recognized, but recognition is modified by the concept of equality: specialists serve the common good and as specialists all are equals. Second, social inequality is reflexively justified. Since social distinctions promote the common good, each man must recognize that social and economic inequalities promote his own good. Or conversely, to demand social equality for all is to act against one's own best interests and to behave irrationally. This idea was worked out in many different ways: from the efficiency of the division of labor in Adam Smith—by way of conceiving economic progress as increasing differentiation—to Talcott Parson's theory that social distinctions operate to simplify complex and obscure relations and so aid people to choose wisely among alternative courses of action. Status differentials are justified on the basis of the common good, and the notion of human equality is retained. John Rawls's theory of justice is a refinement of this conception of justified inequality, inequality that does not harm ultimate human equality.

The second, quasi-Catholic, solution to the problem of the origins of inequality derives from Rousseau himself. Noting that general opinion ascribes the origin of inequality to the institution of private property, Rousseau asks, How did property come into existence? His famous answer appears in *Discours sur l'inégalité*: "The first person who fenced in a piece of land and impudently said, 'This is mine,' and who found people simple-minded enough to believe him, became the true founder of bourgeois society," that is, of the society of unequals. According to Rousseau's hypothesis, the real origin of inequality is the greed of man, his selfish desire to excel, his failure to respect his fellows as equals and his treatment of them as strangers, indeed enemies. Inequality has its origin in man's refusal to treat people as equals; it is the outcome of perverted self-love, of Augustinian original sin. This view again renders the world a vale of tears through which man must pass on his way to the society of equals, in which the will of each is integrated with the will of others in a common law, the general will that both arises from and applies to all. Its very generality enables us to evade our all-too-human partiality.

More significant even than Rousseau's return to Augustine and his revival of the Aristotelian idea of justice as virtue, as a quality of the human will, is his belief that any inequality is essentially inhuman and immoral. Rousseau's conviction of the moral indefensibility of inequality has stupendous consequences. It implies that anyone who strives to excel, although this may be perfectly natural, is acting egoistically and immorally. Conversely, anyone who repudiates excellence is moral. To uphold qualitative distinction is self-discrediting; to fight for equality is the mark of a good and worthy person; and so on. Even doubt about Rousseau's sentiment can be rejected as immoral.

I am not concerned here with the rightness or wrongness of this version of the Fall of Man. Its theoretical weakness was not hidden even from Rousseau's contemporaries. His postulate, that all injustice began when man entered into contradiction with himself, as an explanation has the force of a tautology. But the political consequences of this conception of human nature and society demand our attention.

INEQUALITY AND IMMORALITY

It is true that the conception of the common good undeniably describes the social world in a manner that is remarkably free from contradiction. With its assistance one can even better understand those who fiercely deny social distinctions and yet practice them, who cannot see the irony of a privileged person's waving the flag of egalitarianism. But the justificatory force of the appeal to the common good has diminished. There is much sympathy for alternative ways of life, for the protest against pressure for performance and achievement, and for the escape from social pressures. These attitudes purport to be liberal and generous. But they also evidence uncertainty about the foundation of social order, that is, the presupposition of the common good. This is precisely the doubt that Aristotle failed to put to rest—the doubt whether it is necessary to identify individuals with a given form of life, by way of appraisals of worth, however extolled that form of life may be. Romantic expressivism unleashes anarchic selves, uncomfortable with the discipline that service of a common good requires.

I believe Rousseau's criticism of civilization to be one of the motives for this change of attitude. Others have worked their variations on his theme; one has only to think of Marx and his heirs. All the same, Rousseau's critique of civilization remains more or less ineffective, especially in the sphere to which it was directed. In this economic dimension, the principle of functional distinction remains intact despite strident criticism of capitalism. Two reasons for this can be cited. First, the economy is relatively clearly demarcated, because scarcity is visibly symbolized and morally neutralized in the ubiquity of money. *Non olet.* Money does not stink, it does not betray its origin in shady dealing, and a person having a lot of money need not stink either. Second, the principle of functional distinction has led to a relatively sharp differentiation of roles. Today one can without much scruple dictate to one's secretary over the telephone, rolling along in one's Rolls Royce, that everyone should return to nature and take to foot.

In contrast to the economic realm, Rousseau's conflation of inequality and immorality has deeply penetrated the sphere of education. Here his influence seems enduring. Indeed, Rousseau made organized mass education both possible and necessary; he is, in effect, the father of modern educational theory. With his demand that man attend to man for himself, Rousseau founded both mass education and that openness of the relation between teacher and pupil that allowed instruction and selection to be gradually shifted from class to functional criteria. In the nineteenth century, Rousseau's project was given a new shape by those who related it to the principle of the common good. Mass education was to foster the power and welfare of the nation, an assumption revitalized in the United States by the Sputnik shock of 1957. Fusion of the principles of mass education and the common good was perfected in the twentieth century through application of statistical method.

Statistics showed that this or that group—blacks, Puerto Ricans, or Catholic girls from the countryside—were significantly "underrepresented" in this influential profession or in that famous university, just as eastern WASPs were "overrepresented." A moral transformation of American and German society took place, one outcome of which is the trend toward universal higher education. But the Rousseauan identification of inequality and immorality also made mass education more difficult, placing demands on the educational system that it has proved unable to meet.

Rousseau saw pity and love as the motives for man to turn to man, an appropriate recognition of their common humanity. Indeed, he modeled his proposed relation between teacher and pupil on the relation between father and son. This conception was justified as a counteraction to the class state, the society of unequals, and it was tolerable so long as the principle of the common good modified the principle of common humanity. But the principle of common humanity has led to mass education uninformed by the spirit of a common good that legitimizes distinction and excellence. This situation, in which we now flounder, is an unfortunate feature of Rousseau's legacy, greatly though he would have deplored it.

Hegel emphasizes that education mediates between family and professional life, with family and school differing structurally because of the greater personal distance between pupil and teacher. Mass education must be organized, and organization requires formalization: teachers and students are recruited according to general criteria; students are put into groups according to age; and curriculums are standardized. This structure creates problems for the individual and the principle of common humanity intensifies them, for every failure discredits the pupil as a human being in his own eyes. Similarly, the principle of humanity creates difficulty for the teacher in that he cannot neglect or resist its moral demand without losing respect. His distance from his pupils is much too great, the teacher-pupil relation far too formalized, for him to influence his students as a father does his children. Steadily forced to behave contrary to the standards laid down for his profession, he cannot declare his situation to be impossible without bringing discredit on himself. And once a genuine relation between teachers and students cannot even be openly discussed, the outcome of measures designed to improve education depends solely on chance. Thus the principle of moral equality interpreted as common humanity imposes incoherence on the educational system and hinders its improvement. This is the present outcome of Rousseau's equation of inequality and immorality.

EDUCATIONAL JUSTICE AND COMMON GOOD

The two postulates we have examined are both Christian in origin. The tension between equality and inequality was for a time minimized by viewing each as appropriate to distinct dimensions of life. All individuals were equal in the face of ultimate realities; but qualitative distinction, the quest for and recognition of excellence, was owed to the common good.

Governed by these principles, the concept of society based on class and ascription yielded to a functional and competitive order. Belief in equality generated quantitative expansion of education; the principle of the common good promoted and legitimated greater specialization. Insofar as t' e extension of the market effects a greater division of labor, equality and quality reinforce one another. In a liberal universe equality of opportunity works for the benefit of all.

Today, however, the moral pressure exerted by the postulate of equality works to paralyze and vitiate the energies and the accomplishments that could be expected from the untrammeled mutual accentuation of "quantity" and "quality." The unfortunate Rousseauan identification of inequality and immorality blinds people to the fact that in the modern world some forms of inequality are essential to provide the equality they value most, equality of opportunity, above all equality of educational opportunity.

Modern education, above all higher education, is intended to promote the development of persons. But commitment to equality has precluded many from understanding education's equally important social purpose, that of selection. Yet without selection education is impossible, for every judgment, praise, or criticism is predicated on a selection. However, the state of moral confusion in which we live is such that educational selection is decried as inhumane, and the recognition and reward of the achievements on which society depends, and also the opportunities that it affords its constituent individuals, are deplored as affronts to a common humanity.

This confusion shows itself most starkly in the debate over equality of educational opportunity. Initiated during World War I, this debate has continued, fueled largely by statistics showing that Western educational systems favor the children of the middle and upper classes. New statistics appear in newspapers almost daily, and the pressure of public morality enforces a credulous interpretation of their significance. But such pressure prevents critical attention to an important implication of these statistics, specifically, that the preference apparently accorded by Western education to the middle and upper classes could be mitigated, possibly overcome, by provision of more education. "More and more children, in better and better schools," is the rallying cry for a society of equals. Yet education cannot rid society of the inequalities that the economy produces and requires; this leveling is impossible in the advanced society that Rousseau repudiated and that we cannot repudiate, even if we wished to.

Since every educational system has to select according to certain criteria, it cannot but favor persons with the characteristics and accomplishments that satisfy its criteria. When parents raise their children they are governed by the criteria of their educational system, and the educational system ensures its survival by responding to their attitudes. Thus interaction between people and education generates the classes whose members best meet the common criteria of merit. It cannot be otherwise in a mobile society based on equality of educational opportunity.

A class structure of educational selection is, therefore, necessarily inherent in all education, including mass or universal higher education. If one desires equality of condition or achievement, one must look somewhere else; it cannot be had from an educational system. The statistics simply do not support the equalizing implications commonly drawn from them.

The analysis and discussion by Christopher Jencks and David Riesman in *The Academic Revolution* bolster my argument. They realize that the idea of the equality of man, if strictly applied, excludes selection: "Genes may be somewhat better than parental status, but damning a man for having a low IQ is not in the end much better than damning him for having a black skin or a working-class accent." The authors console themselves by reflecting that nothing would in any case be gained from social mobility. Since the number of higher positions cannot be multiplied at will, every ascent up the social ladder must be offset by a decline. It is much more painful to fall than simply not to rise. So Jencks and Riesman echo the egalitarian demand: the important thing is to restrict mobility and bring about more equality. Thus they try to free the educational system from selection by leveling out social differentiation. But since social differentiations exist, if only because of the division of labor, and since these differentiations cannot be eliminated, Jencks and Riesman can only move selection on the basis of competitive merit out of the schools and into professional life.

If education is impossible without selection on the basis of merit, then teachers must grade their students; the practice is unavoidable. The attempt to evade selection leads, first of all, to the same result as did excessive moral demand: it hinders attempts to improve the educational system. Evasion or suppression of selection also directly harms the system. For if teachers have to grade and rank without any publicly accepted standards of selection, they will use arbitrary criteria, for example, personal prejudices. Then the selection process will be worse than arbitrary, for once criteria, personal and particularistic, are no longer a subject of public discussion, the student must accept a teacher's arbitrary appraisal; he cannot exonerate himself in the event of negative appraisals. Thus, the effort to evade explicit and honest criteria produces only irrational, idiosyncratic, and hence unacceptable policies.

Our real problem is how to reassert and justify the selective function and authority of our educational system. Quite certainly this cannot be done by calling upon the principle of the common good. That principle has exhausted its religious credit and has, so to speak, used itself up in the process. To appeal to the teacher's educational ethos is also of no help. A professional academic ethos exists, but it is not an effective political force. Rather, we shall have to strengthen the capacity of the educational system to control itself.

Now the educational system is certainly autonomous, but unlike the economy it possesses only relatively weak mechanisms of self-control and regulation. The economy regulates itself by way of scarcity, money, and markets—all strategic points for deliberate intervention. Comparable points for leverage do not exist in the educational system: knowledge is not scarce, it can be had and distributed without limit; no child learning Latin loses anything because another also learns it; and one high grade does not preclude other high grades. Still the educational system does have its structural necessities, an inner morality that cannot be ignored with impunity. These necessities, of which there are three, offer a strategy for restoration.

First, a kind of educational justice applies to any learning group. A pupil is naturally annoyed and loses heart if he gets the same "very good" grade for a faultless Latin exercise that another gets for a defective performance. This thoroughly human reaction also explains why the absence of recognized criteria and their honest application is bound to demoralize students. Second, there is an internal organizational differentiation of the educational system. We have schools and grades within schools, that is to say, the educational process is marked by stages, at which selection naturally takes place. And third, there are time limits: primary school lasts four to six years, secondary school seven to nine, and university three to five years. Everyone expects that within these time frames standards of achievement will and must be established. These three structural features derive rationally from the very process of education itself. They are universal because nothing we understand by education can take place without their recognition and institutionalization. They offer the points at which a policy of increased selectivity may be initiated.

Such a policy would consist of two basic activities. We must release teachers from the paternalistic role, into which the principle of common humanity forced them, by now taking account of the proper distance between teacher and pupil that organized mass education requires. We must also create firm and clear rules of competition that students cannot evade without embarrassment.

More precisely a policy of restoration requires the following actions. Educational justice compels the establishment of absolutely firm criteria of educational accomplishment. Nonacademic criteria violate the internal morality of the educational process and must be thrown out: "solidarity," "surmounting of conflicts," "responsible action," and so on. Second, empirically verifiable standards must be established at each point of transition or matriculation. Entrance examinations must be administered and the examiners should not be drawn from among the teachers. Third, we must place clear limits on the time spent at the university, a firm limit on the duration of studies. (Although that is probably a distinctively German problem.)

This policy of increased selectivity would resolve the tension over the issue of quality, even in mass education; indeed, there above all. The policy is just because it institutionalizes the criterion of educational achievement. If we have equality of educational opportunity and fair evaluation no one can rightfully complain about the institutionalization of a criterion intrinsic to the educational process. Moreover, increased selectivity would enable educators to view their students seriously as individuals, not as members of groups claiming special privileges as such.

Many may still object to selection. But for the academic profession there is no alternative to the honest evaluation of educational achievement. In the end, human nature itself demands it.

5

Equality
and the University

JOHN PASSMORE

———

The ideals for which human beings have been prepared to die and to kill, vary with time and place. Loyalty to a liege-lord, liberty, patriotism, and religious zeal have all led men into battle and still do so, in one part of the world or another. For a time, liberty was the ideal that enflamed. But in the more advanced industrial societies liberty came to be taken for granted in the political sphere and frowned upon in the economic sphere. Equality, or its cognate concept, *social justice*, replaced it as the most influential ideal. For all that, there has recently been a revival of libertarianism, often oddly allied with conservatism, and egalitarian impulses still predominate, at least in the thinking of the more conventional sort of radical, who is strongly ensconced in many centers of learning. To be sure, I have yet to hear the battle cry: "Give me equality, or give me death." But men and women have certainly been prepared to kill in the name of equality, sometimes, as in Cambodia, to kill individuals, sometimes, as in our own societies, to kill traditions, to kill institutions.

PURPOSE AND RESPONSIBILITY OF THE UNIVERSITY

Equality is always equality in some particular respect. In the wider social sphere, greater equality of income and greater equality of property have often been taken as objectives. Their advocates have at times attempted to

John Passmore is Professor of Philosophy at the Australian National University.

convert the university into an instrument for achieving these ends, at whatever cost to its traditional character. Not so long ago an American president made an extraordinarily bold pronouncement: "The answer to all our problems," he said, "lies in a single word: education." Lyndon Johnson, to be sure, was a somewhat eccentric president, but in that particular judgment he reflected the illusion of an epoch. The university, to say nothing of the schools, came to be thought of as a place where the problems of society were going to be solved rather than a place for learning and teaching. For the more radical students and teachers, control over the universities was to be the first step in a march through the institutions of capitalism; for proponents of the welfare state, of Lyndon Johnson's Great Society, it was to be the principal means of creating a society at once liberal and humane. These illusions are a primary source of the difficulties from which our schools and universities now suffer. The bubble of illusion has burst, and now the universities are being blamed for not having done what they should never have been called upon to do and should never have thought of themselves as being able to do.

But we must not regard the university in that way. Let us conceive of it, rather, as a place for thinking—for thinking, of course, about society, among other things. Then we can ask what forms of equality ought to prevail in it, without supposing that it has a special responsibility to make of itself an exemplar of equality or even that it is necessarily wrong for it to exhibit any form of inequality that is inadmissible in other institutions outside the university.

Considering the university in this way, we can distinguish at least five types of equality peculiarly relevant to its proper concerns—equality of opportunity, equality of results, participatory equality, equality of esteem, and equality of treatment. We shall look at these in turn, always intent on a single question, Is their implementation, so far as they can be implemented, likely to be detrimental, fatal even, to the proper task of the university, the advancement and the diffusion of learning?

EQUALITY OF OPPORTUNITY: CIVIL JUSTICE

I begin with equality of opportunity, offering a crudely historical account of its interpretation and its application. In so doing, I want to turn a particular eye toward what happened in Australia. Although circumstances, timing, and detail differ from country to country, the order of stages I want to describe has been largely universal in the western world, at least up to a certain point. (Eastern Europe has rejected the wilder forms of egalitarianism and has only to a limited degree accepted its more moderate version.)

At its first appearance, equality of opportunity was identified with the principle of civil justice, which states that when persons are to be selected for entry into a socially central institution (to which only a limited number of persons can be admitted), the sole criterion shall be what the French

Declaration of the Rights of Man calls "virtue and merit."[1] Candidates are to be judged by their capacity to carry on the work of the institution in question at the highest possible level. To put this principle negatively, candidates should neither be preferred nor rejected on such grounds as their social class, parentage, religious or political beliefs, sex, or race.

This principle was originally intended to apply to entry into the civil service but was soon extended to other areas of community life. Universities are, or used to be, very conservative institutions; only relatively recently in their history were they prepared to grant that they had no right to exclude religious dissenters, Jews, women, or blacks from admission as students or apppointment as teachers. Women, to take a notable instance, although allowed to attend lectures, were not admitted as full members of the University of Cambridge until 1947. Elsewhere in the West, the principle of civil justice was recognized at a much earlier date, largely taken for granted not later than the postwar years, with only a very few pockets of resistance, as when children of bourgeois origin were refused admission to socialist universities. Only academic achievement and promise were to count in admission and appointment.

Thus interpreted, equality or opportunity did nothing to diminish the quality of university life, whether in respect to the advancement or the communication of knowledge. Quite the contrary. The universities did not greatly expand to welcome the new classes of students, nor did they modify in any crucial way their institutions or their courses of instruction. The general effect, in consequence, was to replace less able by more able students.

However, virtue and merit were still not the sole determinants of success, whether in relation to university entry or selection as university faculty. Success also depended, to a degree that varied from country to country, on a relatively high income. True, a small number of young men and women won scholarships, but such scholarships were scarce, often bound by restrictive conditions—sometimes absurdly inappropriate as changing conditions made nonsense of the intentions of their donors—and were often too small to serve as anything more than pocket money.

Inevitably, our personal history affects our attitudes. So let me illustrate from my own case, in a society in which social mobility was relatively easy. I could attend university only by binding myself to become a secondary school teacher. That ruled out, of course, such professional faculties as law and medicine. Upon graduation, I could not apply for one of the few traveling scholarships, then the sole avenue to advanced study, since they were not sufficiently well funded to support a student with no other means, and in the dark years of the depression they could not be supplemented by

1. See my "Civil Justice and Its Rivals" in *Justice*, ed. Eugene Kamenka and Alice Erh-Soon Tay (London: Edward Arnold, 1979), 25–49.

outside earnings. I felt no sense of injustice as a result of either of these experiences; I thought of scholarships as a grace, not as a right.

But as the ideal of equality has come to be more widely advocated, it is accompanied by the growing demand that the concept of equality of opportunity, or the principle of civil justice, be reinterpreted. No one, it was now argued, should be prevented from going to university for lack of financial resources. In many countries, scholarships and living allowances were greatly increased in number and value, with no conditions attached to them. They were regularized, instead of being left to the vagaries of private donors. At the same time, the salaries of university teachers were raised to a point at which it was no longer necessary, as it had once been, to undergo a degree of financial hardship in order to accept appointment as a university teacher.

At this stage, few of us saw any signs of danger. Ourselves scholarship boys, we did not wish our successors to be as burdened and confined as we had been, nor did we wish junior lecturers to share what had been our genteel poverty. (Our own prospects, I must add, were enhanced. But it would be too cynical, I think, to suppose that this was the sole motive for our approval.) One voice, it is true, was raised in Australia against the new Commonwealth Scholarships Scheme, the voice of John Anderson, ever mistrustful of the state when it appeared to be bearing gifts. But he was the exception, perhaps the sole exception. Indeed, I should still argue that had the universities refused to expand beyond manageable proportions, the new scheme could only have improved the quality of the university's work, driving out what used to be called the "gilded youth," often far from being either interested or diligent, in favor of the new wave of hard-working scholarship winners.

But soon thereafter Australian demography made necessary the training of a large number of teachers, and the government decided to also seek new experts of every sort. Universities welcomed their expanding population, the multiplication of their staff, as allowing them to appoint new specialists. The ideal of equality continued to gain new ground, prompting a rapid increase in the number of scholarships. At this point, I did raise my voice to assert that growth could be malignant as well as beneficial, but regrettably few of my colleagues concurred, so entranced were they—for reasons not in themselves ignoble even although, in my judgment, wholly ill advised— by the prospect of enlarging their own departments, setting up new options and new specialities.

RAPID EXPANSION AND CONSEQUENT MEDIOCRITY

True enough, Australia, like Great Britain, avoided some of the worst effects of expansion by setting up new universities, enabling the old universities to become more selective, rather than enlarging them to an impossible size. We could not, however, avoid the worst effect of all—the appointment to university posts of large numbers of second-rate people. Although their abilities were considerable enough to earn advanced degrees, they lacked the imagination and the dedication that characterize the best scholars, the best scientists. They were attracted to universities by the charms of a profitable and, as they lived it, not too arduous career. They contributed little or nothing, even when they went through the motions of publishing, to science and scholarship; some of them succumbed either to idleness or to endless political agitation, applying their minds to the construction of amendments to amendments. For them, university teaching was just another job, if one with peculiar advantages.

One must not exaggerate either the glories of the past or the horrors of the present. The prewar universities employed more than enough lazy, uninterested, or incompetent teachers. Not everyone had a first-rate mind or was prepared to exert himself. In the contemporary university, one finds many admirable young people, devoted to their profession, exceptionally able, hard working, conscientious, excellently trained, and possessed of the imagination and the enthusiasm without which training is useless. Their skills can make me feel very humble. By agitating, too, they have sometimes remedied what were real defects in university organization or university teaching.

It would be widely agreed, however, that at a time when brilliant young people are quite unable to find employment as scientists or scholars, our universities are clogged to an unprecedented extent with that sort of person who is most dangerous to university life: the second-rate mind, intellectually dreary, arrogant, cloaking incompetence in empty technicalities or rhetorical verbiage. This is especially so in subjects that have recently expanded with disproportionate rapidity. The old-fashioned lazy teacher was at least readily detectable. The new-style second-rate professional, concealing his weaknesses in jargon or technicalities, attracts his fellows and, in their company, constitutes a formidable barrier to the intellectual flow of university life. But mediocrity is not a necessary consequence of opening the university to wider groups of students. Had the ideal of equal opportunity been conjoined with more rigorous conditions of entry, the outcome could have been very different. But the universities did not earlier argue that they simply could not find staff of a sufficiently high quality to expand at the rate asked of them. Some universities, of course, were mandated by their governments to rapidly increase in size; they had no choice. But universities in other countries could have protested.

The outcome was worst in countries, like Germany, that had no previous experience of mass education; denied the authority to select students, these universities were greatly expanded in size and were particularly subject to doctrinaire demands for equality, not only by students but also by legislators, without any regard either to the resources available or the labor market for graduating students. As a result the students were doubly deceived.

They did not get the university education they hoped for. Rather, like tourists who flock in their thousands to some beach reputed to be peaceful and quiet, their very presence in such numbers destroyed what they sought. And it caused to vanish, too, the careers they had so fondly, and so naturally, expected. If they are profoundly disappointed and discontented, to a degree that may turn out to be much more serious for democracy than the youth movements of the sixties, we ought not to be surprised. The fanatical egalitarianism of that period (a fanaticism that waved aside all talk of consequences as distinct from principles—the radical youth were in this respect true puritans—on the ground that consequences were important only to those who lack passions, to mediocrities, to time-servers) combined with the opportunism of politicians and the weakness of academics to produce our present plight, in which universities, in many countries, stand unprecedentedly low in public esteem.

THE EGALITARIAN IMPULSE INSATIABLE

Our story is still not complete, at least for some countries. Once it was generally assumed that to produce equality of opportunity required only financial support. And this in some measure worked, in that more young people were able to attend university, even if not always the university they had read about or hoped for. But once aroused, the egalitarian impulse was insatiable. It was quite correctly pointed out that lack of money was by no means the only barrier to university entrance or to success within its walls. A student might be unable to compete because he had uneducated parents, or came from a broken home, had been to a poor school or belonged to a disadvantaged social group. The list, indeed, was endless, once this particular line of argument was opened. What was now to be done?

One response, especially in the United States, was reverse discrimination or, as it is euphemistically described, "affirmative action." In defiance of the principle of civil justice that generated the movement for equal opportunity, applicants for university entrance or for selection to university posts could properly be preferred, it was now argued, because they were women, or black, or handicapped, or were members of whatever other social group had the power and the resources to force itself upon the public attention, even if their formal qualifications were inferior. Few individuals were affected, but the effect on university morale was, and is, considerable. Another response, fortunately more often proposed than implemented, was to open the universities to everyone, whatever his qualifications. Where that was impossible, it was seriously suggested that university entrants should be selected by means of a lottery, a procedure that was also advocated as a substitute for university examinations. The goal of not excluding anyone on the grounds of inferior abilities was sometimes approached, especially but not uniquely in the United States, by reducing examination standards to a point at which they became—like referees' statements nowadays—completely meaningless. One cannot but be struck by how little attention was paid by the advocates of such policies to their effect on the quality of the university's work. It was as if quality simply did not matter; it did not matter what sort of education students received, provided only that they could say that they had obtained a degree.

EQUALITY OF OUTCOME: COSMIC JUSTICE

This result was inevitable, an inexorable consequence of the logic of the situation. The university is in no position, nobody is in any position, to remove all sources of inequality. Of course, one can pretend that people are equal when they are not by changing the rules, lowering the standards. Equality of opportunity thus gradually modulates into equality of outcome, equality of results. Implicit in this particular maneuver is a principle of cosmic justice, the principle that since the universe would be an unfair place if people differed in talent, as distinct from differing in respect to their environmental circumstances, it follows that they could not so differ. It is thus quite improper for their university results to make it appear as if they did. The reply that it is unfair to the community at large to pretend that all students have reached the same standard when they have in fact reached quite different standards is then dismissed as gross utilitarianism, an abject surrender to commercial values.

But why single out the university as the place where we should pretend that people have reached the same level who have conspicuously not done so? Why is it *there* that the rules are to be changed, the standards degraded, rather than, let us say, on the sporting fields? For we could all win the marathon race if *winning* were redefined as putting one foot forward—and the seriously handicapped were granted the additional privilege of having only to *wish* to do so. Of course, any such new rules abolish the whole point of marathon races. I simply have to reconcile myself to the fact that I am not as good as other people as a sportsman, a singer, a painter, a carpenter. And that may be partly, for all I know, the result of my upbringing. But I do not therefore demand that I be given the right to take part in the Olympic Games, to sing at La Scala, to join the carpenter's union.

When universities are singled out, one can only conclude regretfully either that legislators—if the singling out is the result of legislation—do not believe that what happens within universities is of any real importance or that academics are too weak-spirited to resist because they do not believe in the real value and importance of intellectual endeavor. Indeed, the public regards marathon running as important in a sense in which science and scholarship are not. Consider: when the Australian government demanded that athletes should not go to the Olympics in Moscow, there was considerable public opposition and agitation. A parallel demand that scientists should sever their contacts with Soviet scientists created no public stir whatsoever; universities protested into the thin air of total indifference.

And no one would for a moment propose that the members of our football teams be chosen by lottery, or that every game end in a draw, or that half of the team members be women.

There is, to be sure, one argument against my analogy that must be taken seriously: competition is intrinsic to sport, whereas it is not intrinsic, is indeed wholly alien to, culture. As a protest against the extremely competitive atmosphere now prevalent in some areas of our culture, with such consequences as that scholars and scientists will not communicate with one another lest their ideas be "stolen," this line of reasoning does not entirely lack force. However, in certain fundamental ways science and scholarship are, and ought to be, as competitive as sport. One ought to constantly strive to improve on what others have done. Merely to write another book without trying to better someone else's book is simply to waste paper.

Fortunately, most countries have stopped short of the bizarre positions I have described. Some individual departments in the humanities and the social sciences have surrendered to doctrinaire egalitarianism, but other departments have stood firm—or as firm as legislators have permitted in their new-found zeal to thrust upon universities the task of compensating for all previous, and subsequent, inequalities. As originally interpreted, I submit, equality of opportunity does no harm to the university—quite the contrary, when it opens up the university to blacks, women, and the religious or politically unorthodox. The provision of scholarships has damaged the university, or so I hold, only when it proceeds at too rapid a pace. But the failure of legislators and academics alike to look with even a minimum degree of consideration at the inevitable consequences of rapid expansion reflects very badly on both of them.

PARTICIPATORY EQUALITY

Let me begin, once more, in an anecdotal manner. As a young lecturer in Sydney, I was relatively lucky. Mine was a university in which there were few hierarchal distinctions at the personal level, in which, over lunch, young lecturers, professors, and university officials talked freely to one another, across departmental barriers and within departments. But at the organizational level the situation was very different; I resented not being a member of the faculty and resented it rather more, if anything, when I was permitted to attend but to speak only when spoken to. Later, in 1937, it was argued that students should be represented on the supreme governing body of the university. I then argued in favor of the scheme, which was indeed accepted.

I am not prepared to grant that the resentment I felt as a lecturer was unjustified, nor that my enthusiasm for the idea of a student senator was a youthful folly. One must, however, distinguish two views: (1) that the older inequalities in status needed to be reduced; and (2) that there should be no difference in rights to participate, at the level of government, between any persons employed by the university or studying within it. The second position, which has been carried to its extreme point in the universities of northern Europe, can fairly be described as doctrinaire. It does not begin by asking what are the advantages, for university life, in lessening inequalities. It begins, rather, from the assumption that every inequality must be removed, at whatever cost. The only admissible assumption, however, is the much weaker thesis: that where a remediable inequality exists, grounds must be given for not remedying it. What form might such grounds take in the present instance?

One can scarcely deny that every person connected with the university, whether as gardener, student, lecturer, professor, or administrative officer has interests, interests the university ought to take into account in its decisions. Furthermore, these interests can easily be overlooked unless they are in some measure formally represented. But students, nonacademic staff, and academic staff do not stand in precisely the same relation to the university's special concern—the advancement and communication of knowledge. Consider first the nonacademic staff. To them, or at least to the majority of them, the university is simply an employer. (There are special categories, like librarians, whose position would have to be separately considered.) They may need to be represented on bodies concerned with conditions of employment, even at the highest budgetary level; at the very least, they should be in a position to make representations to such bodies. Most of the university's affairs, however, are simply not their business. The university is obliged, by its very nature, to take an academic view; gardener and lecturer are not, in its eyes, of equal concern. It should not treat gardeners badly, but nor should it permit them to determine its policy. A university can get along without gardeners, but not without academics.

Now students are for the most part interested in the university as a place where knowledge is communicated. Instruction is clearly part of the university's function, and when it is neglected out of incompetence, laziness, lack of interest, singular devotion to external concerns, or even the undue subordination of teaching to research, students are entitled to protest. Something more than their personal interests is then at stake: the function of the university is involved. And students may be able to make effective representations on such points, to ensure that their rightful needs are not overlooked, only if they are formally represented on some university committees. I do not believe that universities suffer in any way from such limited representation, except when individual representatives are incapable of submitting to the discipline of fruitful discussion.

However, students' commitment to university life is, or ought to be, short-lived. Their experience, too, is very limited. They are likely to be impressed by superficial brilliance, to suppose that they are being well taught when in fact they are being very badly taught, to be caught up by passing fashions, to be attracted to the fanatic or to anyone who promises simple solutions to the problems that properly worry them. All these considerations suggest that their judgment ought not to be allotted the same weight as the judgment of academics, especially in respect to the selection of teachers.

THE PECULIAR TASK OF THE UNIVERSITY

How, I was once asked by a German student, could I justify "one man, one vote" in a political democracy but not in a university? The answer is that a society, unlike a university, does not have a single interest, at least in democratic theory. By giving each person a vote, a democracy enables every interest in the community to be voiced, and no substantial interest is neglected. A university is in a quite different position. It has a *special* interest, the communication and advancement of knowledge. In the language of Plato, it is the best and the indispensable instrument for that purpose. It has a peculiar task to undertake, a task that its traditions and constitution enable it to undertake, a task no one else can so successfully undertake should it falter. Its manner of government should reflect the special character of its task. Arbitrarily to decide, in a conveniently bureaucratic way, that the different elements in the university should be equally represented in the government of the university, as they are in many northern European countries, is to appeal to arithmetical equalities where what is called for, rather, is a functional analysis. The university is not, and should not be treated as if it were, a state in miniature.

I have said nothing, so far, about the case from which I began in telling my own story, the junior member of staff. Unlike the student, unlike the nonacademic member of staff, he is, or ought to be, devoted to the aims of the university; his life consists, or ought to consist, in furthering them. He certainly ought to be able to participate in discussions that may affect his future life as a scholar and scientist. Yet a cautionary note is needed. A young lecturer may be, perhaps ought to be, too deeply wedded to the professional interests of his discipline to recognize that a university has many mansions and that their interests have to be reconciled. This can limit his usefulness as a member of administrative bodies. And although to say this smacks of paternalism, it is, I think, particularly important that young members of staff, in what should be the most productive years of their lives, not be wholly immersed in a network of meetings that can so easily become an excuse for not working.

Just how, in detail, these various considerations can be reconciled, I shall not attempt to say. Let me only put my point thus: the principle that all members of the university whose central concern is the transmission and advancement of knowledge should be represented in the committees of the university does not automatically produce an answer to the question *how far* they should be represented, or on what committees. Once more, a fanatical devotion to equality, a devotion that refuses to take into account the effects of its implementation on the life of the university, can in the end only be damaging to that life. For a government to complain, as I have heard some European government officials complain, that the universities are no longer the center of a great culture when those very same governments have imposed legislation on the universities which destroys all chance of their exercising that role is to be forcibly reminded of Pontius Pilate.

EQUALITY OF ESTEEM AND RESPECT

An equality of esteem is suggested by those who would have the opinions of the student regarded with the same seriousness as the opinions of his teachers, so that, ideally, there will be no teaching but a coming together to exchange opinions, in which each will count as equal. Two arguments are invoked in defense of this ideal. One is that the student is a person and must be respected as such. This we can freely grant, in that a university class is not the place for hectoring, sarcasm, refusing to listen, dogmatic talking-down, or condescension, whether on the part of the professors or on the part of the students. That, unfortunately, needs to be said. The second line of argument is very different and is in essence skeptical. One opinion, it is said, is as good as another. However little a student has read, studied, and observed, however narrow his training and experience, his opinion is worth as much as that of the most learned academic. There are no differences in the quality of activities, either. Bentham's famous dictum, to modernize it slightly, that playing a pinball machine is as good as poetry, quantity of pleasure being equal, is accepted as gospel. (I am setting aside those who argue that playing a pinball machine is actually better, as a proletarian art form, than suspiciously elitist poetry.) So equality of esteem is deduced from the equality in value of all opinions, and from the equal value of all activities and the satisfaction to which they give rise.

Let us look more closely at these arguments. Does respect for persons entail regarding them as equally worthy of esteem? The word *respect* may suggest this; we usually speak of respecting persons only when we esteem them. But in this sense of the word, we do not respect everybody, let alone respect them to the same degree. *Respect*, in this sense, implies discrimination; *esteem* consists in regarding one person more highly than another.

Furthermore, even when we esteem a person very highly, we do not, in academic life, esteem all his opinions, all his activities, to an equal degree. In reviewing his books, in examining his theories, we show our respect by the amount of critical attention we devote to them, not by murmuring that he is entitled to hold a view since that is what he thinks. We certainly would not show our respect for our students by abstaining from criticizing them. Quite the contrary. To respect their opinions, in academic life, is not merely to admit their right to have opinions. Rather, we explain to them that their argument is *not* worthy of esteem if it is badly thought out, is the product of capricious consideration, or is unsupported by appropriate evidence or argument.

SKEPTICISM REJECTED

At this point, however, the second, skeptical, line of argument is often brought to bear. If there is no such thing as evidence, if every assertion is equally warranted, then certainly, every opinion ought to have parity of esteem. But why should we accept this skeptical dogma? It is a view wholly inappropriate to the professional faculties and the sciences. Its home is in literary studies, in social and political theory, in philosophy, and then only when the study of literature is entirely divorced from scholarship and careful reading, political and social theory from empirical research, philosophy from close argument. For only in such stunted cases is it impossible to find good grounds for counting some opinions, but not others, as worthy of esteem. Indeed, there one opinion is of equal worth to another—equally worthless, that is. But this conclusion, generated in such enfeebled studies, must not be allowed to infect areas in which it has no genuine application, as skepticism about science or skepticism about scholarship.[2]

My entire argument, of course, depends on rejecting this kind of skepticism. My premise is that the transmission and advancement of knowledge is both possible and desirable. If this assumption cannot be made, then there is no point in having universities; one might as well transform them into youth clubs, which would be cheaper to run and surrounded by less hypocrisy. Unless one can intelligibly talk in terms of the advancement of knowledge; unless there are some criteria of good science, philosophy, scholarship, and medicine; unless there are people who are especially worth listening to, learning from, then a university is an expensive luxury, which no community can be called upon to support; it would have been better left to the gilded youth as a playground.

THINKING AND THE IDEA OF THE UNIVERSITY

A university is a place for thinking, for thinking seriously in a fashion at once original and disciplined. This purpose does not preclude it, of course, from also being a place where the young can enjoy themselves and find out about the world, other people, themselves. University thinking, too, has to go to the roots of things, to be radical in the etymological sense of the word. At the same time it rests on certain presumptions, and a person who does not share them has no more place in a university than an atheist has in church or a convert to liberalism in a Communist Party. Although these presumptions are much more general than the doctrines of a particular religious or political creed, they do exist, and the simplest of them is that there is such a thing as being learned. The doctrine of equality of esteem tries to destroy this assumption and is thus incompatible with the idea of the university.

2. See my *Science and Its Critics* (New Brunswick, N.J.: Rutgers University Press, 1978).

EQUALITY OF TREATMENT

Now we must consider equality of treatment. Should all students be treated alike? In many countries, they are not. Consider the situation in Great Britain. If a student goes to Oxford or Cambridge he receives individual tuition that is unavailable elsewhere. In Sydney a very sharp distinction used to be drawn between pass and honors students in a particular subject. A great deal more was demanded of honors students, in both attendance at classes and the writing of essays; their level of instruction was very different. They were certainly privileged in being members of small classes, in having much more personal teaching than the bulk of the students. If to a lesser degree, this distinction is still maintained. In the United States, the distinction between undergraduate and graduate work serves the same purpose. Furthermore, universities differ in quality. Some are very selective indeed, and, so far as undergraduate classes go, extremely small. In France, the *grandes écoles* have an aristocratic distinction. In contrast, within the new German mass universities there is no mechanism for singling out the brightest and best students.

Is this separation out of students, whether into highly selective universities or into selected groups within the universities, a gross affront to the spirit of equality? Obviously, it can create problems. In America one sometimes hears the complaint, although by no means in every university, that undergraduates are left to the uninterested mercies of young assistants preoccupied with the completion of their theses, that the students have no contact with the great scientists, the great scholars.

In other American universities, however, as in Australia, this does not happen. The convention has been, indeed, that the outstanding scholars shall devote part of their time to teaching relatively elementary classes. That, I think, is right. Those who go to a university to learn are entitled to have some contact, even if it be limited, with the ablest of its inquirers. From the university's point of view, it is in this way that students are most likely to acquire enthusiasm for their subject—provided the teaching is not merely a desultory exercise. From the students' point of view, they are otherwise being cheated.

RELEVANT REASONS AND DIFFERENCES

With that reservation, I should still wish to argue there is no good reason for attempting to make all universities equal and no good reason why, within the university, all students should be treated in the same way. There are relevant differences among students, differences of which the university may properly take account. Some will wish or will be able to participate much more fully than other students in the academic life of the university. Not every student is, or wishes to be, a scholar. And the attempt to make all universities equal will be impossible so long as there are great teachers, geniuses, traditions, more pleasant and less pleasant locations. Equality could be achieved only by demanding that the universities should dismiss any teachers who rise above the level of mediocrity, or by insisting that the poorer students go to the universities where the good teachers are. But countries that do their best to ensure that excellent teachers and students are unable to seek out one another are doing fatal damage to science and scholarship.

TEACHING AND RESEARCH

Another possibility is to remove the best scholars and scientists to research institutes, so that they will not by their presence affect the equality among universities. This is far from an imaginary danger. For the last quarter of a century I have been a member of such an institution, my contact with students restricted to a few exceptionally able young people writing theses for the doctorate. I do not apologize for that fact and do not regret it. The sort of work I have been doing is, for the most part, unsuitable for ordinary university courses, and it is very demanding of time and requires extensive international contacts—none of these compatible with the manifold duties of a professor in an Australian university. Fortunately, our research schools have not taken from the universities all their best people or even a considerable proportion of them. Nevertheless, it is not an example I should wish to be universalized. But there are signs that in northern Europe, as an attempt to repair the damages of egalitarianism, it may come to be universalized. The serious work will be done only in what are substantially refuges from the university.

THE DISTINCTIVE NATURE OF THE UNIVERSITY

One of the most obnoxious of the many obnoxious concepts the last decades have generated is *tertiary education*, taken to include not only universities but any form of post–secondary school education, from trade courses to business schools. It is obnoxious for two reasons, first as disregarding the distinctive nature of universities, their contribution to the advancement of knowledge; second, in assuming that university education is essentially similar to, although subsequent in time to, primary and secondary education. This development is particularly disastrous in countries whose high schools are by no means the equivalent of the older French *lycée* or German *Gymnasium*. It suggests that the university is *essentially* a place for teaching, that university instructors should devote all their time to teaching and are to be judged solely by their success in it. (In Sweden, this doctrine has been carried so far that a special class of university teachers are expected to devote their time entirely to teaching.) One might attribute these developments simply to a reaction to the fact that teaching has often been unduly neglected in universities. But, more accurately, they represent a general process of leveling within the educational system. Their effect on the university, as an institution devoted to both teaching and research, can only be calamitous. I do not believe that only those who are actively engaged in research can teach. There are good teachers who read widely but do not feel any impulse to do research; Oxford and Cambridge have always contained many such teachers. One may well wish that there were more of them, confronted as we sometimes are by insignificant research conducted only for the sake of creating a reputation for doing research. Nevertheless—a much weaker thesis—students do need to have *some* contact with men and women who are genuinely devoted to research, who are working on the frontiers of knowledge.

HUMAN INEQUALITY, ACADEMIC EXCELLENCE, AND INTELLECTUAL PROGRESS

A broader question, at what point abler students should be separated out for special treatment, is not so easily settled. The current tendency is to postpone that separation, in the supposed interests of equality. In England the only educational issue that seems to arouse any real feeling turns around the question of whether selective grammar schools should be turned into comprehensive schools, with the odd complication that many of those who say most strongly that they should be continue to send their own children to private schools. In Australia, the selective high schools have come under attack, with the same consequence of strengthening the position of the private schools. But the partial destruction of the grammar schools in England is already having the effect of making it harder for children of working-class origin to enter Oxford and Cambridge. Yet none of these facts is likely to deter the egalitarian. The solution, he will argue, is to abolish the private schools. He is quiet indifferent to the effects his policies are likely to have on English cultural life. The egalitarian, as I said, is a man of principle, for whom consequences are irrelevant.

In an ideal world everyone would have contact with scientists and scholars of real excellence. Television, the nearest one can come to this, shows great men, but only as pundits rather than as engaged in inquiry. There is no substitute for working with or under such people. Television cannot be a substitute for daily discussion, for sudden inspiration arising out of casual conversation. Unequal treatment, unequal access to great scientists and scholars, is, I believe, in this sense a necessary condition of intellectual progress, unequal treatment in centers of excellence. But in university classes that influence can be somewhat more broadly expanded.

I have tried to suggest that the attempt to secure absolute equality in all respects—an attempt which Aristotle long ago saw as the besetting vice of democracies—can be destructive of excellence. Different countries, working in different traditions, with different institutional patterns, will have to cope with the resulting problem in their own ways. But unless they see it as a problem, unless they are prepared to deviate from doctrinal egalitarianism in the interests of excellence, our universities cannot but rapidly decline.

Our story illustrates a very familiar caution, The road to Hell is paved with good intentions. It is a story without villains, a story about the damage idealists can do, when an ideal is fanatically interpreted as necessary and sufficient for salvation. To which I should add Virgil's apothegm: "It is easy to descend into Hell, but to arise again, that is the really difficult labor!"

PART II

The Pursuit of Truth

6

Research and Teaching in the Universities

JOSEPH BEN-DAVID

The research university based on the principle of the unity of research and teaching is threatened today. In the 1960s universities considered as their main task enlarging their advanced research and training facilities, in response to the rapidly growing demand for training of students, and increasing funds available for research. By the mid-1970s the situation had changed dramatically: universities were hard put to maintain their research facilities and rarely dreamed of expanding them. They now concentrate their efforts on maintaining enrollments, and they are willing to cater to practically any demand for any kind of study, without paying much attention to its scientific content.

Although, in principle, universities are still committed to research, they feel they can do little about it and leave responsibility for the advance of research to governments and individual initiative. Universities' revenues and operations, which depend usually on the numbers and kinds of students, are today less conducive to research, for students are much less interested in research than were their predecessors fifteen or twenty years ago. Catering to the demands of these new students, universities find it increasingly difficult to treat teaching and research as organically related functions, and so the two tend to drift apart.

I am indebted to Bruce L. R. Smith, Edward Shils, and John Wilson for their comments on the first draft of this chapter, and to the Spencer Foundation for support of my research.

Joseph Ben-David is George Wise Professor of Sociology at the Hebrew University in Jerusalem and Professor of Education and Sociology at the University of Chicago.

The question I want to address is whether this drifting apart of teaching and research is likely to become a long-term trend that may result in the migration of basic research to nonuniversity institutions, or even in the absolute decline of research. Or is this trend a temporary and reversible phenomenon? To answer this question, I must first describe in some detail recent changes in higher education.

RECENT CHANGES IN HIGHER EDUCATION

Student enrollments continued to increase during the 1970s, but at a slower rate than in the 1960s, and in some countries they have declined temporarily. However, if all postsecondary and not only university education is considered, growth has been much greater. In the United States total postsecondary enrollments grew by 31 percent between 1970 and 1976. But in degree-granting institutions the increase was only 16 percent, compared with 69 percent in two-year institutions. Another trend harmful to research is the redistribution of students among disciplines. In the United States between 1970 and 1976 graduate enrollments declined in engineering (12 percent), arts and letters (14 percent), mathematics (34 percent), natural sciences (9 percent), and social sciences (12 percent). The percentages of students electing science declined also in Austria, Belgium, Finland, Italy, and Britain between the mid-sixties and the mid-seventies, but there were small increases in Germany and Sweden. Student demand shifted to less research-intensive subjects, such as business and management studies, communications, public administration, the law and health professions, of which only medicine is research oriented. Between 37 and 71 percent of all American institutions added to their curriculums different kinds of professional or vocational programs and courses. But only between 12 and 37 percent added programs and courses in the arts and sciences—the highest percentage representing courses in fine arts—from 1970 to 1978.[1]

Indications are for a change for the worse in the qualifications of entering students. In the United States average scores of high school seniors taking the College Board Scholastic Aptitude Test (SAT) declined from 460 to 429 on the verbal, and from 488 to 468 on the mathematical part between the academic years 1969–70 and 1977–78. In fact, 85 percent of American colleges and universities now offer compensatory or remedial programs. That these signs of decline in the quality of students are not reflected in

1. Data are from the following sources: on two- and four-year U.S. institutions, Carnegie Council on Policy Studies in Higher Education, *A Classification of Institutions of Higher Education*, rev. ed. (Berkeley: University of California Press, 1976), pp. xi–xiv; on U.S. graduate enrollments, Verne A. Stadtman, *Academic Adaptations: Higher Education Prepares for the 1980s and 1990s* (San Francisco: Jossey-Bass, 1980), p. 38; on European enrollments, Organization for Economic Cooperation and Development (OECD), Committee for Scientific and Technological Policy, "The Function of Scientific Research in the Universities," mimeographed (Paris: OECD, 1980), p. 57; on additions to American curriculums, Stadtman, *Academic Adaptations*, p. 142.

grades, which have somewhat improved, can only be interpreted as a compromise of standards. Furthermore, American institutions of higher education of all kinds are trying to recruit dropouts, and evening, adult, and transfer students, as well as several other categories unlikely to go into research. This situation contrasts sharply with that of the late forties to the sixties, when qualifications of entering students constantly improved. The number of American colleges joining the College Entrance Examination Board rose from 79 in 1948 to 707 in 1966. The minimum SAT scores for entrance rose everywhere, in some institutions by as much as one hundred points from 1958 to 1965.[2]

Concern about students uninterested in research extends to Europe as well. Some institutions of higher education have even abandoned research. The most conspicuous move in this direction occurred in Sweden, when a 1977 "reform" transformed the universities partially into community service institutions that cater to all the educational wants of the adult population in their regions, while continuing to teach undergraduates and graduates along more or less traditional lines. Adult learners and most of the undergraduates are taught by lecturers who are not expected to do research and hence are required to teach far longer hours than docents and professors, who are expected to be engaged in research.

The Swedish development does not differ much from the situation in the United States. In both countries higher education in the seventies created new educational opportunities for new types of students, many of whom take sub–college level courses; undergraduate enrollments in vocational fields in which there is no unity of teaching and research have grown; and the recruitment of teachers who are not researchers into institutions of higher and postsecondary education has increased. The difference is that in the United States these new functions have been performed partly by community colleges, partly by specialized professional schools, and only to a smaller extent by colleges and universities, which have begun to place more emphasis on professional training and nontraditional students. In Sweden the new functions have resulted in drastic changes in university structure.

None of these developments is quite new. American universities have been pioneers in the introduction of subjects with little scientific basis, but in the past the universities insisted on subsequently creating a scientific basis for the new subjects through the initiation and encouragement of research.[3] This emphasis on research was characteristic of American univer-

2. On compromise of standards, see Stadtman, *Academic Adaptations*, pp. 21–22; on recruitment, see Stadtman, pp. 128–29. Data on SAT scores from Gerald Grant and David Riesman, *The Perpetual Dream: Reform and Experiment in the American College* (Chicago: University of Chicago Press, 1978), pp. 198–99, 406–7.

3. See Eric Ashby, *Any Person, Any Study: An Essay on Higher Education in the United States* (New York: McGraw-Hill, 1971); Abraham Flexner, *Universities: American, English, and German* (New York: Columbia University Teachers College Press, 1967); and Joseph Ben-David, *Trends in American Higher Education* (Chicago: University of Chicago Press, 1981).

sities until the late 1960s, but it has considerably weakened since then—a
new development.

WEAKENING COMMITMENT TO RESEARCH

The weakening commitment to research is also evident in university finance. Expenditures for research grew faster than enrollments in the sixties,
but barely kept pace in the seventies. Current expenditure per investigator
remained more or less constant, or has declined between 1970 and 1976 in
the majority of countries belonging to the Organization for Economic
Cooperation and Development (OECD). But capital spending per research
scientist declined considerably in all during the same period.[4] These data
confirm the impression gained from student statistics. In contrast to the
sixties, when research led the development of higher education, it now
trails growth in student numbers. The stagnation or decline of spending
per researcher permits no leeway for the rising costs of books and increasingly sophisticated equipment. Resources for innovation that is the
lifeblood of research have seriously declined.

The picture is even bleaker if one examines the use of research moneys
that come from the universities' own resources. These are practically all
expended on staff salaries, which means that universities have abandoned
maintenance and improvement of laboratories, libraries, and other facilities. This trend began in the sixties when universities—owing to
the abundance of outside research funding—became accustomed to defray
research-related expenses from those funds rather than from the regular
budget. In consequence, responsibility for the allocation of research funds
and maintenance of research facilities has been shifting from universities to
research councils and other public or private agencies.[5]

However, during the sixties these developments did not diminish the
feeling that research was a most important university task. Creation of
structures for research and graduate education were among the principal
concerns of university administrators. They used outside money because it
was available, not because they thought research peripheral to the teaching
mission of the university. The insidious and unintended consequences of
this practice became visible in the seventies when external funding declined. By then universities found themselves ill equipped to cope with the
problem and accepted curtailment of research as inevitable. They did little
to find new institutional sources of support and concentrated their effort on
educational expansion without much concern for the scientific implications
of the new programs and kinds of students. It seems as though some

4. Data from the following sources: on expenditures in 1960s and 1970s, OECD,
"Scientific Research," p. 13; on expenditure per investigator, D. Wolfe "Forces Affecting the
Research Role of the Universities," in *The State of Academic Science: Background Papers*, ed.
Bruce L. R. Smith and J. J. Karlesky (New York: Change Magazine Press, 1978), pp. 14,
18, 20, 22.
5. Wolfe, "Forces," p. 13–24.

universities and systems of higher education deserted the ideal of the unity of teaching and research, despite their continuing lip service to it.

SEPARATION: A LONG-TERM TREND?

Let us return to the question of whether this separation of research from teaching is likely to be a long-term trend that might lead, perhaps, to their total separation. We must now inquire into the causes of the decline in support for university research. The immediate cause seems to have been the reduced demand for new academic staff in higher education. Between 1966 and 1969 some 102,000 new academic positions were created in the United States, and American universities granted 88,131 doctorates. But between 1976 and 1978 only 28,000 new academic positions appeared, while 109,400 new doctorates were granted; that is, there were more than four times as many graduates as new positions. Probably a similar decline in demand explains the strange phenomenon in Sweden of an increase in doctoral candidates combined with a sharp decrease in doctoral degrees awarded between 1969–70 and 1977–78.[6] Facilities for graduate training and research were expanded in both countries, and in most others, during the sixties to meet the demand for researchers, of which a large and highly valued fraction was for new university teachers. This demand fell sharply during the seventies, partly because the greatly expanded universities could easily assimilate a large part of the increasing undergraduate enrollment, and partly because the new enrollment consisted mainly of nontraditional students, unlikely to become candidates for research degrees, and often interested in remedial, vocational, and other subacademic—or, in the best case, professional—programs. Needless to say, these programs provide little opportunity for basic research.

Of course, universities had not expanded solely to meet the demand for more university teachers. There was also increasing demand for qualified graduates outside the academic system, and this demand is worth analyzing. No evidence exists that, prior to the expansion of the fifties and the sixties, there was much demand for liberal arts graduates, or for researchers in the basic arts and sciences. In the fifties and sixties industry and government probably could have done with a much smaller crop of graduates in most of these fields. Indeed, decisions to found new universities, to encourage high school graduates to continue their studies, and to increase support for basic research were taken on the basis of circumstantial and incomplete evidence. This included the balance of international trade in technological knowledge, comparisons of competitiveness of science-based with non–science-based industries, and analysis of the sources of long-term growth of the American economy. It was understood that these analyses were in-

6. Data on American doctorates from Lionel S. Lewis, "Higher Education in the Lower Depths," *Contemporary Sociology* 9 (July 1980): 508; on Swedish doctorates, OECD, "Scientific Research," p. 12.

conclusive and did not demonstrate that investment in research always pays off.[7] Still the belief was that research would produce long-term benefits. Since Western economies were thriving in the sixties, and no serious shortages of anything existed, expectation of distant benefits seemed to warrant investing in science. Governments did not have to decide to shift limited resources to research, only how best to allocate surplus funds for the improvement of society's future. The purposes competing with research and education were a variety of welfare programs, which received a considerable share of the surplus.

The availability of financial support, in addition to directly stimulating the growth of higher education and research, also fostered the introduction of more highly educated researchers into industry and government. Educational upgrading of the professional, administrative, clerical, and technical workforce was general,[8] and many firms and government departments initiated research and development activities.

Evidently, this scientific subsidy could not grow at a pace faster than the population and economy for more than a short time. By the late sixties rapid growth came to an end, first in the United States, where it all began, and subsequently in other countries. Although the slowdown of academic expansion was inevitable on purely demographic grounds, its effects were aggravated by the economic stagnation of the seventies. Surplus funds seeking worthwhile public objectives disappeared. Governments were no longer worried about creation of centers of excellence in scientific research, or about finding and financing research in fields that promised fundamental breakthroughs. Rather they were concerned with paying their oil bills and fighting unemployment and inflation. Higher education and research now had to compete with vital everyday needs. Furthermore, research—by the mid-sixties quite a sizable operation—was suspected of serving special interests. Governments and corporations became reluctant to finance projects that did not have foreseeable pay-offs, and they demanded economies and strict accounting for every penny spent on research. Universities had to adjust to a market in which there was no new demand for training and

7. Such analyses include: E. F. Denison, "Measuring the Contribution of Education (and the Residual) to Economic Growth," in *Study Group in the Economics of Education: The Residual Factor and Economic Growth* (Paris: OECD, 1964); G. Freeman and A. Young, *The Research and Development Effort in Western Europe, North America, and the Soviet Union: An Experimental International Comparison of Research Expenditures and Manpower in 1962* (Paris: OECD, 1965); W. Gruber, D. Mehta, and R. Vernon, "The R and D Factor in International Trade and International Investments of United States Industries, *Journal of Political Economy* 75 (1967): 20–37; D. B. Keesing, "The Impact of Research and Development on United States Trade," *Journal of Political Economy* 75 (1967): 38–48. Reviews of the inconclusiveness of these analyses include Joseph Ben-David, *Fundamental Research and the Universities: Some Comments on International Differences* (Paris: OECD, 1968); and Alvin M. Weinberg, *Reflections on Big Science* (Cambridge: Massachusetts Institute of Technology Press, 1967).

8. M. Ushiogi, "A Comparative Study of the Occupational Structure of University Graduates," *Developing Economist* 9 (September 1971): 350–68.

research in basic fields. They were forced to explore the possibility of serving a new clientele, with constricted intellectual interests. They faced a new market in which short-term economic or other practical usefulness became an increasingly important criterion for curriculums and for the allocation of research money. Suddenly, the glamour disappeared from study and research in the basic fields.

STAGNATION OF ACADEMIC RESEARCH IS TEMPORARY

This analysis suggests that the stagnation of support for academic research during the seventies is not necessarily the beginning of a long-term decline. The events of the seventies seem primarily a reaction to accelerated growth, an adjustment to economic stringency. Our society has not become disillusioned with science; indeed surveys show continuing belief in the importance and potential utility of science, and general industrial and applied research. The only major problem attributed to science is pollution, but even here people trust science to find solutions. According to American surveys from 1976, 45 percent thought that pollution was created by science, but 56 percent held that science and technology could make major contributions to reducing pollution.[9]

Thus, fundamentally, the causes of present problems are two: the cyclical academic slowdown following accelerated growth was inevitable on the basis of demographic trends; and the effects of this slowdown were reinforced by international economic difficulties that precluded investment in the unpredictable future benefits that might derive from basic research. But this interpretation of the decline in university research as a cyclical phenomenon does not imply that all we should do is wait for the cycle to enter a new phase. Cycles do not always have predictable courses. While the present downturn is caused by predictable and predicted demographic and economic trends,[10] its end cannot be foreseen in the same way. For just about the time the deceleration began—first in the United States in 1966–1968—the situation was complicated by the worldwide outbreak of student disturbances, triggered mainly by American political and military failure in Vietnam. The disturbances were accompanied by the rise of ideologies hostile to science and the Westen cultural heritage.

Although these events are not intrinsically related to the fate of university research, they continue to have a profound effect on the prospect of cyclical upturn. Student unrest, particularly the assaults on research by some students and faculty, followed by the worldwide economic crisis of the 1970s, raised questions everywhere about the utility and rationale of basic

9. National Science Foundation, *Science Indicators 1976: Report of the National Science Board, 1977* (Washington, D.C.: U.S. Government Printing Office, 1977), pp. 176, 179. See also pp. 168–79 for survey results.

10. Derek J. De Solla Price, *Little Science, Big Science* (New York: Columbia University Press, 1963).

88   JOSEPH BEN-DAVID

research. The suitability of the university as the place for research also came
into doubt. Had there been no student outcry or economic malaise, European countries, in which higher educational enrollments during the sixties
did not exceed, and were in most cases well below, 20 percent of the age
group, and which invested only 1 to 2 percent of their gross national
product in research and development—compared to more than 3 percent in
the United States—could probably have continued to expand their university research to catch up with American standards. Similarly, university
research is now lagging in nations such as Germany and Japan, which had
supported research at a growing rate in the seventies.[11]

Too, the questioning of the legitimacy of basic science depressed the
morale of the scientific profession. Had the downturn in university research
in one country been offset by continued growth in others, as it once was, few
would have taken seriously those who now speak of the impending—and
well-deserved—doom of Western science. Everyone would have recognized
that the troubles were due to overexpansion and would have sought rational
ways to adjust to the new conditions. The international nature of the crisis,
however, lends credence to the prophets of scientific disaster. Thus even
people who have reservations about the denigration of science spend more
time debating the alleged sins of the universities than advancing the cause
of research.

To ward off these critics—most of whom come from the ranks of faculty
and students—and to satisfy a public alerted to charges of university waste
and eager for savings in a time of economic distress, so-called reforms were
legislated, which only added to the plight of the universities. In several
European countries laws provided for participation of students and nonacademic employees in decisions affecting university research. And in the
United States recipients of federal funds had to comply with new regulations concerning the preparation of proposals and reports, accounting for
time and effort, evidence of expenditure, and observance of so-called equal
opportunity criteria—all of which are costly, unproductive, and time consuming.[12] Instead of responding to scarcity with an increase of efficiency,
governments and universities adopted policies that render even more problematic the prospects for recovery.

PROSPECTS FOR RECOVERY

The prospects for recovery are not easy to assess. One can argue that there is
no ground for pessimism about the future of university research. The
slowing down of the growth of investment in science was, after all,
inescapable. Today's difficulties are only the consequences of the precipi-

11. National Science Foundation, *Science Indicators 1976: Report of the National Science
Board, 1978* (Washington, D.C.: U.S. Government Printing Office, 1979), p. 6.
12. Wolfe, "Forces"; Sanford A. Lakoff, "Accountability and the Research Universities,"
in *State of Academic Science.*

tate, and in many ways unwarranted, expansion of the late fifties and early sixties. Public support for science and the vitality of science-based industry—electronics, genetic engineering, and so on—are signs that sooner or later enthusiasm for university research will return. Deterioration of the university research environment and the obsolescence of laboratory equipment are, of course, serious matters. But one can take comfort that some universities and some outstanding university projects are doing well. This may indicate a new trend toward differentiation, in which some universities do advanced research in all fields, while others specialize or become mainly teaching institutions.[13]

This optimistic assessment is bolstered by the observation that universities have learned to live with the legacy of political disruption. The campuses are now quiet, and research is conducted undisturbed. One may contend that universities have adjusted to the new climate of sentiment and have returned more or less to normal. But although some adjustment had undoubtedly taken place, it remains to be seen whether this represents an injurious truce or promises a restoration of vitality and health.

Symptoms of permanent damage are not lacking. Regulatory burdens have been imposed under pressure for both students and faculty. And despite relative calm and absence of violence—by no means at all universities—an internal threat of political interference with freedom of research persists. In many a European, Australian, and Latin American university belief in some version of Marxism is almost obligatory in the social sciences and in some of the humanistic studies. The situation in the United States is better, but even there a degree of ideological pressure exists. While most social scientific research is ostensibly apolitical, nevertheless a strong bias toward Marxist-inspired themes is evident. Inequality is analyzed in conceptual frameworks that accept unquestioningly the Marxist meanings of *capitalism*, *imperialism*, and *exploitation*. There is also a fair amount of ritual reference to Marx and an etiquette of deference to him. Sometimes it seems that every social scientist, past and present, can be ignored or criticized, but not Karl Marx.

IDEOLOGICAL AND POLITICAL PRESSURES

The ideological pressure that prevails in European, Australian, and Latin American universities is reminiscent of the climate in continental Europe—outside the USSR—of the 1920s. Academic freedom seemed to obtain, and by and large research was conducted objectively, dispassionately, and frequently brilliantly. But an unwritten rule permitted professors and students of certain political persuasions to use lecture halls and the university as forums for ideological propaganda and political recruitment. Occasionally this license for the use of terror was abused. Certain political and religious doctrines were treated as beyond dispute. In sensitive fields—

13. Smith and Karlesky, *State of Academic Science.*

history, literature, and the social sciences—appointments were rarely made of those professing the "wrong" political views. This ideological license was granted to the parties of the Right, and the fascists greatly exploited it to their political advantage. Today it is the Left that benefits from license.

Some natural scientists and university administrators are not greatly worried by these developments. They hold research in social science and the humanities to be of doubtful validity anyway. Political compromise at the expense of these disciplines, they think, is a small price to pay for academic peace, which allows undisturbed research in the real or "hard" sciences.

This is an ill-informed and shortsighted attitude. Whatever one thinks of the logical and empirical standing of the social sciences, the opportunity to study and discuss social and political issues in an atmosphere of dispassionate tolerance and objectivity is crucial. If this opportunity is withheld at the university there is little hope for tolerance outside, in politics or in the streets.

Furthermore, the threat of political pressure is far from absent in the natural sciences. I do not take a stand on the issues involved. But the *means* used by some members of the universities against research they deem politically unacceptable or harmful, and against researchers, shows that there are people who will not refrain from coercion and terrorism. I have in mind recombinant DNA research, investigation of the genetic components of intelligence, and research related to the military. One is reminded again and again of Nazi and Bolshevik intrusions into biology and other fields of science, and their victimization of scientists with "undesirable" racial characteristics or ideological views.

FINANCIAL WORRIES

Last but not least, American universities, including some of the most prestigious, are facing formidable financial challenges. In medicine and several branches of other fields, especially physics, up-to-date research requires equipment and facilities that individual universities are unable to afford. They are increasingly less fit to compete with industrial laboratories and a small number of specialized research institutes. Financial difficulties also beset some relatively inexpensive fields—language and areas studies, for example—that have very few students, for universities allocate funds on the basis of enrollments.

These are the kinds of problems that European universities faced a long while ago. In the last decades of the nineteenth century, they debated how to accommodate scientific research that requires a lot of money and bureaucracy. They turned to governments and private benefactors and specialized research institutes were established. These institutes—Institut Pasteur in France; Physikalisch Technische Reichanstalt and the Kaiser Wilhelm (now Max Planck) Institute in Germany; and the British research councils—reduced the importance of universities as centers of research.

The only significant exceptions to this trend of separating research from teaching were the American universities. Their graduate schools could accommodate new fields and—by the standards of the times—large-scale research organizations, which Europeans saw as threatening to their traditions and organizational balance. The question is whether American universities will be willing and able to adhere to their institutional resolve. Can they serve as centers for all kinds of basic research and devise new forms of organization and cooperate for that purpose? They did so in the fifties and sixties for high-energy research. Or will they divest themselves of responsibility for research and, weakened by the legacy of internal conflict, follow the European path of abandoning certain fields to specialized research institutions?

THE FUTURE OF TEACHING AND RESEARCH

In the light of my analysis it is not easy to feel assured about the future of university-based research in the 1980s. A distinct possibility is that the separation of research from teaching will continue and accelerate. Of course, we would still have research and scientific advance, but the nature of research would probably change.

Pursuit of spontaneous basic research has been made possible by close ties between research and teaching. The location of advanced research in independent and competing universities, in each of which there has been a constant flow of new researchers, has served effectively to enforce high intellectual standards, to recognize originality, and to ensure the circulation of ideas to students, and through them to society at large. Severance of the connection between research and teaching would eliminate these highly desirable incentives to both intellectual and cultural vitality.

7

The Natural Sciences

SJOERD L. BONTING

To say anything of significance on so broad a topic it is necessary severely to limit the points to be considered. Although it would be desirable to discuss scientific research in the Communist countries and in developing nations, I shall confine myself to the West and in particular to western Europe. I want to examine the tremendous growth in scientific research during the 1960s and early 1970s and its consequences, considering promises fulfilled and unfulfilled, effects good and bad, societal and governmental reactions favorable and unfavorable, and scientists as heroes and villains. In addition, we must notice the recent radical changes in economic and social conditions in the West and their effect on scientific research in the universities.

ORGANIZATION AND FINANCE

A recent study by an official of the Netherlands government provides information on six representative western European countries—Belgium, Italy, the Netherlands, Norway, the United Kingdom, and Switzerland.[1] In these countries university research is almost completely financed by the government, both directly, through general university funding, and indirectly through research councils. By way of contrast to the United States, private foundations play a very minor role, funding only 2 percent or less of all university research. In these European nations the ministry of education is solely or largely responsible for university funding; although in the

Sjoerd L. Bonting is Professor of Biochemistry at the University of Nijmegen.

1. W. van Rossum, *The Organization and Financing of (Para)-University Research in Western Europe: A Comparative View* (The Hague: Netherlands Government Document, 1979).

United Kingdom a university grants committee receives, budgets, and disburses the money.

All these countries experienced a substantial growth from the 1950s to the 1970s in both manpower and money for scientific research in general and for university research in particular. Table 1 illustrates this development in the Netherlands. Responsible for this munificence were western European affluence, the large increase in student enrollment and consequent increase in staff, and probably defense spending. Table 2 shows that rapid growth was general throughout western Europe, although data for only the latter half of the period are available. When we add to this expenditure the many European joint research installations and ventures— such as the European Nuclear Physics Institute (CERN), Euratom, the European Space Agency (ESA), and the European Molecular Biology Labo-

TABLE I

Growth in manpower and funds
for science research in the Netherlands, 1959–1976

	Manpower (1000 man-years)			Funds ($ million)		
	1959	*1979*	*ratio*	*1959*	*1979*	*ratio*
Universities	3.6	9.2	2.6	28	376	13.4
Industry	18.4	27.2	1.5	146	1115	7.6
Government institutes[a]	8.0	12.8	1.6	55	472	8.6
Total	30.0	49.2	1.6	230	1963	8.6

[a]Government institutes include the intramural and extramural (university grants) expenditure of the national research council.

TABLE 2

Manpower and funds for university science research,
ratios of 1975 levels to 1967 levels

	manpower	*funds*
Belgium		4.2
Italy	1.7	3.9
the Netherlands	1.3	2.6
Norway	1.4	2.8
Switzerland	1.9	2.2
United Kingdom		2.4

TABLE 3
Distribution of science research expenditure
over university, governmental, and industrial laboratories
as percentage of total national research and development budget in 1975

	university	*government*	*industry*
Belgium	32	68	
Italy	17	23	60
the Netherlands	20	20	59
Norway	28	20	51
Switzerland	16	7	77
United Kingdom	8	28	64

TABLE 4
Percentage of science research funds
received by universities from national research councils,
1970–1975

	%
Belgium	25
the Netherlands	12
Norway	14
Switzerland	22
United Kingdom	59

ratory (EMBL)—we may conclude that European scientific research potential now equals that of the United States, although actual scientific productivity is another question.

Expenditures for scientific research in the universities as a percentage of total national expenditure for research and development varies considerably among European countries, as shown in Table 3. The lower percentages result from large expenditures for research in industrial laboratories and in nonuniversity government research institutes, as the last two columns of Table 3 indicate.

Table 4 shows a considerable range in the percentage of university research financed by national research councils as distinguished from general university funds. The lowest percentage is that of the Netherlands, namely,

TABLE 5

Expenditure for research in science and in humanities and social sciences
in the Netherlands

	1969			1976		
	Science[a]	Humanities and Social Sciences	Science	Science	Humanities and Social Sciences	Science
	($ in millions)		(% of total)	($ in millions)		(% of total)
personnel	82	23	78	237	87	73
material	30	4	88	78	13	86
operational costs	123	29	81	423	125	77
total	235	56	81	738	225	77
	(number per year)		(% of total)	(number per year)		(% of total)
doctoral degrees	489	139	78	613	195	76

[a]Science includes technical, medical, and agricultural research.

12 percent. However, the Netherlands government is now increasing the funding of projects through the national research council at the expense of direct university support. In the United Kingdom the percentage of research supported by various research councils has always been high; a substantial part of this money is allocated to the research council units and groups at the universities. However, the situation in these countries differs considerably from that in the United States, where nearly all university scientific research, except for faculty salaries, is directly financed by external agencies.

Several significant differences are not apparent from the data in the tables. For example, the national research councils in the Netherlands and Belgium support only basic research, whereas in Britain up to 25 percent of council funds support applied agricultural, medical, and environmental research through government departments' contracting with university research groups for applied research projects. In the Netherlands the national research council is now starting to support applied as well as basic research. Furthermore, the national research councils in Belgium, Norway, and Switzerland have no research institutes of their own, whereas the councils in Italy, the Netherlands, and Britain have their own institutes. In the latter three countries these institutes receive from 25 to 86 percent of the research council moneys, depending on country and field of research. This percentage is tending to rise, which could be detrimental to university research. Finally, Britain and Norway make their national contributions to international research organizations like CERN and ESA from their research councils' budgets; such contributions represent as much as 26 percent of a council's budget.

Traditionally scientific research has received the lion's share of university research expenditure, although in the last decade the proportion allotted to the humanities and the social sciences has increased somewhat. Data illustrating this trend in the Netherlands are displayed in Table 5. Interestingly enough, the proportions of doctorates awarded, taken as a research output indicator, are nearly the same as those for funding.

SCIENCE POLICY

Given the rapid growth of government expenditure for research in the universities and the deterioration of national economies since the mid-1970s, it is small wonder that most governments have tried to obtain more control over the cost and direction of university research. This greater measure of supervision, called *science policy*, takes various shapes in different countries, but always involves more bureaucracy in the form of studies and reports compiled by various offices. Unavoidably, such monitoring places some constraints on the autonomy of the university and on the freedom of individual scientists.

However, the effect of science policy on the direction of scientific development is rather slight, as Derek De Solla Price shows by means of extensive statistical studies, presented in a lecture that is reported in a Netherlands government publication. He finds that a country's total spending and manpower devoted to scientific research is closely tied to its gross national product (GNP). The higher the GNP, the higher also is the percentage of GNP spent on research. And there is a remarkable proportionality between this percentage and the country's scientific manpower, as is displayed in Figure 1. He also finds that the number of doctorates granted annually in the United States did not rise sharply in response to the creation of the National Science Foundation or to the Sputnik launching. However, degrees awarded fell sharply after the great depression and at the beginning of World War II, indicating that economic factors mainly determine scientific productivity.

It is well to have in mind De Solla Price's sobering conclusions as we review the directions science policy has taken in some countries. The goals of science policy are usually defined as follows: first, to improve research efficiency, and second, to make scientific research more responsive to social priorities. To achieve these objectives governments use either a coordinated or decentralized form of organization. The former combines a ministry of scientific policy and a national research council, as is the case in Belgium, the German Federal Republic, and France. In the latter model, used by the

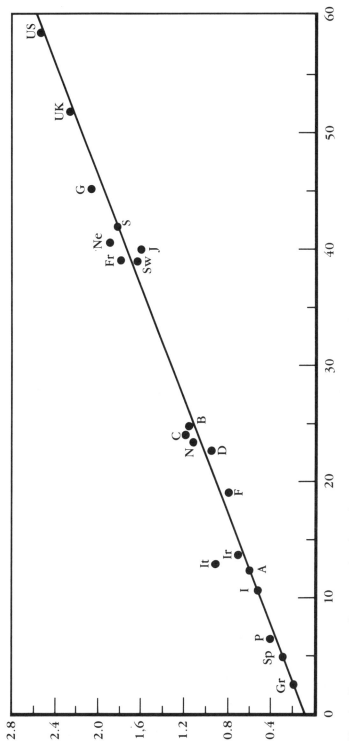

Fig. 1. Percentage of gross national product spent on research plotted against scientific manpower per 10,000 population for twenty countries.
(Gr = Greece, Sp = Spain, P = Portugal, I = Iceland, A = Austria, It = Italy, Ir = Ireland, F = Finland, D = Denmark, N = Norway, C = Canada, B = Belgium, F = France, Sw = Sweden, J = Japan, Ne = Netherlands, S = Switzerland, G = West Germany, UK = United Kingdom, US = United States)

United States and the United Kingdom, research is handled through various government departments and research councils. In practice, of course, there are hybrid forms of organization. For example, in the Netherlands from 1977 to 1981 the minister of science policy had only a very small budget, but he had authority to coordinate the scientific activities of the various departments. And in the United Kingdom there is some coordination among the departmental chief scientists and also among the five research councils.

Improvement in research efficiency, the first objective of science policy, is usually pursued through policies of selectivity—the competitive grant system with peer review—and financial concentration on centers of excellence. For example, the Netherlands research council awards 83 percent of its funds in three- and four-year project grants through a large number of national research communities. Usually these communities are organized on the initiative of leaders of university research groups in highly specific fields, for example, nucleic acid, bacterial cell walls, membrane transport, hormonal action, and so on; their members discuss and evaluate one another's proposals. For many years this system worked very well and stimulated research while providing maximum autonomy to the scientists. However, competition began to threaten cooperation once the resources of the national research council ceased to rise, and competitiveness intensified as the number of proposals submitted increased owing to the decrease in university budgets. Moreover, the advocates of science policy rightly feel that the second objective of policy, rendering research responsive to social needs, is hardly met by this structure of organizations and procedures.

To achieve this second policy goal ministers and the research councils are often authorized to concentrate their moneys on particular fields or in special forms. As an example, I point to the research units, research groups, and program grants of the Medical Research Council (MRC) in the United Kingdom. The *research units* are established around a professor of proven outstanding ability. He appoints a number of staff members who are employed and supported by the MRC. The research unit has indefinite tenure which means it usually lasts for the duration of the active career of its director. In contrast, a *research group* has limited tenure. Its staff is employed by a university, which is expected eventually to incorporate the group and support it from university funds. A *program grant* is awarded to a series of linked projects, usually coordinated by one investigator, at a university. In addition, the MRC awards project grants and graduate student stipends.

In 1975–76 the Medical Research Council funds were allocated as follows: intramural research, 18 percent; research units, 43 percent; research groups and program grants, 16 percent; project grants and graduate stipends, 21 percent. Clearly this system affords considerable opportunity to direct research according to social priorities. Moreover, up to 25 percent of research council funds may be used for contracts that permit individual government departments to sponsor applied research on selected topics in university laboratories.

In the United Kingdom, the Science Research Council, which supports only basic research, has allocated 60 percent of its money for computer science to three universities, namely, Cambridge, Edinburgh, and Manchester. The council's purpose was to impede development of this field in other universities in order to have three first-rate, large-scale centers. The council also operates a program of awards to graduate students who carry out joint research projects, the parties to which are industries and university departments.

In the Netherlands the national research council has pursued the second goal of science policy in a very modest way by setting aside a small portion of its funds for projects of national priority such as energy and aging. For these subjects proposals may be submitted directly, that is, not through a research community.

FURTHER DEVELOPMENTS

There is no doubt that science policy, especially in its objective of making scientific research more responsive to social priorities, will play an increasing role in European university laboratories in the eighties. Three developments in the Netherlands illustrate this prospect.

First, the national research council is now being authorized to finance applied research, for which proposals must contain a clear description of the expected use of the findings by an industry or another "customer." Second, the government is planning to reduce the direct financing of university research over the next nine years by 50 percent of the present amount. Of these funds one-third will be used to double the research council's budget for project grants in both pure and applied research. The remaining two-thirds will finance university research groups earmarked by the minister of education and sciences, acting upon the advice of the academic council. So far this council has served only as a consultative body of the universities and as an advisory body of the minister in the educational sphere; it has had no prior experience of research management. Hence it is still unclear how this system of earmarked financing will work. In addition, university research groups may undertake contract research for industry and government.

Third, a Netherlands government report on technological innovation enumerates the research areas to be stimulated—microelectronics and biotechnology, for example—and the means by which this is to be done. The universities will be involved in three ways: contract research performed by university laboratories; special grants to university research groups; and establishment of "transfer points" at some universities for scientific and technological information to be utilized by industry, especially small and medium-sized industries.

These and similar developments elsewhere raise questions as to the future of university scientific research. Our forecast must consider the effects not only of science policy but also of other important changes in our societies.

In seeking to improve the efficiency of research, science policy has had profound effects through the national research councils and the various forms of competitive research grants. The positive effects are immediately and highly visible: in the well-staffed, well-equipped, and well-supplied laboratories; in the many able young scientists trained on these projects; and in the steady increase of scientific publications issuing from these laboratories. The requirements to explicate research objectives and to become more time- and cost-conscious have certainly been salutary. However, the grant system can unquestionably become a serious administrative burden for the scientist. The often lengthy administrative procedures can hinder free, inventive basic research, which is not only an end in itself but also the wellspring of successful applied research. Fund raising and proposal writing may force investigators to divert attention from their real scientific interests.

The economic depression, coming after a long period of growth, is causing a good deal of harm. The need to reduce personnel costs in the universities especially affects temporary junior staff positions and thus increases the teaching and administrative load of the senior staff. In the Netherlands, the norm for research time of university staff members has decreased from two-thirds in 1969 to less than one-third in 1980. Since the great increase in staff appointments in the sixties and early seventies has been reversed so suddenly, there is soon bound to be a general aging of senior staff coupled with immobility. Moreover, the steady flow of new young scientists, equipped with the doctorate, is now leading to unemployment and inappropriate employment. The makers of science policy should now lend financial support to postdoctoral fellows rather than to new doctoral candidates.

Another set of difficulties for scientific research in the universities is produced by the drastic changes in society heralded by the "student revolution" of 1968 through 1970. The call for "democratization" of the European university system has generated a cumbersome bureaucracy composed of many councils and even more numerous committees. A burgeoning officialdom deluges us with reports and requests for reports. In some universities there is politicization, which is inimical to good science, although probably less so in the natural sciences than in the social sciences. Furthermore, an atmosphere of mistrust and fear of science pervades our society, which has seen too many instances of dual potentials of science: nuclear science yields sophisticated medical treatments but also causes fatalities by radiation in war or accident; biomedical science produces life-saving drugs but also deadly chemical-biological agents; and chemistry gives us useful products but also causes environmental pollution. Even the responsible attitude of molecular biologists, displayed in their call for a voluntary moratorium on recombinant-DNA experiements until safety guidelines had been formulated, worked against them. If this climate of mistrust and fear persists, it could do great damage, not only to university science but also to social welfare.

RESPONSIBILITY OF SCIENTISTS

European university scientists certainly have every reason to be grateful for all that Western society has provided them since World War II. This munificence certainly places them under obligation, now that the economic tide has turned, to cooperate with their governments to use their scientific capabilities for the public good.

There are several ways in which scientists should help to make science policy effective. They should try to overcome their customary disdain for applied research, while continuing strongly to defend the need for spontaneous and innovative basic research as intrinsically valuable and as the foundation for useful applied research. At the same time scientists should critically appraise the aims and methods of science policy and its results. Then they should try to persuade the responsible government officials to frame their policies so that what is achievable can be achieved with a minimum of bureaucratic hindrance. And officials should recognize that novel and useful ideas are not generated in weighty advisory bodies, but rather in the mind of a bright scientist having a lively discussion with some colleagues. Scientists should caution against the trend to enlarge the number and size of nonuniversity government research institutes at the expense of scientific research in the universities. At stake here is both the quality of university research and, even more importantly, the educational mission of the university.

Another important obligation of the scientists is to help dissipate the public's distrust of science. They should take part in explaining to the public and its elected representatives scientific findings and their broader implications. For only then can we expect legislatures and government ministers to make informed decisions about the regulation and application of scientific inquiry.

8

The Social Sciences

MARTIN BULMER

University social science research is a development of the twentieth century, particularly of the period since 1945. I will briefly sketch the origins of this research, some problems it poses for university organization, and the recent trend of conducting large-scale research outside the university. I am concerned with three particular questions. In what way, and with what success, can large-scale, organized, social inquiry fit into the structure of the modern university; to what extent can it be successfully institutionalized? What are the implications of increased expenditure by government for social science research, both within and outside the university? What effect has increasing government interference had on the conduct of research in the university?

The place of *research* in the social sciences in universities is central to the long-term health of these disciplines, but it has received less attention than the place of teaching, relations between teachers and students, the government of universities, or the politicization of social science faculties. Research is less glamorous, less controversial, lends itself less to polemic than these other issues. Nevertheless, if the research bases of the various social sciences do not flourish, those subjects will either atrophy or more probably come to occupy a position in universities analogous to more marginal subjects such as social work or journalism. My aim here is less to explore in detail the position of particular countries or disciplines than to raise general questions for consideration.

Martin Bulmer is Lecturer in Social Administration at the London School of Economics and Political Science.

My focus is on *large-scale* and *organized* research in the social sciences, in which a considerable number of auxiliary staff is employed, in which there is division of labor and hierarchical organization. It entails collecting and processing large amounts of data and elaborate statistical analysis or mathematical modeling. Some of it has predominantly a theoretical interest, other parts are predominantly descriptive. My survey ranges over both basic and applied research, with examples drawn from each, although the applicability of the distinction made in a hard-and-fast manner has been questioned: "The adjectives 'pure' and 'applied' imply a division where none should exist and their use can be harmful."[1] My examples are drawn principally but not entirely from Britain and North America.

THE AMBIVALENT PLACE OF RESEARCH

A basic theme of my analysis is the ambivalence that universities display toward large-scale research. On the one hand, "big social science" is fostered because of its intellectual importance (for example, economic modeling), the resources that it brings, and the benefits that follow from having a complex research organization to complement the teaching staff. On the other hand, large-scale research meshes uneasily with departmental structures, makes demands on teachers that they are not always willing to meet, and may elevate technique and efficiency over the values of careful scholarship and thought. Some parts of large-scale research are boring and trivial, and some academics feel that the presence of this research (for example, social survey research) dilutes their universities. Moreover, some large-scale research requires the employment of large numbers of nonacademic staff, whose presence at the university prompts considerable resistance and scrutiny of their status in relation to academic staff. Large-scale research enhances the reputation of universities and furthers their scholarly objectives, but it also represents an intrusion that some deem undesirable. Hence large-scale research is increasingly carried on outside universities.

HISTORY OF SOCIAL RESEARCH IN UNIVERSITIES

The historical origins of research in modern universities are relatively well known. The influence of the late nineteenth-century German university and its later American counterparts is a familiar theme of the history of universities and of research. With the founding of Johns Hopkins University in 1876, "perhaps the single, most decisive, event in the history of learning in the Western hemisphere,"[2] research came to have an importance at least equal to teaching. The foundation of Clark University (1889) and the University of Chicago (1892), together with enlargement of graduate

1. F. Dainton, "The Future of the Research Council System," in *A Framework for Government Research and Development* (London: Her Majesty's Stationery Office, 1971), p. 3.

2. E. Shils, "The Order of Learning in the United States," in *The Organization of Knowledge in Modern America*, ed. A. Oleson and J. Voss (Baltimore: Johns Hopkins University Press, 1979), p. 28.

work at Harvard and Columbia, transformed the American university system and laid the foundations for its international preeminence in the present century, particularly in the natural sciences. The emphasis in both German and certain American universities upon the advanced seminar and graduate instruction testified to the crucial position of research.

If the seminar was the characteristic mode of instruction in this research-oriented system,[3] "the wheel within the wheel, the real center of the life-giving, the stimulating, the creative forces of the modern university," as E. R. A. Seligman put it in 1892, the setting in which serious scientific investigation was conducted, was the laboratory. At least, this was so in the natural sciences; its equivalent in psychology was Wundt's laboratory in Leipzig, opened in 1879. What, however, of the other social sciences whose methods were nonexperimental? Where did the political scientist, economist, or sociologist go to conduct research? The answer, for the most part, was to the library or to the study or to the archives, to work on printed materials and unpublished documents. Firsthand inquiries in the field were unusual but not unknown.

Beginning around World War I, the methods of research, its organization, and its financing all began to change significantly. These changes had a far-reaching effect on universities. In the first place, social scientists in several disciplines became much more interested in the firsthand gathering of data. Malinowski's sojourn in the Trobriand Islands became the prototype. In American political science, Charles Merriam headed a movement for the direct observational study of political behavior. In sociology, W. I. Thomas and Robert Park similarly turned toward observing, interviewing, and studying unpublished documents. In psychology, J. B. Watson's behaviorism was an aggressive statement of an approach already well established. Wesley C. Mitchell in economics used statistical data in new ways to observe the workings of economic institutions.[4] The study of society became more systematically empirical, relying more on direct contact with the subject matter, rather than on archival data or on qualified informants such as clergymen, magistrates, or other middle-class officials.

Changes in the organization of research followed. At several American universities in the 1920s centers of social science research began to develop, consisting of a loose organization providing support staff, aid for graduate students, subsidies for publication, and released-time for teaching staff to conduct research. The Local Community Research Committee, set up at the University of Chicago in 1923, provides one example;[5] other important

3. L. R. Veysey, *The Emergence of the American University* (Chicago: University of Chicago Press, 1965), pp. 153–58.

4. On Merriam, see B. E. Karl, *Charles E. Merriam and the Science of Politics* (Chicago: University of Chicago Press, 1974), especially pp. 100–17. On Mitchell, see D. Ross, "The Development of the Social Sciences," in *Organization of Knowledge*, pp. 125–30.

5. M. Bulmer, "The Early Institutionalisation of Social Science Research: The Local Community Research Committee at the University of Chicago 1923–30," *Minerva* 18 (1980): 51–110.

centers were established at Pennsylvania, Columbia, Harvard, and North Carolina.

A necessary condition of this change was outside financial support. Before 1930, little government money was available for social science research in any country. Early nineteenth-century social investigators were men and women of private means. In the early twentieth century, philanthropy became important, especially through bodies like the Russell Sage Foundation and the Laura Spelman Rockefeller Memorial, which in the decade after 1923 put millions of dollars into basic research in America and western Europe.

By 1930, other sources of funding for social research appeared. During the 1930s, particularly after Roosevelt's election, federal government support for research began to grow rapidly, and private philanthropy, although it remained important, was no longer the only source of support. Moreover, foundations altered significantly their grant-giving policies during the decade. Whereas hitherto they had made large general-purpose grants to universities, the increasing growth of social science coupled with financial stringency during the Great Depression led to the project-grant system. Scholars seeking support were required to specify much more carefully their aims and interests. The decision as to which scholars received support moved from the university to other organizations.[6]

At the same time that the social sciences began to rely more on the firsthand collection of data and to create simple research organizations to facilitate such tasks, forward-looking scientists and foundation officials shared a belief that social science could prove useful in making a "massive attack" on social problems. The social sciences thus entered a phase when the results of research were believed to be socially useful.[7] How social science would influence policy was not very clearly articulated. Sometimes, as in President Hoover's Committee on Recent Social Trends, great reliance was placed simply on the comprehensive collection of authoritative social facts. Increased resources for research, coming initially from foundations, greatly enlarged the scale of, and led to some changes in, the organization of research. A few bodies, such as the Brookings Institution, were created altogether outside universities.

The increased scale of financial support and the size of projects and of ancillary staff raised problems of integrating research with teaching and the advance of knowledge. Countries differ markedly in the extent to which the direction and finance of scientific research is centralized and in the extent to which teaching and research are combined.[8] An important feature of the

6. See R. E. Kohler, "The Management of Science: The Experience of Warren Weaver and the Rockefeller Foundation Programme in Molecular Biology," *Minerva* 14 (1976): 279–306.

7. See M. Bulmer, *The Uses of Social Research: Social Investigation in Public Policy-Making* (London: Allen & Unwin, 1982).

8. J. Ben-David, *The Scientist's Role in Society* (Englewood Cliffs, N.J.: Prentice-Hall, 1971), p. 174.

developments in the United States between 1860 and 1920 is that there was
no "establishment," no sole authority; rather competition existed among
different kinds of institutions supported in various ways. Nevertheless,
universities became the dominant centers of natural scientific research by
the early twentieth century.[9] Independent research institutes were either
under their influence or so small that they could not compete effectively
with the more dominant university departments. By contrast, there developed in Germany after 1911 the Kaiser Wilhelm Society for the Promotion
of the Sciences (now the Max Planck Gesellschaft), with its own highly
specialized extrauniversity research institutes directed by leading scientists
and staffed by scholars free of teaching duties. In Britain and France,
research institutes in science and medicine were established outside the
university, such as the National Physical Laboratory and various centers
supported by the Conseil National de la Recherche Scientifique, which was
established in 1939.

In the social sciences, developments were not so rapid, though basic
questions concerning institutional integration persisted. Was large-scale
social science research promoted most effectively in or outside the university? If within, how should it be integrated with teaching responsibilities and the conventional structure of academic departments? Before
the post–World War II expansion, several different arrangements were
tried. Outside the university were bodies such as the Brookings Institution
in the United States and Political and Economic Planning in Britain.[10]
Within the university a variety of different types of research centers flourished, some integrated within teaching departments, some semiautono-
mous. Of the latter, some were specialized by function (like the Columbia
Bureau of Applied Social Research), some by intellectual orientation (like
the Frankfurt Institut für Sozialforschung.[11]

Growth of American university science between 1860 and 1920 was the
result of a hunger for fundamental knowledge, fostered by a competitive
and decentralized system. Though elements of this system persist, notably
its competitive hierarchy of universities, public and private, growth in
academic social science after World War II was, as in Europe, supported by
government and seen as an integral part of national economic policy. Convinced of the usefulness of social science research, governments injected
resources on an ever-increasing scale.

LOCATION OF LARGE-SCALE RESEARCH

In the 1920s and 1930s, when foundation support was decisive, the social
sciences were just "taking off." After 1945 the base from which growth

9. Shils, "Order of Learning."

10. See J. Pinder, ed., *Fifty Years of Political and Economic Planning: Looking Forward
1931–1981* (London, Heinemann, 1981).

11. On the Frankfurt Institut, see E. Shils, *The Calling of Sociology and Other Essays on the
Pursuit of Learning* (Chicago: University of Chicago Press, 1980), pp. 188–93.

continued was larger, and the problems associated with growth were on an altogether different scale. Though never on the scale of "big science" in the natural sciences, the postwar period began the era of "big social science," posing new intellectual and organizational problems for social scientists and for those supporting social science. The Rockefeller contribution was effective because it began from a very small base, and allowed universities to expand this base modestly and gradually over a fifteen- or twenty-year period, in conjunction with graduate teaching, without being over-whelmed by the expense or scale of activity. With increased government concern for research and increased reliance on government as the chief paymaster, the scale of research grew. To some extent objectives were modified toward more applied studies, and different types of research or-ganizations were created (some outside the university) to foster social sci-ence research. Examples of such organizations include the National Opin-ion Research Center and the Michigan Institute for Social Research in the United States, and the National Institute of Economic & Social Research and the Tavistock Institute in Britain.

The precise level of financial support by governments in the 1970s is difficult to establish. Global estimates have been put forward of U.S. federal government expenditure in excess of $500 million on all social science research, and British government support of about £50 million. (These estimates relate to direct support for research staff and activities in univer-sities and in nonacademic institutes.) The actual magnitude is in any case less important than the dramatic dependence of social science on govern-ment. Although private foundations still provide significant support for research in social science, its scale has become relatively modest compared to that provided by governments. Other sources of finance are of marginal importance. Fee income is not an adequate base from which to finance large-scale academic research, while the commercialization of research within universities has been traditionally proscribed. We will return to these problems of relations between universities and the state, but first let us consider the internal weaknesses of universities as settings for large-scale research.

Though the idea of the unity of teaching and research has been almost universally accepted, its practice has posed severe problems. Research and teachable academic disciplines do not necessarily fit easily together.[12] The intellectual and organizational relation between large-scale research and individual research and teaching of academics is problematical. Of course, large-scale research is not only conducted in universities but also by in-house government research divisions (e.g., U.S. Bureau of the Census; Office of Population Censuses and Surveys, and the Central Statistical Office in Britain); in independent, nonacademic, nonprofit research organizations

12. J. Ben-David, *Centers of Learning: Britain, France, Germany, United States* (New York: McGraw-Hill for Carnegie Commission, 1977), p. 102.

(e.g., Mathematica, and Stanford Research Institute in the United States; Social & Community Planning Research in Britain); and in commercial firms (notably market research in many countries, and in American social research firms such as Abt Associates). Universities nevertheless retain distinct advantages as places in which to conduct research, since they form a public network. Their number gives

> the impression of a mighty concourse . . . reinforced by the linkages and interchanges between the members of various learned societies. A trans-local identification was strengthened in the minds of those who experienced this plurality of connections and thus felt themselves to be engaged in a vast national and international movement of the spirit. Despite the specialization of research, the co-existence of practitioners of disciplines within faculties, and of faculties themselves within universities, created a diversity and radius of intellectual intercourse which supported the general conviction that the advancement of knowledge was an end of the highest value.[13]

Even so, not all basic scientific research activity in Europe has been incorporated in the university; for example, the Kaiser Wilhelm (now Max Planck) Gesellschaft and the independent research institutes supported by the British research councils are centers of basic research located outside the academic sphere. Independent institutes such as Brookings, National Institute of Economic & Social Research, and Political and Economic Planning (now part of the Policy Studies Institute); centers for survey research; and independent research contractors constitute organizations for applied social research external to the university.

What determines where research is conducted and how it is organized? Basic research is likely to be conducted at universities, while very large intelligence and monitoring activities, such as the census and large continuous surveys, are always likely to be carried out by government. We will not, however, further discuss in-house government research. Though often demonstrating great strengths in methodology and technique, this research suffers from the overriding disadvantages of subjection to direct political control, lack of real intellectual freedom, and sometimes lack of intellectual power. Government organs are therefore unsuitable locations for much basic and applied social science research, a judgment reflected by the preference of governments for contracting out even highly applied research, a trend that began in the United States during World War II.

The most critical questions concern the capacity of academic institutions to absorb large-scale research. Although universities are seemingly the natural locus for most basic and applied social research, in recent years a good deal of research has moved away from the university. This trend reflects both the universities' view of large-scale research and the fact that

13. Shils, "Order of Learning," p. 31.

academic organization has features that constrain the relation of research and teaching. There is no doubt that universities and large-scale research do not fit comfortably together. To understand why we shall consider the different ways in which social research can be institutionalized.

INSTITUTIONALIZATION OF LARGE-SCALE RESEARCH

Large-scale research requires considerable resources: staff, equipment, and materials. As the scale of research activity increases, qualitative changes occur. Staff need to be employed, both trained researchers and nonacademic personnel with secretarial, clerical, computing or routine survey skills. A division of labor emerges, together with some sort of organization to manage the enterprise and administer the funds. Small projects, involving one or two people, may be run partly by the principal investigator, partly with the aid of central university services. Increases in scale, however, require more complex organizational forms of various kinds.

The simplest of these is the *collegium*, an informal group of colleagues of equal status, who meet to discuss ideas and engage in cooperation on ad hoc projects. Usually decision making is democratic and fairly consensual, and the group has little or no formal authority over the activities of its members (except the right to admit or exclude individuals). Members of a collegium may come from more than one university, from several departments within one university, or from a single department. The learned society is the best example of the interuniversity collegium. Within universities, the degree of organization may be informal, as with "journal clubs" or formal, as with a body like the Society for Social Research at the University of Chicago in the 1920s, which served as an underpinning for the Chicago School of Sociology.[14]

A more complex form is the *research committee*, a group of persons pursuing their individual research interests within an overall focus and framework provided by the committee. The main advantages of this organization lie in providing a letterhead, secretarial and clerical services, influence in the university and weight with grant-giving bodies.[15] Often having *center* or *committee* in their titles, these groups may have members from one or several departments. They offer a forum for sharing common interests, have graduate students attached to them, and usually have a director or chairman. The latter, however, is likely to have little authority other than over the disposal of the minor services that the center or committee commands.

Such bodies do not fundamentally modify the departmental structures of British and American universities. At the London School of Economics, the Population Investigation Committee is a distinguished example of such a

14. M. Bulmer, "The Society for Social Research: An Institutional Underpinning to the Chicago School of Sociology in the 1920's."

15. See P. H. Rossi, "Observations on the Organization of Social Science Research," in *The Organization, Management and Tactics of Social Research*, ed. R. O'Toole (Cambridge, Mass.: Schenkman, 1971), p. 159.

body. More recently, the International Centre for Economics and Related Disciplines draws its members from several departments. At the University of Chicago, the well-established committee system (e.g., the Committee for the Study of New Nations; the Committee for South Asian Studies) crosses departmental lines. Very occasionally, committees evolve into departments or quasi departments (e.g., the Committee on Statistics; the Committee on Social Thought). Committees offer opportunities for fruitful exchange and confer diplomatic and strategic advantages, but they essentially do not direct the activities of their members. They merely provide a convenient framework within which university teachers can pursue their research, sometimes in collaboration with colleagues of similar interests.

A more complex structure is the *university research institute*, situated within the formal structure of the university but having an existence distinct from departments. Membership in many cases overlaps, but the institute is a distinct entity, with its own board, director, budget, and staff (though these vary in number). Institutes command considerably greater resources than committees, mostly derived from grants from outside sources (government, research councils, and foundations). They have their own offices, perhaps their own equipment, and staff to direct and conduct research (some of whom may be university teachers on leave or on part-time appointment) together with graduate students writing doctoral theses. The director of an institute may have some real authority, although subject to various checks and balances.

Institutes vary in their organizational complexity. Some coordinate activities spread over different departments, as does the Institute for Research in the Social Sciences at the University of North Carolina, founded by Howard Odum in 1924, which claims to be the oldest university-associated social research organization in the United States.[16] This pattern was followed in the recent initiative by the British Social Science Research Council to establish designated research centers designed to strengthen research in particular fields by means of large program grants. Such centers have their own budgets, but are headed (with two exceptions) by academic teaching staff for whom the centers are a way of consolidating their own research interests.

Some institutes may be formally autonomous within a university. The British Social Science Research Council supports several research units (in industrial relations, race relations, and sociolegal studies) that are led by a senior academic, but have their own full-time research staff with some ancillary support. The work they perform, however, does not differ much from that done by academics with a large program grant, and such units were set up primarily to stimulate research in particular fields, rather than

16. G. B. Johnson and G. G. Johnson, *Research in Service to Society: The First Fifty Years of the Institute for Research in Social Science at the University of North Carolina* (Chapel Hill: University of North Carolina Press, 1980).

because of any organizational necessity for such a structure. Senior members of the staff are research managers, but in the main they supervise the work of junior colleagues.

By contrast, the most complex form is the *nonprofit research enterprise*, an organization with a large professional and ancillary staff attached to a university. Much larger than a research institute, the research enterprise involves a very elaborate division of labor, hierarchy of authority, and virtually complete independence from the departmental structure of the university. The prototype is the large American survey research center: the National Opinion Research Center at Chicago, the Institute of Social Research at Michigan, and the former Bureau of Applied Social Research at Columbia.

Directors of these enterprises are research managers running complex organizations whose form is entirely different from that of an academic department. Conduct of social surveys requires the most extensive division of labor in the social sciences. Staff are needed with specialist knowledge of sampling, questionnaire construction, interviewing, data processing, and data analysis. Coordination of the work of research specialists, technical personnel (in fields like sampling and computing), and field staff for interviewing (most of whom are geographically distant from headquarters) is a completely different sort of activity from that of the scholar-teacher. It is one, moreover, for which many academics are singularly unsuited either by vocation, location in a university teaching department, or temperament.

> Essentially, an academic department is a collection of scholars whose work is only minimally integrated in a division of labour sense. . . . When an academician refers to the independence of academic life, he is usually referring to the fact that once he has met his teaching obligations (over which he has a great deal of control) he is free to pursue his own intellectual interests within the limits set by local production standards and the amount of research funds he is able to obtain. Indeed, so pleasurable is the lack of a defined division of labour that any attempt to engage in large-scale research enterprises has led to the grafting on university structures of organisational entities in which such a division of labour is possible, rather than imposing such a division of labour upon existing departmental structures.[17]

BUREAUCRATIC RATIONALITY AND ACADEMIC FREEDOM

The largest American survey organizations began as independent agencies that later were grafted on to universities. The National Opinion Research Center is still somewhat separate from the University of Chicago, although located on its campus, while a very large number of the university's social science staff hold positions as senior study directors at the center. The

17. P. H. Rossi, "Researchers, Scholars and Policy-Makers: The Politics of Large-Scale Research," *Daedalus* 93 (1964): 1149–50.

management of such an organization entails the difficult reconciliation between the value of individual autonomy, which holds sway in the university, and the principles of centralization and hierarchy. However, unlike a commercial firm, the effectiveness of the enterprise rests ultimately on expert social science knowledge. In a survey the most important decisions of last resort lie with the scientific director of the study, rather than with the project manager who administers the survey through its various stages. As a former director of the National Opinion Research Center has observed, it is very hard to recruit people who have both analytic ability and skills in managing complex survey operations. To administer such an organization involves ensuring harmony among various specialists, reconciling scientific and managerial responsibilities, and balancing centralization and autonomy: "Research administrators do something more than 'chair,' something less than 'direct.'"[18]

The career of Paul Lazarsfeld, founder of the Columbia Bureau of Applied Social Research, suggests the importance also of entrepreneurial spirit in such enterprises. Much of a director's time is spent in trying to secure the future of the organization, which is largely dependent on grants. Lazarsfeld was adept at persuading commercial firms to entrust semi–market research inquiries to him, then riding more fundamental social science research work on their backs. The many skills needed for success in this position are not widely found among academics.

Furthermore, the intellectual and organizational relationships between the nonprofit research enterprise and the university are complex. A social survey research organization employs many persons who are not academics, and there are perennial problems about the integration of large numbers of nonacademics into the university. Some scholars go further and question the intellectual merit of survey research as an academic activity. They do not question its value as a tool for data collection, but some wonder whether it properly belongs in the university setting.

Even if its legitimacy is acknowledged, the nonprofit research institutes encounter intractable problems in reconciling scholarly autonomy with the bureacratic rationality necessary for effective performance of large-scale survey research. These problems are compounded by their employing persons with academic training who have no clear academic status. Moreover, the presence of such centers of survey research may bias the training of graduate students toward survey-based projects for which financial support is readily available. Or it may warp the intellectual fabric of departments by affecting emphases in appointments. And although these problems arise particularly in survey research, other large-scale research centers, such as the Institute of Human Relations at Yale, have encountered difficulties in surviving in the face of departmental antagonism. Trying to marry certain sorts of large-scale research to social science departments may cause the

18. K. Prewitt, "Management of Survey Organizations," in *Handbook of Survey Research*, ed. P. Rossi and J. Wright (New York: Academic Press, forthcoming), p. 34.

academics to dislike the outsiders, to distrust their work, or to envy those who spend all their time on research. Thus members of institutes and especially enterprises are sometimes concentrated elsewhere on the campus and spend most of their time with one another, although this weakens their links to departments.

To sum up, the more complex and large-scale a research organization becomes (as in an enterprise), the more uneasily it fits within the traditional departmental structure of universities. Indeed, so severe can be the strains that enterprises may flourish more successfully outside the university altogether. In the recent past, other forces have also encouraged such separation.

INCREASING GOVERNMENT DEMANDS FOR SOCIAL RESEARCH

Recent trends in social science research are not simply a function of the internal structure of universities, which are after all institutions for the pursuit of truth. My second theme, increasing government support for research, comes to the fore at this point. For governments have in the last thirty years sought increasingly to commission research of all kinds from a variety of different sources. The movement of large-scale social science research outside the university—the expansion of bodies such as Brookings, the National Institute of Economic & Social Research, the Policy Studies Institute, and the units of the Conseil National de la Recherche Scientifique—is in part a response to the difficulties just discussed but is also an effect of governments' decisions as to where to award grants and place contracts. Even in the United States, research and teaching activities, usually thought to be complementary, particularly at the graduate level, are becoming separated and their numerous connections weakened. Teaching and research are not necessarily still mutually reinforcing:

> The United States is beginning to resemble the Federal Republic (of Germany) in having substantial research effort concentrated within institutes or centres attached to universities but with little organized relationship to the teaching functions of the university. The pressure towards more reliance on user groups and national facilities for expensive lines of inquiry could even move research to some extent off the campus, although to date most national facilities have been largely controlled by university-based scientists.[19]

An increasing demand for policy-relevant research has generated new institutions altogether external to the university. In the United States, "just as market research moved in large part (though never entirely) outside academic institutions to commercial organizations, public-policy research has begun to move outside universities to non-profit and profit-making

19. B. L. R. Smith, "The Changing Role of Research at American Universities" (Paper delivered at the Second International Conference of the International Council on the Future of the University, Toronto, Canada, 1977), p. 5.

organizations, each having its own distinct character." [20] These include the Rand Corporation, Abt Associates in Cambridge, Mathematica at Princeton (but independent of the university), the Stanford Research Institute (which severed its links with the university), Batelle at Seattle, and Westat (a consulting firm set up by former employees of the U.S. Bureau of the Census). To take one example, Abt Associates between 1970 and 1980 increased its staff from 200 to 1,100, and its annual revenues from $3.5 to $27 million. Its 1980 report is that of a very successful and enterprising commercial company (which it is) whose business is applied social research. In Britain, although market research is dominated by commercial interests, nonprofit organizations are more characteristic of social science research outside the university. They are funded partly by endowments, partly by grants from foundations and research councils, and live to some extent on contract research from government. Quite significant contributions to the social sciences have originated from the Tavistock Institute, the Institute of Community Studies, the Centre for Environmental Studies and the Institute of Economic Affairs (though the latter has political affiliations); the National Institute of Economic & Social Research has played a major role in economic research. More recently the Policy Studies Institute has concentrated on research on social policy. Though academics sit on their boards as individuals, all are formally independent of universities. [21]

J. S. Coleman speculates that the general trend in audience, market, and now public-policy research is for the initial exploratory stages to be conducted in the relatively unstructured university setting, but that the university is "too irregular, irresponsible and unpredictable" for the most efficient execution of policy research. [22] So it tends to move off campus. Academic social scientists would of course question whether efficiency is a relevant criterion for judging the worth of research. It is more likely to be salient in large data-gathering activities. Policy research is only one type of social science research, and there is clearly scope for specialization of function between universities and other research bodies. It seems, however, that quite significant amounts of analytical social research (not just census and survey taking) which governments consider useful are now conducted outside the university. The quality of much such research is questionable, and many of the controls provided in universities by open publication or collegial criticism are absent. But the trend seems clear.

RECENT GOVERNMENT INTERVENTION

Let us now turn to our third theme, the influence of government on the university. In several ways in recent years, governments have interfered

20. J. S. Coleman, "Sociological Analysis and Social Policy," in *A History of Sociological Analysis*, ed. T. Bottomore and R. Nisbet (New York, Basic Books, 1978), p. 699.

21. See M. Bulmer, ed., *Social Policy Research* (London: Macmillan, 1978), pp. 27–39.

22. Coleman, "Sociological Analysis," p. 699.

with and regulated the activities of social scientists. Intervention may take the form of government-mandated change in the fundamental internal governance of universities, of which the Dutch university reforms of 1970 are the most flagrant example.[23] Changes in arrangements for university finance can be abrupt. In Britain, the unprecedented increase in fees for overseas students will have a potentially severe effect on recruitment in the social sciences; it has plunged into crisis faculties with large numbers of foreign students. Immigration rules in the United States, Canada, and Britain now make it more difficult to appoint foreign social scientists to permanent academic positions, thus impairing the international character of scholarship. Governments can also hinder research. For example, federal regulations in the United States, originally imposed in biomedical research, have been progressively extended to the behavioral and social sciences. That American universities are required to constitute institutional review boards, which vet individual research projects through a local peer-review system, represents major government interference with free scholarly inquiry.[24]

DEPENDENCE ON THE STATE

The most serious issue, however, is the universities' dependence on state support. When resources were plentiful and expansion continued, universities did not suffer when some resources were directed to extrauniversity research enterprises. Indeed, some welcomed such actions as protecting the university from contamination by too much applied work. However, the era of government faith in the economic benefits of expanded social science now seems to be at an end in several countries. In a climate of economic stringency, how will universities adapt? The dependence on government support, so welcome in times of plenty, may turn out to be a considerable liability. The most serious direct effects seem likely to be felt in graduate teaching and the level of support for basic research.

At the graduate level, universities regenerate themselves by training future scholar-teachers. But when appointments for the immediate future are likely to be so limited, either the attractiveness of graduate study may diminish or departments may feel pressured to tailor curriculums to the job market. In America, for example, one observes significant increases in courses in applied sociology and in public policy. Alternatively, prospective social science researchers may be trained in other ways, for example, by apprenticeship in research organizations. Research institutes and enterprises have always been able to offer financial support to graduate students.

23. H. Daalder, "The Dutch Universities Between the 'New Democracy' and the 'New Management,'" in *Universities in the Modern World*, ed. P. Seabury (New York: Free Press, 1975), pp. 195–231.
24. See M. Wax and J. Cassell, eds., *Federal Regulations: Ethical Issues and Social Research* (Boulder, Colo.: Westview Press, 1979).

In the absence of other sources of finance and academic posts, many young researchers may seek training in research organizations. Of course, some see this as desirable for those intending to pursue a research career. Discussing European doctoral programs, in which a higher degree is commonly awarded without the required coursework customary in the United States, a former member of the British Social Science Research Council and chairman of its sociology committee has asked whether the doctoral program is the best mode of educating postgraduates: "I do not question its value as an intellectual experience. Its value, however, as a preparation for a research career, particularly outside the strictly academic world, is questionable."[25] Universities uphold the scholarly ideal in part by offering the ablest among the young the opportunity to become scholars themselves. What will be the effect on graduate study if this inducement is severely contracted as a result of declining government support for the social sciences?

In the conduct of social science research, alternatives to the financial dependence on government are not obvious. Large-scale social science research began in the university with foundation support, but foundations cannot today supply the necessary resources. Nor can universities fund large-scale research out of their own endowments or current income. For example, if social surveys cost approximately $50 per interview, a sample of 1,000 interviews will be far beyond the normal budget of most universities, which make little or no provision for such costs. Commercial sponsorship is also unlikely to be a particularly hopeful or acceptable source of support, except perhaps in certain fields of economics. There are few people who can, like Paul Lazarsfeld, walk the fine line between the academic and commercial worlds.

ACADEMIC INTEGRITY

One possibility might be for universities to go into business. But this runs entirely counter to the academic ethos, and introduces extraneous values into the academy that may damage its deepest purposes. Of course, individual social scientists can and do engage in extramural profitable activities, particularly through writing and research consultancies. Bringing such activities into the university in an organized form is quite another matter, as Harvard recently discovered when it considered creating its own genetic engineering company. This proposal was dropped after protests from the faculty. President Bok is reported as saying "the preservation of academic values is a matter of paramount importance to the university, and owning shares in such a company would create a number of potential conflicts with these values."[26]

25. R. Illsley, *Professional or Public Health: Sociology in Health and Medicine* (London: Nuffield Provincial Hospitals Trust, 1980), pp. 169–70.
26. "Genetic Engineering Plan Dropped," *Times Higher Education Supplement*, 28 November 1980.

In the immediate future, maintaining universities as institutions for the pursuit of truth and promotion of learning will be a difficult task. In the social sciences the outlook is unclear, because of difficulties in incorporating large-scale research in universities, and the problems posed for graduate education by a shrinking job market. Universities are now paying the price for having become dependent on government in a period of expansion. Large-scale social science research, particularly applied, is not necessarily best conducted in a university context. Should universities continue to accommodate it, in order to maintain the prosperity of their social science departments? Or should they recognize that in the present economic situation, social science departments and the scale of their graduate teaching and research activities will have to decline for the sake of academic integrity?

9

A Conversation
about the Humanities

WALTER RÜEGG

In chapter 12 of this book Allan Bloom argues that "the humanities above all should be the source of standards for the university. . . . For we can only recognize that there is an intellectual crisis in the light of the standards they provide." Bloom offers four reasons to explain our present crisis, all of which apply directly to problems of research. I shall consider and comment on his diagnosis, for I am convinced that one of the main reasons for the weakness of the humanities is the lack of real conversation among humanists. I write to encourage more conversation.

THE CRISIS OF THE HUMANITIES

According to Bloom, toward the close of the eighteenth century, the belief arose that "the human sciences . . . were to provide the rational basis for the understanding of man and the answers to the questions of greatest concern to him. Under the influence of this inspiration the great nineteenth-century scholarship flourished." But something went wrong: "The aimlessness and dispiritedness of the human sciences were powerfully diagnosed by Nietzsche . . . as early as the 1870s." What went wrong? Why this disappointment? Why did the work of the nineteenth century become spiritless?

The standard answer refers to historicism, that is, to the displacement of cognitive authority in the humanities by concentration on the historical process itself. I wish to take this explanation one step further and state as my

Walter Rüegg is Professor of Sociology at the University of Berne.

main thesis that the nineteenth-century crisis in the humanities was caused by the displacement of the program of *studia humaniora* by the German invention of the *Geisteswissenschaften*. The former constitute studies through which men could learn to behave more humanly; the latter are inspired by a conception of the "spirit" of humanity as expressed in its total historical reality.

A NEW CONCEPT OF HISTORY

At celebrations of the commencement of the twentieth century, official speakers in German universities, usually professors of humanities, were especially proud to point to German accomplishments in science and technology. Speaking in Berlin, Ulrich von Wilamowitz-Moellendorf said that Germany, by its nineteenth-century achievements, had only "paid back the debts of gratitude which it owed to nations of older civilizations and finally became their peer."[1] Wilamowitz was one of the most distinguished humanist scholars of the age. His views are typical of the self-understanding of the humanists who had fallen into disgrace with Nietzsche.

For German scholars of the nineteenth century, scientific work was not so much a personal endeavor as performance of a national duty. This duty derived from a secularized form of absolute truth, the objective spirit of world history. The humanist had to reveal through scientific investigation the ideal forms and eternal laws of history that are hidden behind worldly manifestations and differentiations. Hence research in the humanities acquired new significance. Cultures remote in time and space were to be understood as emanations of the "world spirit" in specific historical and geographical contexts.

This new concept of history, which had its origins in the work of Vico and Herder, could be described as the secularized form of the Christian vision of history. It had special significance for Germany. For there intellectuals and political elites during the Napoleonic wars were opposed to French cultural domination and so tried to create a national self-consciousness that depended mainly on evoking tradition. But Germanic tradition offered little intellectual nourishment for national unity. The only traditions in which intellectuals could find principles of unification were in the humanities. Therefore, the *Geisteswissenschaften* derived initially from a new relation of German thinkers to classical antiquity.

CLASSICAL SCHOLARSHIP AND NEO-HELLENISM

Classical scholarship developed into *Altertumswissenschaften*, founded by Winckelmann, who gave a new meaning to the humanities. A whole

---

1. Ulrich von Wilamowitz-Moellendorf, *Erinnerungen 1848–1914* (Leipzig: Koehler, 1928), p. 246. I have dealt with this centenary speech in my essay "Die Antike als Leitbild der deutschen Gesellschaft des 19. Jahrhunderts," in *Bedrohte Lebensordnung. Studien zur humanistischen Soziologie* (Zurich: Artemis, 1978), pp. 93–105.

generation of German intellectuals, inspired by his work, found in antiquity a spiritual home in which national self-consciousness could arise. This new approach to classical antiquity sprang from the new conception of history. Winckelmann was not interested primarily in human triumphs as displayed in literary and artistic works. Rather he found in these works, especially in the concreteness of sculpture, religious revelation of divine forces and transcendent ideals. In this light, to imitate the ancients does not refer to style and form; Winckelmann explicitly defines *imitation* as becoming intimate with inimitable and therefore divine images. This intimacy should be so perfect that a scholar could make his own what a Greek said to an ignoramus about Zeuxis's portrait of Helena: "Take my eyes and a goddess will appear to you."[2] To use his eyes to discover and reveal the divine aspect of worldly phenomena is the task of the scientist, the goal of his research.

Winckelmann discovered in Greek art the famous "noble simplicity and serene greatness."[3] These ideals could be identified with the ideal of youth. In fact, Greek art represented youth as harmony in the same way that Greek poetry and philosophy were seen by Herder and Hegel as harmonious products of a nation in the youth of human history. The German nation was taken to be young in comparison with others.

Youth, natural beauty, harmony, originality, freedom, and patriotism were the principles by which the Greeks could help to shape a fresh German *Volkstum*. This would be purified of the artificial, unoriginal, and rhetorical Roman tradition and its offspring, French civilization. Professors of classics such as Friedrich Ast (Landshut), Reinhold Bernhard Jachmann (Danzig), Franz Passow (Weimar), Friedrich Jacobs (Munich) found in this affinity of Germans and Greeks the philosophical and historical rationale for a German national education based on learning Greek.[4]

This neo-Hellenism, as Rudolf Pfeiffer accurately designates the new epoch of classical scholarship,[5] was in the Platonic idealist tradition. But in contrast to earlier forms of idealism, the new scholarship did not take its image of man from a transcendental world of ideas or the heavens. Nineteenth-century neo-Hellenism, which spread out from Germany, found its ideal embodied in the historical model of Greek youth. Therefore,

2. Johann Winckelmann, "Gedanken über die Nachahmung der griechischen Werke in der Malerei und Bildhauerskunt [1755]," *Sämmtliche Werke*, vol. 1, ed. Josef Eiselein (Donauöschingen, 1825), p. 8.

3. Ibid., p. 30.

4. See Friedrich Paulsen, *Geschichte des gelehrten Unterrichts auf den deutschen Schulen und Universitäten vom Ausgang des Mittelalters bis zur Gegenwart. Mit besonderer Rücksicht auf den klassischen Unterricht*, vol. 2, 3rd ed. (Berlin: De Gruyter, 1921), pp. 229–241; Ast, Jacobs, Evers, Jachmann, eds., *Dokumente des Neuhumanismus I*, 2d ed., (Weinheim: Beltz, 1962), p. 9; Franz Passow, *Vermischte Schriften* (Leipzig: F. A. Brockhaus, 1843), pp. 15–19.

5. Rudolf Pfeiffer, *History of Classical Scholarship from 1300 to 1750* (Oxford: Clarendon Press, 1976), p. 167.

to develop into an authentic modern man one had to know through research the concrete realizations of the Greek *Volksgeist* as found in its history, geography, law, philosophy, literature, language, fine arts, medicine, and so on.[6]

NEO-HELLENISM: POSITIVE AND NEGATIVE CONSEQUENCES

In both positive and negative ways neo-Hellenism was fundamental to the development of the human sciences in the nineteenth century. Since the humanities aimed at the education of modern man through familiarity with historical instances of a philosophical idea of man, the Greek ideal inevitably came into conflict with other ideals of man and their historical exemplars. Romanticism opposed the pagan ideals by emphasizing the spirit and the men of the Christian Middle Ages. In particular, Romantics promoted all kinds of studies whose purpose was to reveal the *Volksgeist* of the modern nation itself.

The search for alternative models of man was constrained by the process of research, for research demonstrated that all abstract models were one-sided and incomplete. Nevertheless, historical research is the foundation of the admirable scholarship of the nineteenth century. This was the positive outcome of the idealistic origins of the *Geisteswissenschaften*.

The negative consequences of neo-Hellenism may be illustrated with the history of the term *humanism*. By its semantics *humanism* shows the fundamental change brought about by the shift from the "humanities" to the "human sciences." The humanities studied human works as expressions of human self-understanding. The human sciences pursue universal principles that should explain and direct human history. As is the case with all isms, *humanism* was coined as a battle-cry, first by Niethammer, a friend of Hegel's. In opposition to a progressive educational program established by the *Philanthropinum*, a school that claimed to develop the natural properties of man and to provide training in useful skills, humanism was to be grounded in the government of mind over nature, and it was to foster idealistic rather than materialistic values. Since man shared natural needs and utilitarian attitudes with all animals, contrary to its name the *Philanthropinum* was devoted to animality; only humanism could promote humanity.[7] Because the fundamental values of humanity had been presented in classical antiquity, the intellectual class that is to translate the classical ideal into public functions would be educated in the classics.

The younger generation of Hegelians abstracted from antiquity the notion of human evolution as a process of cumulative rationalization. Humanism became identical with industrialism and democracy, with "govern-

6. August Böckh, *Enzyklopädie und Methodologie der philologischen Wissenschaften*, ed. Ernst Bratuschek (Leipzig: Teubner, 1877).

7. Friedrich Immanuel Niethammer, *Der Streit des Philanthropinismus und Humanismus in der Theorie des Erziehungs-Unterrichts unserer Zeit* (Jena: Friedrich Frommann, 1808), p. 8.

ment of the people and of all human beings over the rigid nature within and outside man," in the words of Arnold Ruge, one of the first editors of Karl Marx. The realization of Greek ideas was to be found not in ancient Greek society but in "democracy as envisaged by the North Americans." The human ideal was no longer the Greek youth, but rather the self-made man of liberal capitalism: "Humanism in opposition to Christianity proclaimed universal education and the rights of man"; "The old form of religion in the Christian faith or the old Christianity is the old religion. The new religion is Christianity realized or Humanism."[8]

HISTORICAL ABSTRACTION AGAINST THE HUMANITIES

In his early writings, Karl Marx appropriated the term *humanism*, but he emphasized another principle in the idea and history of man. The dialectic between nature and man was given objective reality in the concept of work. Humanism had to be "real" or "concrete." Humanism involved elimination of man's economic alienation that arose with the division of labor and private property: "Communism as a positive elimination of private ownership, as human self-estrangement and therefore as real appropriation of the human being by and through the man. . . . This communism as perfect naturalism equals humanism, as perfect humanism equals naturalism."[9]

The three varieties of humanism have in common an abstract idea of man that could be developed through scientific research into a rational program for moral education and political action. But if the research is carried out in a scientific manner, it is bound to destroy the inspiration on which it is based. For example, by investigating the Greeks' "noble simplicity and serene greatness" classical scholarship soon compromised the idealistic image of the Greeks. Moral and political values to which liberalism and industrialism are related, and which were expressed openly in the nineteenth century—even in encyclopedias and political dictionaries[10]—came into question as supposedly authenticated by the historical, social, and political sciences.

So far as scholarship has as its purpose moral and political edification, its consequences are disastrous. The abstract idea of man taken as an absolute idea paves the way to ideologies, which pretend to supply religion on a

8. Quotations from Arnold Ruge, "Ernst Moritz Arndt [1840]," *Sämmtliche Werke*, vol. 4, 2nd ed. (Mannheim: J. P. Grohe, 1847), p. 90; "Eine Wendung in der deutschen Philosophie [1842]," *Sämmtliche Werke*, vol. 10 (1848), p. 444; "Was wird aus der Religion [1841]," *Sämmtliche Werke*, vol. 3 (1847), p. 224.

9. Karl Marx, *Oekonomie und Philosophie* [1844], in *Der historische Materialismus: Die Frühschriften*, vol. 1, ed. S. Landshut and J. P. Mayer (Leipzig: Kröner, 1932), p. 294. See W. Rüegg, "Zur Vorgeschichte des marxistischen Humanismusbegriffs," in *Anstösse, Aufsätze und Vorträge zur dialogischen Lebensform* (Frankfurt am Main: Alfred Metzner, 1973), pp. 181–197.

10. C. F. L. Hoffmann, *Vollständiges politisches Taschenwörterbuch* (1849; reprint ed. München/Gütersloh: Bertelsmann, 1981).

rational basis but in reality undermine respect for human ambivalence and complexity. This danger is even present in some of the great achievements of nineteenth-century scholarship, for example, Theodor Mommsen's *Roman History*. Mommsen's depiction of Cicero is a caricature because he ignores the ambivalence and complexity of human personality.[11] On a lower level, reduction of the humanities to a simplified ideal of personality is represented by the German *Bildungsphilister*.

Thus the dispiritedness of the human sciences, on which Nietzsche remarked, resulted from the emphasis that the *Geisteswissenschaften* put on the "spirit" of world, nature, and man. The crisis of the humanities did not come from the distinction between nature and freedom, or between nature and history, as Bloom would have it. The *Geisteswissenschaften* in practice operated to impoverish understanding of human nature. Their penchant for historical abstractions in the service of political or national purpose deprived the humanities of authenticity and deflected them from their true purpose, self-appreciation and understanding.

FURTHER EXPLANATIONS OF THE CRISIS

The second reason that Bloom offers for the crisis of the humanities is that "nobody is quite sure what they are." Whereas the natural and social sciences can give an account of themselves, "the humanistic part of the university . . . is just a heap of departments without any discernible order or vision of a whole of which they are parts, no account of what kind of knowledge they are seeking or what they contribute to the education of the whole man." Third, the humanities "do not have the authority of science, and they are somehow connected with tradition, style, and form—all of which are contrary to the taste of democracy and anathema to the radical movements." And lastly, to attempt to justify the humanities on utilitarian grounds is profoundly corrupting: "Their highest vocation in a democracy is to present alternatives to the dominant views of man and the good life for the sake of freedom of the mind." But democrats value utility first and foremost.

Bloom's first line of thought suggests that we distinguish between the lack of any order and the kind of knowledge that the Renaissance sought in the humanities. Then the humanities were the leading program of inquiry and higher education, conceived in opposition to the scholastic ordering of knowledge. Although the humanities always lacked any unity of substance, they had a clear vision of the knowledge they were seeking and transmitting to educate the whole man. This program can be summarized in the notion of the *studia humanitatis*, from which the humanities as we know them are derived. By studying human works, one studies to become more fully human. At the close of the fourteenth century, Coluccio Salutati, the

11. Theodor Mommsen, *Römische Geschichte*, vol. 3, 6th ed. (Berlin: Weidmannsche Buchhandlung, 1875), pp. 619–621.

founding father of humanistic studies, defined the task of the *studia humanitatis*. They serve "ad recte scribendum quandam ianuam aperire quo per te possis in alia diviniora et magis ardua penetrare,"[12] that is to say, the humanities should open a kind of entrance to the correct writing by which man on his own can penetrate to other more divine and arduous fields of knowledge. The site of research in the humanities is not the shrine of ultimate truth, but rather the atrium in which men of different condition, birth, power, goals, and faith have to communicate, to compromise, and to cooperate with one another on equal terms. This they do through the correct use of language and common sense. From interactions among individuals a consensus on fundamental values emerges. And they, in turn, maintain a continuing conversation with the authors of their language.

It seems that recent developments in philosophical anthropology have revitalized the old-fashioned idea of the humanities. Since this renewal emphasizes the verbal dimension of culture, it is interrelated to Bloom's arguments that the humanities lack authority and are connected with tradition, style, and form. And so far as this relation is based on an analysis of everyday life, research and education in the humanities should recover their importance for the life of liberal democracies. Even their usefulness for the good life of democratic citizens would be restored. In this way Bloom's fourth reason for the crisis in the humanities would be dealt with.

I propose to illustrate four common aspects of the old and the new conceptions of the humanities by commenting on Bloom's humanistic dimensions of style, form, tradition, and utility. The aspects that I have in mind are the following: the understanding of man as the "language animal," or in a larger view, man as the "symbolic animal"; the dialogical structure of communication; the impact of translation and interpretation for the understanding of tradition; and the common sense of everyday life.

LANGUAGE AND SYMBOL

According to Buffon, "le style c'est l'homme même." This discovery of the fundamental relation between language and man characterizes far better the humanistic movement of the Renaissance than does emphasis upon the so-called rebirth of antiquity. Already Isocrates had supplemented the myth of *homo faber*—who constructs the world through his reason—with a definition of man as a being endowed with the gift of speech. For the humanistic tradition—from Isocrates and Cicero to the humanists of the fourteenth through the eighteenth centuries—only through language does reason become a moral force.

While Winckelmann seeks divinity in sculpture, Petrarch, the initiator of the Italian Renaissance, is impressed by his reading of ancient authors, for their styles reveal their personalities. Petrarch discovers in the written

---

12. Coluccio Salutati, *Epistolario*, vol. 3, ed. F. Novati (Roma: Istituto Storico Italiano, 1896), p. 614.

word the emotional and rational expression of another human being in all his richness. If man is conceived as identical with his writings, then orthography, grammar, rhetoric, poetic theory, literary and textual criticism, and other disciplines dealing with language and style, all gain an anthropological and even a philosophical dimension. Research on the correct spelling of a name can become important; misspelling would be offensive to the person. Research on style or the authentic text is justified, because wording not only portrays facts or thoughts but also represents the self-understanding and self-display of a distinct personality. Moreover, research helps to understand the place of the author in his world.

The object of research is neither the author's world in its objectivity nor the absolute truth of the author's position. The grasp of language as the symbolic form by which man expresses his thinking occupies in the Renaissance a philosophical location somewhere between realism and nominalism. Language is regarded neither as a purely subjective invention nor as a manifestation of an objective reality. Rather language is the essential human activity by means of which men try to define their situation in nature and society.[13]

The fundamental importance of language as the symbolic form of human self-assertion and action is now accepted by many anthropologists, sociologists, and philosophers. For example, according to Paul Ricoeur, "human sciences may be said to be hermeneutical (1) inasmuch as their *object* displays some of the features constitutive of a text as a text, and (2) inasmuch as their *methodology* develops the same kind of procedures as those of *Auslegung* or text interpretation."[14] Also notice that Michael Polanyi attempts to bridge the partly artificial gap between Lord Snow's "two cultures" by analyzing knowing as an active comprehension of the things known and as an anticipation of unknown true implications through personal participation. Personal participation is made possible since "by the invention of symbolic forms man has given birth and lasting significance to thought."[15]

Research into the significance and influence of texts through an appreciation of rhetoric can be placed with focus on form and style as an expression of a personal quest for truth. Rhetoric even turns the table on philosophy in Chaim Perelman's thesis that all philosophical proofs are rhetorical in nature. Perelman argues that rhetoric must regain its central position in a humanistic philosophy that is based on generally accepted knowledge, formulated in common sense and the commonplace.[16]

13. See Rüegg, *Anstösse*, especially pp. 9–48, 91–167.

14. Paul Ricoeur, "The Model of Text: Meaningful Action Considered on a Text," *Social Research* 38 (1971): 529–562.

15. Michael Polanyi, *Personal Knowledge: Towards a Post-Critical Philosophy* (London: Routledge & Kegan Paul, 1962), p. 265.

16. Chaim Perelman, "Philosophie, Rhetorik, Gemeinplätze," in *Der Mensch: Subjekt und Objekt*, ed. T. Borbe (Vienna, 1973), pp. 237–246; reprinted in *Seminar: Die Hermeneutik und die Wissenschaften*, ed. Hans-Georg Gadamer and Gottfried Boehm (Frankfurt: Suhrkamp, 1978) pp. 381–392.

THE DIALOGICAL STRUCTURE OF COMMUNICATION

The dialogical structure of communication is the second fundamental feature that characterizes the old conception of the humanities and its renewal. It stems from a change in social structure, from a highly stratified society in which each group had its own function, norms, models, and symbolic forms to a more open society in which social role and cultural orientation are less determined by filiation and tradition. The epistemological and social cleavages between the "I" and the "Thou," between insiders and outsiders, between brothers and strangers, can no longer be bridged by public institutions, for these lack unity and authority.

The political, social, ecclesiastical, and intellectual schisms of the late Middle Ages gave birth to the university. It was conceived as an institution for the education of professionals charged with the tasks of finding and applying rational solutions for conflicts and disturbances in both society and nature. Scholasticism aimed to rectify a disturbed order by eliminating opinions that deviated from objective truth, and the dialectical process was the means to this end. The humanists took everyday experience into account, accepting the diversity of perspectives and actions in the pursuit of personal, social, and transcendental goals. They understood society as oriented toward greater individual freedom; they welcomed greater equality and opportunity; and they looked to conquer and exploit the unknown.

This is the reason why scholastic dialectics were replaced by humanistic dialogue both within and without the university as the fundamental structure of the pursuit of truth. Personal experience and perspective complemented purely rational deliberation in the confrontations of thinkers and speakers. Informal colloquies in Italian gardens and cloisters inaugurated the formalized dialogue in the scientific societies and academies that spread all over Europe from the fifteenth to the eighteenth century. This oral dialogue was paralleled by an epistolary style of writing in the presentation of scientific findings. Findings were published in the form of letters addressed to specific persons, relating the personal experiences of the writer and reader to the topic under consideration. The style of communication was differentiated in accordance with the personal and social characteristics of the readers. These letters were published as a conversation between persons who comment on each others' thoughts and statements.[17]

The actuality of this dialogical structure of communication is so obvious that the only question we have to raise is, Why has use of the term *dialogue*, as in the phrases "dialogue between nations," "dialogue between confessions," or "dialogue between humanists," become so hollow and meaningless? This question leads us to my third concern, the influence of translation and interpretation on the tradition of values.

17. See my *Anstösse*, especially pp. 135 ff.

TRANSLATION, INTERPRETATION, AND TRADITION

I said that the dialogue between different interests, values, and scientific perspectives has its locus in the atrium and not at the shrine of truth itself. This conversation requires mutual respect from the participants as good listeners and truthful speakers who are willing to learn from one another and to persuade without resort to lies, threats, or subterfuge. When these attitudes are absent or when fundamental issues are at stake—issues that belong not in the lobby but at the shrine of truth—no dialogue will take place. Moreover, dialogue also risks becoming meaningless if it asks for continuing translation and interpetation of the ineffable individuality of others in the context of the actual situation.

This interpersonal process can be described as a tacit integration of small but still significant differences into "personal knowledge." Michael Polanyi illustrates this process with the example of stereoscopic views in which the viewer integrates different images into a single novel image. Our conception of human nature is formed in a similar manner through silent integration of innumerable experiences with quite different personalities.[18] But this tacit integration of stereoscopic views, or novel experiences, presupposes in addition to the differences a prevailing similarity of meaning that informs the outlook of the participants. When this similarity is not guaranteed by an oral tradition, as is the case in closed social groups, participants can combine the visual and experiential differences only if they learn by the translation and interpretation of past experience—stored in written tradition—to understand the meaning of what is expressed by others.

The third humanistic discovery—and therefore the third fundamental element in the humanities—is a new understanding of tradition. Modern man can learn from tradition, but not necessarily because the past offers models for imitation. In the first *querelle des anciens et modernes*, which took place between 1400 and 1600, humanists like Salutati, Bruno, Valla, and Erasmus made quite plain that modern man must express himself differently from the ancients, precisely because language derives its meaning from the common use and common sense of a specific community.[19] Still modern man can enter personally into conversation with educated men of the past. Through interpretation and translation of their experiences into his own, the modern person can come to understand man in a situation different in time and place from his own. Erasmus praises the use of letters and the art of printing as the most useful inventions for the benefit of mankind. He says they allow you to "converse as much as you like with the

18. Michael Polanyi, "Sinngebung und Sinndeutung," in *Seminar*, p. 126.
19. See J. E. Seigel, *Rhetoric and Philosophy in Renaissance Humanism: The Union of Eloquence and Wisdom, Petrarch to Valla* (Princeton, N.J.: Princeton University Press, 1968), pp.

most eloquent and holy men. And to get as much acquainted with the
mind, the attitudes, thoughts, endeavours and deeds of men that lived so
many years ago as if you would have been associated with them for many
years."[20]

In a society in which traditional values are no longer taken for granted,
moral education, political responsibility, and ultimate value orientation all
gain from translation and interpretation of documents from the past.
Where philosophies of life are no longer transmitted orally from one generation to the next, we have to rely on indirect interaction with the founding
fathers of our culture in its institutional and symbolic forms.

THE COMMON SENSE OF EVERYDAY LIFE

German scholars used to reproach the Renaissance humanists for their lack
of philosophical thinking and their emphasis on commonplace and common sense. It is true that in general the humanists preferred the *saluberrimae
leges vitae* of the Hellenistic morality, represented in the writings of Cicero
and Plutarch, to sophisticated syllogisms. If humanistic skepticism and
morality did not promote philosophical thought, still they had great influence on the formation of urban elites. Frederick A. Olafson draws attention
to "the deep affinities which bind the language of history, literature, and
philosophy to the world of myth, on the one hand, and to that of common
sense, on the other." By the world of common sense he means "a world of
persons," "a world of human purpose and agency," "a world in which one's
most significant vis-à-vis is another person and in which the mode of
understanding appropriate to a human life as well as to human relationship
retains the dramatic and narrative form that characterized myth."[21] The
emergence of a world of common sense from the realm of myth characterizes
the humanities of the Renaissance as well as their modern renewal.

Everyday life and ordinary language have become so popular, even fash-
ionable, in recent philosophy and sociology that one has to be somewhat
skeptical about the ramifications of this trend. Nevertheless, the everyday
life of the mass of mankind, to which Allan Bloom refers in contrasting the
utilitarianism of democracy with the values of the humanistic tradition,
possesses a "prescientific common sense" that "radiates," as Olafson says,
"out from the concept of the persons as knowers and agents."[22]

63–98; Jan Lindhardt, *Rhetor, Poeta, Historicus. Studien über rhetorische Erkenntnisse und Lebens-
anschauungen im italienischen Renaissancehumanismus* (Leiden: E. J. Brill, 1979); Marc Fuma-
roli, *L'âge de l'éloquence rhétorique et "res literia" de la Renaissance au seuil de l'époque classique.
Hautes études médiévales et modernes 49* (Geneva: Librairie Droz, 1980).
    20. Erasmus, Preface to an edition of Cicero's *Tusculanae Quaestiones*, in *Opus epistolarum*,
vol. 5, ed. P. S. Allen and H. M. Allen (Oxford: Clarendon Press, 1924), p. 340.
    21. Frederick A. Olafson, "Humanism and Humanities," in *The Philosophy of the Curricu-
lum: The Need for General Education*, ed. Sidney Hook, Paul Kurz, Miro Todorovich (Buffalo,
N.Y.: Prometheus Books, 1975), pp. 53–74; quotations taken from p. 53.
    22. See Hans-Georg Gadamer, *Wahrheit und Ideologie* (Tübingen: I. C. B. Mohr, 1960),

HUMANISTIC RESEARCH AND THE FUTURE

At the beginning of the liberal epoch, the humanities were successful because they helped societies, in which new economic forces challenged traditional structures and values, to transfer and to adapt the old values to new social structures. I am confident that in our modern societies the humanities will play an even more important role, because future societies will rely even more on the use of symbols. Humanistic understanding will be so fundamental for the future of mankind that humanistic research will necessarily expand in both scope and depth.

In recent decades research in the humanities has made important advances by applying techniques imported from other disciplines, for example, dendrology and radiography in archaeology, and sociology and economics in history. Humanistic studies have also advanced by exploiting the store of nineteenth-century knowledge while discarding its presumed ideological implications. Here I point to the German *Rezeptions-* and *Begriffsgeschichte*, the French schools of Annales and Maison des Sciences de l'Homme, the Warburg Institute, and the Renaissance studies in the United States. These occupy the same place today that classical philology did in European investigations of cultural history.

THE TASK OF THE HUMANITIES

Between 1939 and 1944 a committee appointed by the American Council on Education explored the situation of the humanities in twenty-two selected institutions. This committee came to almost the same conclusions as Allan Bloom and other scholars who deplore the lack of unity in the humanities.[23] Humanistic self-criticism appears to me to be something of a cognitive lag insofar as the apparent lack of educational value of the humanities can be placed in historical perspective. It is simply one of the negative consequences of the nineteenth-century *Geisteswissenschaften*, an outlook or a philosophy of life that we no longer subscribe to.

A new anthropologically and philosophically grounded orientation to the fundamental importance of language and other symbolic forms for the understanding and forming of man has arisen. This new humanism begins to revive and enlarge the traditional goals of the humanities through use of the positive results of nineteenth-century scholarship. The humanities have, so to speak, descended from the nineteenth-century mountain top of supreme scientific authority to their former preparatory level. We retreat

---

chapter 1, on "the importance of the humanistic tradition for the *Geisteswissenschaften*" and the relation between the rhetoric tradition and the "sensus communis." For more details on common sense, rhetoric, and the humanities in the Renaissance see my essay "Cicero, orator noster," in *Entretiens sur l'antiquité classique*, vol. 28, *Cicéron et la rhétorique*, ed. Olivier Reverdin (Vandoeuvres-Genève: Fondation Hardt, in press).

23. Harold B. Dunkel, *General Education in the Humanities* (Washington, D.C.: American Council on Education, 1947).

from the shrine to the atrium. But by exploring the foundations and manifestations of man's pursuit of truth, research in the humanities will fulfill a more humble but no less important task for the other sciences and for humanity.

10

The Mediterranean Experience

JULIO R. VILLANUEVA

Today no one can question the important role played by universities in scientific investigation. But concern is increasing in many countries about the future of academic science, that is to say, the research function of the university. This concern focuses on two main issues, both of which are of major importance to higher education. First, the total funds for research allocated by governments have declined in many countries in recent years. Second, the proportion of funds allocated to universities and to research institutes directly sponsored by governments is changing. In several countries, certain nonuniversity institutions are receiving an increasing share of government money, and in some cases, for example, research in space exploration and military development, their work is classified. These projects require large amounts of money, full-time staff, and specialized equipment that cannot be duplicated on many university campuses. Such developments clearly affect the relation of advanced research to teaching and the responsibilities of faculty. Radical changes in the performance of research could seriously alter this crucial relation and transform the training of future scientists.

UNIVERSITY AND NONUNIVERSITY RESEARCH

One of the fundamental problems facing European universities today is the consolidation of their role as centers for basic research. A general agreement

Many thanks are owed to Professor Sofia Corradi of the University of Rome and to Professor Demetris Deniozos of the Scientific Research and Technology Agency, Athens, for sending me documents and for their valuable comments on the state of research in Italian and Greek universities, respectively.

Julio R. Villanueva is Professor of Microbiology, University of Salamanca.

that one of the university's main tasks is to conduct basic research of high quality is countered by pressures to withdraw research from the university and to direct it to applied and utilitarian projects.

In some European countries, the science budgets of government departments provide selective financial support for university research through a research council system. These expenditures, for both the universities and the research councils' own institutes and laboratories, are intended to provide a sound scientific and technological base, including a supply of trained manpower, that will meet each nation's needs. The councils' objectives are to foster research and postgraduate training in their specific fields, to carry out research on problems of national and scientific importance, to develop the sciences as such, and to maintain a basic capacity for research.

Various international organizations have expressed concern that the research function of the university is indeed undergoing a series of profound changes induced by social, economic, and political forces. The university's capacity to do high-quality research depends on the maintenance of scientific standards; the provision of the skilled manpower required by government, industry, and other sectors of society; and more fundamentally, the accumulation of knowledge and understanding. Current constraints on these needs include: fluctuations in student enrollments; slowdown in the growth of finance; government pressure for socially relevant research; and changing social values. In addition, many note a lack of innovation, the difficulty of initiating research under optimal conditions of staffing and instrumentation, and pressures on researchers to conduct projects that may not be of the highest scientific importance.

To this situation the universities have responded in ways governed by local circumstance; in adversity, some have been more resourceful than others. These responses have been recently analyzed by the Committee for Scientific and Technological Policy of the Organization for Economic and Cooperative Development (OECD). The committee reports four general areas of response: new modes of distributing resources, separation of teaching and research, stratification of institutions and staff, and recruitment and mobility.[1]

What is striking and gives cause for worry is that only one or two governments have begun to develop policies to address the dangers created by a scientific cadre that is growing older, and becoming less mobile and more demoralized every year.

BASIC AND APPLIED RESEARCH

There is also great anxiety in many European countries about the kind of investigation conducted in the universities. Some fear that the balance between fundamental and applied research is tipping too much toward the

1. Organization for Economic Cooperation and Development (OECD), "The Function of Scientific Research in the Universities" (Report of the Committee for Scientific and Technological Policy, Paris, 1980); subsequent in-text references to OECD are to this report.

latter in an effort to meet current social and economic needs. With the exceptions of the Deutsche Forschungsgemeinschaft (DFG) in West Germany, and the Zuiver Wentenschappelijk Orderzock (ZWO) in the Netherlands, whose priorities are essentially scientific, our universities are in danger of becoming too involved in short-term work. For example, the research councils in the United Kingdom are under increasing pressure to fund investigations relevant to policy objectives, and Canadian universities are becoming centers for applied research. As affirmed by the OECD, government research priorities should be established in consultation with the scientific community; officials must develop new modes of participation in decisions and resist the natural bureaucratic propensity to centralize control. For today governments understand better than ever that science is fundamental to economic power. The energy crisis provides new tasks for science and technology, and the latter is drawing more and more on basic research. In many countries the national economy benefits from the capacity of universities to serve as agents of innovation.

The significance of university research is not merely that it is research—mainly basic or long-term—or that it plays a crucial part in preserving the balance and quality of a nation's overall research and development effort. Its importance resides in the fact that it fulfills a number of unique functions that pervade the economic, social, and cultural dimensions of life. But the traditional view that university education and research are inseparable has been challenged not only by economic stringency but also by governments, legislatures, and members of the public. Research and teaching are tending to grow apart as the distinction hardens between research-based institutions and the rest. Further, in some countries the increase in student enrollment in the 1960s was accompanied by an even greater expansion of the non-university sector of higher education. Today a declining proportion of students attend institutions in which any research is conducted, and a declining proportion of all teachers engage in research. Mass education has increased the burden of teaching and has caused some universities to compromise their standards in hiring new faculty. Both the increase in instruction and the deficiency in recruitment have had detrimental effects on the quality of research.[2]

In some countries of southern Europe the renewal of the technical infrastructure on which contemporary science is based is meeting with serious problems. Conversations with scientists reveal that universities are increasingly unable to maintain sufficient equipment out of their normal operating budgets.

ADVANTAGES OF THE UNIVERSITY

As a setting for research, the university has several advantages over other academic or industrial institutions: it is closer to basic research; its reserves

2. F. Gonzalez, "Basic and/or Applied Research," *Abstracts of the VII General Assembly of the CRE* (Helsinki: Council of European Rectors, 1979), p. 147.

of talent include teaching staff and graduate students; it offers a propitious
setting for collaboration among several generations of scientists; and its
great diversity offers many opportunities for interdisciplinary work.[3] Further, the university's permanence and longevity permit development of
long-term projects. Information and cooperation are the university's main
priorities, and investigation is absolutely free and open, under standards
controlled by the international scientific community.

It has been generally accepted that a close connection between teaching
and research is an essential principle for all universities. High-quality
instruction is closely associated with high-quality research, an association
that benefits the teacher, the investigator, the student, and society. Indeed,
the greatest responsibility of a genuine university lies not merely in the
transmission of information, but in the creation of new knowledge, in the
search for truth, and in the advance of science. Thus universities must
encourage the association of teaching and research.

Unfortunately, many professors find little support from colleagues or
society, and often renounce their ambition of achieving better research
conditions, as information on the allocation or availability of funds for
research may be hard to come by. Others are defeated by a scarcity of
equipment and inadequate maintenance, little flexibility in the recruitment of specialized staff or in requisition of materials for laboratory experi-
ments, the unavailability of grants for travel, poorly managed libraries and
data centers, and the like.

SCIENTIFIC RESEARCH IN SPAIN

The major obstacles to scientific research in Spain are inadequate funding
and student enrollments that demand greater attention to teaching (see
Table 1). Too, Spain is a country with a weak research tradition. As a
consequence, there is no social conscience to support research and scientific
development in general; many people are insensitive to the need to develop
science. Even worse, our situation is marked by disinterest on the part of the
government and politicians.[4] But Spanish society recognizes that the university is the ideal place for the creation of new knowledge. Spanish universities are deeply involved and committed to the current national reconsideration of values; they are spreading new ideas and locating people of talent.
Thus university professors are playing an important part in national
renovation.

In 1964, Spain began development plans that have led to spectacular
economic growth. Now continuous growth depends on scientific advance,
which is the key to technological development. If Spain is to compete in

3. M. Malita, "Universities as Centers of Research," *Higher Education in Europe*
[Helsinki] 5, no. 2 (1980): 34.

4. J. R. Villanueva, *Universidad, Investigación y Sociedad* (Salamanca: Ediciones Universidad de Salamanca, 1980).

TABLE I
Growth of higher education in Spain,
1960 to 1980

	1960	*1970*	*1980*
Number of Universities	14	23	32
Students	76,362	184,261	650,000
Faculty	9,625 (1966)	21,589 (1975)	34,774

world markets, her assimilation of foreign technology must be followed by the development of her own technology. The government must take an interest in and become responsible for scientific and technological progress.

In recent decades Spanish universities have suffered from a sheer lack of funds, which made it difficult for researchers to form teams with sufficient continuity. However, more recently the equipment of many departments has been considerably improved, and the research, though not the technical, staff has been enlarged. Several important research teams of international renown have been formed, and the creation of many new universities has opened opportunities for young professors. Unfortunately, expansion and mobility discourage team stability. Too, Spanish universities do not now receive sufficient research funds to train graduate students and to offer services to society similar to those provided in other countries.

Financial sources for research at the department level are various, including grant programs for graduate students with parallel research support; research support for lecturers; grants to projects from the Comisión Asesora de Investigación Científica y Técnica; support from private foundations; foreign funding, mostly from the United States; and contributions from industry or the government for specific projects. The first of these sources deserves special comment. The grant program for predoctoral students was established in 1967 on the occasion of the beginning of a national development program (Plan for the Formation of Teaching and Research Staff). On the basis of an open public examination 860 grants were awarded that first year to the most brilliant graduates of all Spanish universities. These renewable grants, which are still awarded annually, include support for the department in which the student is to do his work, and renewals depend on reports issued by the research commission of each university. Many graduate students, possibly more than 8,000 between 1970 and 1980, have been able to complete their doctorates with this assistance, and the vast majority have obtained positions as assistant professors and assistant full professors. This is a very important infusion of competent researchers into the university.

There is no question that the advance of scientific research is already producing tangible results. Above all, it encourages Spanish society to appreciate science. Only such a change in the climate of opinion can help to correct serious imbalances that have appeared during the recent spectacular economic developments, including the chronic deficit in our balance of payments. This deficit is, of course, the direct consequence of importing foreign technology.

Reports of the Comisión Asesora de Investigación Científica y Técnica and of the OECD confirm that the research potential in Spain is very low, namely, only .6 per thousand of the active population. This failure endangers the growth of our entire research and development system, although efficient use of our potential could contribute decisively to the regeneration of both scientific and technological advance. Nevertheless, in Spain there is still a lack of respect for science. It is significant that there is no systematic and rigorous study of the deficiencies of the research system.

THE THREE-YEAR PLAN OF RESEARCH ADVANCE

The Spanish government is now considering a three-year plan for the advancement of scientific and technical research. This plan places special emphasis on strengthening the basic structure of the national research system. Also modest, but not negligible, programs of applied research and development would be initiated to quickly contribute important economic and social benefits. Additional funds—more than 70,000 million pesetas for a three-year period—would be used principally to deepen the foundation of the research system in both the universities and the state-managed research centers.

Specifically, the three-year plan has four goals. First, advance of research in the public sector; the objective is to consolidate the national infrastructure of research and development. Here the plan contemplates formation of research staff through assignment of 3,300 new scholarships during the three-year period. At the same time, the intention is to adequately endow research centers. Funds are earmarked for renovation of equipment and for expansion of the centers that warrant it. The three other goals of the plan concern the improvement of research and development in the business sector, the development of technical scientific services and activities related to research, and the participation of Spain in the international scientific community. All these activities promise important benefits.

Today nearly all the Spanish provinces have one or more institutions, or centers, of higher education, and the regional balance is very good. However, as a consequence of this great expansion and the high mobility of faculty, it is difficult to organize research groups, even small ones, on a stable basis. In the state research centers, notably the Superior Council for Scientific Research, the problem of staffing is, if anything, even more grave. After vigorous initial growth, this center lapsed into total stagnation through the aging of personnel. Moreover, many of the activities of these state centers have dissipated because they lacked a policy of progressive growth. Fortunately, the three-year plan provides for an important increase in the centers' teams. Similarly, the plan provides for improvement of the university research potential, mandating the creation of 2,076 posts for technical and auxiliary research staff, of which approximately half will be assigned to the universities.

THE UNIVERSITY AUTONOMY ACT OF 1982

The University Autonomy Act envisages research as a basic activity of the university, one that should be underwritten by the public authorities, and in which society should collaborate effectively. Thus an opportunity is offered whereby the universities can establish collaborative relations with private and public businesses or with any other organizations interested in the development of science and technology. The intent is to afford more freedom for research, without neglecting the responsibility to employ growing resources in the most efficient manner.

The act specifies that a national scientific policy must focus on the research effort at the universities; they should be given the structures and equipment necessary to carry out their mission. It recognizes that scientific research constitutes a primary function of the university and that it is a faculty right. The act also provides for freedom of choice of objectives of individual research, which must be coordinated with research projects undertaken by the universities.

In 1979, the Ministry of Universities and Research was created, separate from the Ministry of Education and Science established in 1964. However, the new ministry has not been effective in rising above the bureaucratic shuffle; it is now being restructured as the Ministry of Education, Universities, and Research. The only really positive action of the Ministry of Universities and Research was the authorization of 1,800 professorships and 1,800 assistant professorships to be allocated among the universities, an important step toward improving teaching and research. We may hope and expect that Spanish society and government will continue to acquire increasingly positive attitudes toward the university and higher education.

THE ITALIAN UNIVERSITIES

Past and present tensions in the Italian universities have complex causes. The Italian system of higher education was transformed in the 1960s to meet the needs of the masses rather than those of an elite. However, facilities, faculty, and social services were not adequately expanded. This incongruity has led to strain in student-professor relations, and a concurrent sharp rise in youth unemployment has lowered expectations and bred resentment among graduates. These circumstances have compelled the Italian government to give university problems high priority.

Many of the problems facing Italian universities are in the area of research; they are common to Mediterranean universities, and we have met with them in our examination of Spanish higher education.

In Italy, scientific research is carried on mainly in three sectors: university departments, centers of the Consiglio Nazionale delle Ricerche (CNR), and state-run or private industry. Research has always been an important feature of the Italian university, and the CNR supports a large proportion of the research done in university departments. Most of the equipment in their laboratories has been purchased with money from the CNR, and university professors are in charge of most of the CNR's own research centers.

In 1980, the research budget of the CNR amounted to 250 billion lire, with an additional 60 billion for applied research. The CNR has 2,188 investigators, 2,498 technicians, and 192 auxiliary staff. By way of comparison, the Italian universities have 16,249 researchers, 1,047 technicians, and 2,528 auxiliary personnel. Most university people apply to the CNR for research grants.

In 1978, the Ministry of Public Instruction gave Italian universities 24 billion lire for research, although they had asked for seven times as much. In 1979, the funds allocated for university research were 33 billion lire, and the CNR provided 230 billion.[5] A great change came in 1980 when legislation dealt with the universities' strong request for more direct funding from the government. Research funding by the ministry increased from 33 to 91 billion lire. In 1981 the research figure stands at 141 billion, and in 1982 the proposal is for 191 billion.

Two policies—advanced study abroad and distinguished foreign scholars in Italian universities—constitute innovations of the utmost importance that augur great possibilities for the future of research in Italy. Nor can one overlook the strides the CNR is trying to make in applied research. Among the most promising aspects of these developments is the cooperation effectively established among the universities, the CNR, and Italian industry.

An important step forward for Italian universities is the establishment of an information center for ongoing research, to which each university must report on its activity; this information is the basis for future funding. It has been suggested that the Consiglio Universitario Nazionale, as the consultative board of the Ministry of Education, establish objective criteria for future funding. The board will administer 40 percent of the government funding, while the rest will be distributed directly to the universities.

The most basic deficiency in the Italian research system is the lack of a doctoral program designed to further the education of researchers and specialists. Italian professors do basic research with the help of assistants, whose low morale reflects their inadequate pay. It will be most important for the government to establish a research doctorate and a fellowship program to send Italian students abroad, which would allow study abroad to become a keystone of the national research system. Among the many other

5. S. Corradi, "Towards a Redevelopment of Italian Higher Education," *CRE Information* no. 51 (1980), pp. 91–104.

problems with respect to research in university departments is the universities' lack of control over the activities of researchers, who cannot be fired for inefficiency, and whose careers are governed by seniority. Unfortunately, Italian industry has shown little or no interest in university research, as is the case in most Mediterranean countries.

Italian research is in the forefront in a number of fields, including gravitation, the structure of matter, nuclear and energy physics, nuclear medicine and medical pathology, nuclear biology, genetics, archaeology, and agriculture. Italians are doing work of international importance despite difficulties and, at times, virtual institutional anarchy. But conditions have vastly improved, and the forecast for the near future must be that research will continue to be a dynamic force in the Italian university.

THE GREEK UNIVERSITIES

Greece has fourteen universities and institutions of higher education. The first university was founded in Athens in 1837, on the German model, as a center for scholarship and science. Between 1915 ad 1930, six more universities were created, and five more since 1964 in response to the increasing demand for higher education. The same model was used for all these institutions, and is still in use, despite attempts at reform.[6] Only the two most recent institutions, founded after 1973, have been erected on principles that are distinctly American. However, in the last five years, efforts have been intensified to rework the operational structure of the universities and to integrate them into their social environments.

The 1978 act on university reform, which has been widely contested, above all seeks to improve university efficiency. The act proposes replacement of the traditional professorial chairs by American-style departments, seeks an increase in the turnover of assistant staff, and introduces more stringent study regulations. Early drafts of the act designate research as one of the main functions of the university, a political choice of major importance.

The Greek reform ensures participation of students and assistants in policy making, especially in areas related to teaching and research. Creation of a national council for higher education should constitute a valuable new connection between the universities and society, while vacillations in policy resulting from frequent cabinet changes should be reduced. However, the council may adversely affect university autonomy, for it has authority over the creation of new institutions of higher education, schools, and departments. Its authority also covers the allocation of annual budgets, the general orientation of research, the construction of new campuses, and so on.

6. L. Mavridis, "Reform and Development of Tertiary Education in Greece" (Report for the Ministry of National Education and Culture, Hellenic Republic, 1979); D. Deniozos, "Improving the Research Capacity of the Universities in Semi-Industrialized Countries, the Greek Example," *CRE Information* no. 50 (1980), pp. 68–81.

Unlike many western European nations, Greece has no national scientific policy. In Greece, as in other developing countries, university research is identified with basic or fundamental research; it is not viewed as a function of national or regional needs. Recently, various professors (most of them educated in western Europe and the United States) have become more conscious of the distance between the university and society, and they have begun to establish contacts with industry and public authorities.

Finance for university research is provided mainly by the state. A limited number of research programs are financed by various foreign institutions or international organizations. University moneys tend to be used for fundamental research, external funds more frequently for applied research. In 1977 the total budget for the universities amounted to 8,508 million drachmas (about $230 million), nearly 1 percent of Greece's gross national product.[7] However, unable to break this figure down between teaching and research, we must seek a measure of the Greek research effort in an oblique manner. A 1976 survey of research activities in a number of institutions by a branch of the Ministry of Culture revealed about 2,500 projects in progress; universities accounted for 1,100 projects, or 44 percent of the total.

A national research foundation promotes research, in both the natural sciences and the humanities, in the university and elsewhere. Applications for grants are evaluated by groups of experts. In 1976 the foundation spent 30 million drachmas on more than 100 projects, most of which were in the universities. The foundation also supports a number of research institutes and maintains the largest library of scientific journals in Greece. Additional support comes from a state scholarship foundation that provides funds for graduate study in Greece and abroad. In 1978 almost 100 new scholarships were awarded.

In Greece's science and technology centers, much of the departments' equipment and facilities is used for both teaching and research. Graduate students often develop projects under the direct supervision of staff members. As a rule, all departmental staff must distribute their time between teaching and research. In addition, a number of research centers have recently been established. These include the Institute for Modern Greek Studies in the University of Thessaloniki, the Institute for Regional Development in the Panteios School for Political Science, and the Center of Byzantine Research. In these institutions the faculty is completely devoted to research, engaging only in some highly specialized teaching.

A service for research and development has been established in the Ministry of Culture and Science to promote and finance scientific research and development. There is also an interministerial committee on scientific research, and a service for scientific research and technology is located in the

7. Data in this and the following paragraph from M. L. Batrinos, "Scientific Research in Greek Universities" (Report for Division of Higher Education and Research, Council of Europe, Strasbourg, 1978).

Ministry of Coordination. According to recent information, this latter committee is responsible for formulating a national research program and for establishing research priorities. Such planning will repair a serious deficiency.

Greece is now a member of the European Economic Community (EEC). Greek universities will have to evolve and improve to the level of the European universities, especially with respect to scientific research. Meanwhile, the present failure to adapt higher education to social development represents a serious handicap for Greece. Higher education and scientific research have to become important political priorities—backed by massive financial resources—if Greece is to participate in the EEC on an equal footing.[8]

8. J. Siotis, "L'enseignement supérieur en Grèce à l'heure européenne," *CRE Information* no. 48 (1979).

11

Research in Italy

JOHN A. SCOTT

Research has always been an important part of Italian university life. Even in 1980, a professor may think little of canceling classes or of beginning the academic year two or three weeks behind schedule; if he has produced a weighty volume he will feel that he has more than earned his keep and the respect of colleagues and students.

To obtain an overall picture of the importance and achievements of academic research in Italy, it is essential to take account not only of work done in universities but also that undertaken in research centers financed by the state, chiefly through the Consiglio Nazionale delle Ricerche. This council finances a great deal of the research carried out in universities (providing about 90 percent of scientific equipment in university laboratories), while its research centers are for the most part under the direction of professors.

ADMINISTRATION OF RESEARCH

The Consiglio Nazionale delle Ricerche (CNR) is a massive organization with over 5,700 research workers. In 1978, 230 billion lire were allocated by the CNR, and 24 billion lire by the Ministry of Public Instruction for research.[1] Most faculty apply to the CNR for grants. There are eleven

John A. Scott is Professor of Italian at the University of Western Australia.

1. Figures for 1980 staffing were supplied by Dr. M. Moretti, Secretary General of the CNR. In the *Relazione generale sullo stato della ricerca scientifica e tecnologica in Italia per l'anno 1978 (Atti parlamentari, VII Legislatura: Camera dei Deputati)*, doc. 13, n. 3–bis (Rome, n.d.), p. 47, the figures for 1978 are broken down as follows: CNR—2,188 researchers, 2,048 technicians, 192 auxiliary staff; university—16,249 researchers, 2,047 technicians,

consultative committees (eight for the sciences, three for the humanities and social sciences). In theory, anyone can apply, but in practice three-quarters of the funds go to the sciences; and, while university assistants (*borsisti, contrattisti*) may apply, they must be sponsored by a professor. However, no one teaching in a university or a public high school may be paid for his services, as this would contravene an Italian law designed to prevent payment of two salaries to an individual. Hence, money from public sources must be spent on equipment, travel, and ancillary services.

A law passed in February 1980 provides for increased expenditure on research by the Ministry of Public Instruction: 90 billion lire in 1980; 140 billion in 1981; and 190 billion in 1982. Of these moneys, 40 percent will be administered by the newly constituted Consiglio Nazionale dell'Università, while the remaining 60 percent will be distributed directly to the various universities.[2] The probable result will be that, whereas in the past the CNR has supported basic university research, in the future it will tend to concentrate on setting up and maintaining centers of excellence and special long-term projects of an applied nature. It is impossible to forecast what shifts will occur in the distribution of CNR funds (at present, approximately 15 percent for humanities, 8 percent for social sciences, 77 percent for natural sciences).

IMPORTANT DEFICIENCIES

On both the CNR and the universities, strong pressure is exerted by trade unions and young researchers to have temporary positions transformed into permanent ones. There is very little control over research workers, who cannot be fired for inefficiency and whose careers are governed by seniority. This leads to unproductive creation of lifelong *ricercatori* who accomplish little or nothing, while the situation is static: the average age of people in research is constantly increasing—a fact bewailed by many directors of research centers—and there is virtually no turnover and no new blood. Trade unions in the universities may hinder technicians from cleaning laboratories or feeding animals. Italian industry has shown slight interest in scientific research in the universities: large firms either do their own research and train their personnel in their own laboratories or they rely heavily on foreign patents.

2,528 auxiliary staff. Data on 1978 budget from *Relazione*, pp. 385ff. In 1980, the research budget of the CNR consisted of 250 billion lire plus 60 billion lire for *progetti finalizzati* (applied research).

For the total number of projects financed by the CNR, with a brief description of each, see: *Ricerche finanziate dal CNR (anno 1975)*, 2 vols., (Rome: CNR, 1978), which lists 2,890 projects. See also (for 1978): *Annuario degli organi di ricerca*, 3 vols., (Rome: CNR, 1978). It should be noted that, in 1978, the Ministry of Public Instruction gave Italian universities 10.45 billion lire for research, whereas they had requested 70.37 billion lire (*Relazione*, pp. 393–395).

2. For the composition of the Consiglio Universitario Nazionale Provvisorio, see the *Gazzetta ufficiale della Repubblica Italiana*, 10 February 1979, pp. 1340–1341.

Until now, however, the most basic deficiency in the Italian research system has been lack of any equivalent to a doctoral program, which should be an important supply of personnel while the next generation is being trained by apprenticeship. Thus large programs of both basic and advanced research have had to be carried out by professors, or entrusted to assistants (*contrattisti*, *borsisti*, *assegnisti*: the so-called *precari*) who, though employed to do research, have all too frequently been preoccupied with their own precarious situation.[3] They have also had to take classes scheduled for professors and help conduct examinations (a Herculean task in Italy), frequently to an extent that has interfered with their research. This has given rise to further discontent and also to an unjustifiable expectation that a research assignment to work on a particular research project should result in a permanent position.

SIGNIFICANT INNOVATIONS

Despite these problems, Italian research is effective. For the future, most important is the establishment of a doctoral program with a research degree (*dottorato di ricerca*). The Legge Valitutti of February 1980 specifies that this will be a purely academic title, that is, it will not confer any professional advantage or privilege outside the universities; it will require a minimum training of three years and all candidates will receive a scholarship. A highly significant feature is that no less than a quarter of these scholarships will be set aside for research to be undertaken in foreign universities.[4] What has been tolerated and occasionally encouraged in the past—advanced study abroad—will now become one of the linchpins of the Italian research effort. A parallel development is a provision for university teachers and experts from other countries, who may now be invited to teach for a period of months or even years in an Italian university with rank and privileges equivalent to those held abroad. (Hitherto, only Italian citizens have been allowed to hold official teaching positions in Italian universities.) These two measures—advanced study abroad and provisions for distinguished foreign scholars to teach and undertake research in Italy—constitute innovations of the utmost importance that should open up immense possibilities for the future of research in Italy.

Another highly significant innovation is the introduction of the *progetto*

3. The *contrattisti* were introduced in 1973 by the Legge Malfatti: their contracts were originally for four years. *Borsisti* were introduced later and given a *borsa* (scholarship) for one year. *Assegnisti* were supposed to be given a stipend for two years. However, hitherto governments have regularly renewed all contracts, scholarships, and stipends of this group, who form the majority of the *precari* ("precarious ones"). The Valitutti Law of February 1980 intends that they should disappear, for the most part by assimilation into the new category of *ricercatori* (researchers). The trade unions and the *precari* themselves are unwilling to accept the possibility that some of them may not be judged fit (*idonei*) to continue in a university career. The situation is further complicated by the effects of a falling birth rate, which mean that employment in the secondary school system is virtually impossible as an alternative.

4. The text of the Legge Valitutti has been published in the *Atti parlamentari (Camera dei*

finalizzato, which groups together various projects or subprojects (*sottoprogetti*) for specific areas of applied research. As elaborated by the CNR, the *progetti finalizzati* now cover some twenty-five sectors of research, all clearly linked to the needs and problems of Italian society: for example, the conservation of energy and discovery of alternative sources, preventive medicine, ecology, agriculture, and air traffic. The general commission set up to oversee this new structure includes a majority of university professors as well as representatives of Italian industry.[5] So far, the CNR has spent more than 160 billion lire on these projects: 20 billion in 1976; 35 billion in 1977; 45 billion 1978; 60 billion in 1979. This increase in expenditure was prompted by an increasing awareness of the importance of projects that have proved to be a highly flexible instrument for rapid discovery and realization of new lines of research. One of the most promising aspects is the cooperation effectively established between the CNR, universities, and Italian industry. For example, in 1978, seventeen *progetti finalizzati* involved 9,759 research workers: 1,690 from the CNR, .6,570 from the universities, 440 from industry, and 1,059 from other organizations.[6]

RESEARCH FRONTIERS

Italian research is in the forefront in a number of fields. Fundamental work on gravitation and the structure of matter is being done at the University of Rome and at the nearby Istituto di Fisico Nucleare. Important connections with Euratom and the Centre Européen de Recherche Nucléaire (Geneva) help to maintain high quality, which is also stimulated by centers such as the Centro di Cultura Scientifica Ettore Majorana at Erice (Sicily), to which leading scholars from all over the world are invited. Important discoveries have been made by the observatory at Asiago (Vicenza). The CNR's Istituto di Fisiologia Clinica (Pisa) has brought together a team of doctors, surgeons, mathematicians, engineers, and technicians to collaborate in solving problems in nuclear medicine. Computers are used for their work on the pathology and surgery of the human heart, echocardiography, and metabolism of certain proteins. The importance of this exploration was recognized by the award of an international prize at Tokyo in 1974. As is so often the case, this independent center (financed and controlled by the CNR) is under the direction of an academic expert, L. Donato, who also holds the chair of

---

Deputati), *VIII Legislatura: Disegni di legge e relazioni*, documenti, n. 810-B, pp. 1–35. The section on scholarships abroad is on p. 23.

5. See: Consiglio Nazionale delle Ricerche (Servizio affari scientifici e tecnologici), *I progetti finalizzati* (Rome: CNR, 1979), pp. 8–13. The commission calls on the expertise of eleven consultative committees (p. 12).

6. Ibid., p. 9. Rather than the number of researchers involved, the importance of the role played by Italian industry in the *progetti finalizzati* can be judged from the distribution of funds in the same year: CNR, 7 billion lire; universities, 15 billion; industry, 13 billion; other organizations, 3 billion; administrative expenses, 3.25 billion; scholarships, 2 billion (ibid., pp. 124–125).

special medical pathology at Pisa. Contacts with the Scuola Normale di Pisa (a prestigious institution founded by Napoleon on the lines of the École Normale Supérieure) are also important, while students in both institutions can find a more practically oriented environment and help with their *tesi di laurea* (and, in future, the *dottorato di ricerca*). The Istituto di Fisiologia Clinica is the only research center to have patients; much of its work is directed toward preventive medicine and discovery of techniques for monitoring patients' progress without introducing cumbersome equipment into the body.[7]

Another important development is the Area della Ricerca di Roma, which covers seventy hectares, some thirty kilometers to the northeast of Rome. Organized and funded by the CNR, it provides a centralized service area (for example, in laser research and spectometry) for the University of Rome. The center has eight laboratories; six for chemistry (including nuclear chemistry), one for agricultural science, and one devoted to research into archaeological problems (for example, the preservation of ruins and buildings from the effects of atmospheric pollution; also, a Sabine necropolis is on the site). There are accommmodations for visiting scholars from overseas: the International Congress of Photochemistry was held there in October 1979, the International Congress on the Chemistry of Oxides of Carbon in February 1980.

As mentioned, one of the problems is the general aging of research workers: in September 1980, national *concorsi* to take on new staff were organized, the first in many years, designed to give a total of 1,800 new research posts to the CNR over the next three years.

COMPUTERIZATION

Use of computers by the Istituto di Fisiologia Clinica in Pisa may provide us with a bridge between research in the sciences, medicine, and the humanities. Italy has the distinction of being the only country to have created a uniform system for its computers. In 1965, IBM offered a new type of advanced computer system (7090) to the University of Pisa, which was chosen because of its airport and its central location. Symbolically, it was decided to use one of the most sophisticated products of modern science to produce the most comprehensive concordance of Dante's *Divine Comedy*, in honor of the seventh centenary of the poet's birth. In 1949 Professor Roberto Busa, S.J. was the first to use mechanical equipment for a concordance, in his work on Thomas Aquinas. In 1964, the Accademia della Crusca decided to start work once more on its famous dictionary. It was decided to transfer all this mechanical work to the new Centro Nazionale Universitario di Calcolo Elettronico (CNUCE) in Pisa.[8] The need for a

7. Further details in: Istituto di fisiologia clinica (CNR), *Programmi di ricerca* (Pisa: Istituto di fisiologia clinica, 1980).

8. A further example of the interchange between the state university system and the CNR may be found in the fact that the name "Centro Nazionale Universitario" has been left

specialized link between scholars and machines was quickly perceived and provided. This was organized and eventually became a separate center under the direction of Professor A. Zampolli.[9] In June 1978 the section was detached from the CNUCE and became the CNR's Istituto di Linguistica Computazionale (ILC). The ILC provides essential services between computers and some fifty research centers, chiefly in the fields of philology and linguistics. Much of the work consists in providing lists of word frequencies, concordances, incipits, and the like. An electronic library has been set up, with 8,000 magnetic tapes of texts in many languages, converted into machine-readable form. Important links have been formed with similar centers abroad, as the European Economic Community is constructing a computer network with an international linguistic bank. Current pioneering work at the ILC also includes studies in lexicography, dialectology (The *Atlante Linguistico Italiano*), linguistical statistics, and the problems of machine translation. Research projects include the *Dizionario Macchina dell'Italiano* (with about 1,000,000 forms), which will reduce the time necessary for lemmatization; an automatic analysis of Italian syntax; the provision of new models for statistical linguistics and help for studies in psycholinguistics. Work is being extended to Spanish and Sanskrit, as well as an etymological dictionary for Gaelic. Most noteworthy is that the ILC is the only center in the world to combine text processing with the manifold dimensions of computational linguistics.

The computers at the ILC are used by scholars all over Italy. One of the most interesting ventures was launched by the Centro del Lessico Intellettuale Europeo, another research center of the CNR, directed by Professor Tullio Gregory of the University of Rome. It aims to provide a history of the cultural terminology of the Mediterranean world, with particular emphasis on the language of philosophy in the seventeenth and eighteenth centuries (when the vernaculars took over the function of Latin in this area). A comprehensive analysis of Giordano Bruno's lexicon has just been published;[10] monographs are being compiled on the history and evolution of certain terms and word-groups; and three international congresses on intellectual lexicography have been organized (in 1974, 1977, and 1980). The center's work forms a unique marriage between lexicography and the history of ideas.

---

unchanged, though the center is officially detached from the university system and is now wholly dependent on the CNR.

9. For a detailed description of work accomplished in 1974–1976 and plans for the future, see: A. Zampolli, "Division Linguistique du CNUCE. Activités de 1974 à 1976," in *ORDO. II° Colloquio Internazionale del Lessico Intellettuale Europeo*, vol. 2, ed. M. Fattori and M. Bianchi (Rome, 1979): 817–818 (with bibliography).

10. M. Ciliberto, *Lessico di Giordano Bruno*, 2 vols. (Rome, 1979). For a summary of the center's activities, see: T. Gregory, "Rapport sur les activités du 'Lessico Intellettuale Europeo,'" in *I° Colloquio Internazionale del Lessico Intellettuale Europeo*, ed. M. Fattori and M. Bianchi (Rome, 1976), pp. 21–43; also, the same author's "Lessico Intellettuale Europeo (1974–1976)," in *ORDO* 2:779–785.

The computers at Pisa have also helped to transform the venerable Accademia della Crusca, which is now situated in the bucolic setting of a Medici villa outside Florence. Founded in the 1570s, the academy produced the first great dictionary of a European vernacular in 1612 and inspired the creation of both the French and the Spanish academies. It now has three research centers, concentrating on lexicography, philology, and grammar, each with its own annual journal. Conferences are organized with participants from abroad. In 1964 work on the famous dictionary was resumed under the leadership of the great scholar Giacomo Devoto. It was decided to begin with the medieval period from the origins of the Italian vernacular to 1375 (death of Boccaccio and the explosion of Latin Humanism). Now under the direction of Professor D'Arco Silvio Avalle, the scope of the work undertaken is unique in its effort to expand lexicographical research to include every aspect of the Italian language (instead of attending only to the literary tradition and code, as in that great monument to premechanical lexicography, the *Oxford English Dictionary*). Twenty million occurrences have been collected so far; work is estimated to take another ten years to complete. One of the problems in such a long-term venture is that computers evolve, with the ensuing danger that all work done may become obsolete. However, a new and highly sophisticated system of computer programing has been set up for this purpose in collaboration with the ILC at Pisa.[11] A parallel venture is the series entitled *Concordanze della Lingua Poetica Italiana delle Origini*, for which photographs of all known manuscripts have been gathered from many countries. Accompanied by the decision to use only those manuscripts that can definitely be ascribed to the period before 1300, the resulting synoptic view has led to some illuminating results in the redating of manuscripts and in an understanding of their place in medieval culture, which was dictated by specific cultural policies.[12]

BRIGHT PROSPECTS

Other important domains of Italian research include biology (genetics and the structure of molecular biology), art history, medieval and Renaissance culture, Roman law, classical philology, and archaeology. Etruscology has a leading center at the University of Rome. The University's Institute of Archaeology was responsible for the momentous discovery in 1977 at Ebla, Syria, of a hitherto unknown Semitic language. The deciphering of Linear B in 1953 was quickly exploited by Italian scholars, who have helped to

11, See: D'Arco Silvio Avalle, "Il lessico italiano delle origini e l'informatica linguistica," in *ORDO* 2:749–760, and the same author's *Al servizio del Vocabolario della Lingua Italiana* (Florence, 1979).

12. This kind of ambitious project is all the more precious and extraordinary when one considers the difficulties that face scholars who have to use Italian libraries, and the lack of any adequate general catalogue (see Professor Denys Hay's criticisms in "Storici e Rinascimento negli ultimi venticinque anni," in *Il Rinascimento. Interpretazioni e Problemi* [Bari, 1979], pp. 20, 31, 40).

revolutionize our understanding of the second millenium B.C. One center for such studies is the Istituto di Studi Micenei (the only CNR institute in the humanities), directed by Professor Saccone of the University of Rome. This institute organizes archaeological missions for the eastern Mediterranean basin and Mesopotamia, publishes Greek incunabula with the collaboration of foreign scholars, and arranged the first International Congress of Mycenaean Studies in 1967.

Modern techniques in archaeology and work with computers by the Accademia della Crusca are striking examples of the way Italian genius combines the best of two worlds, by grafting innovations onto the oldest university tradition in Europe. Fears have been expressed that the new law (Legge Valitutti of 1980) will widen the separation between research and teaching, but it is too early to tell. It must be acknowledged that the proliferation of research centers outside the universities (though usually under the direction of university professors) may lead to an unhealthy split between the overcrowded and at times poorly equipped universities and the relatively peaceful research havens. However, the law now makes it possible for state universities to decide whether or not to create a system of departments, organized according to local needs and resources. This new option goes against the faculty chair system and indeed the whole tradition of Italian bureaucracy;[13] it may be well or ill used. There should be little doubt, however, that Italian scholars have continued to produce work of international importance, despite great hindrance and at times virtual anarchy in the universities. On the whole, conditions have improved, and the forecast for the 1980s must be that research will continue to be a dynamic element in the Italian university system. Determined efforts are being made to rationalize this system, especially insofar as research is concerned. If these are carried through successfully, some brilliant achievements may be expected—perhaps on a par with the legendary group led by Enrico Fermi in the 1930s.

13. Compare Giovanni Sartori, "The Italian University System," in *Universities in the Western World*, ed. Paul Seabury (New York: Free Press, 1975), pp. 246–56.

PART III

Academic Standards
and University Organization

12

University Standards and the Decline of Humane Learning

ALLAN BLOOM

———

We may begin a consideration of the problem of standards in universities with the most obvious, the most quantifiable (the fact that the quantifiable is the only persuasive thing to us is a symptom of the problem) change in standards during the last twenty years, undergraduate grade inflation. Although professors may no longer be very sure about what they measure themselves against, students do know that they are measured by those A, B, C, D, and F's, or rather those A's and B's, and the grade-point average which sums up their total achievement at the end of four years. In even the best universities the inflation in grades has matched that in the economy, with the difference that in the academic economy there is no way to inflate the A; it cannot be surpassed, so that among students there are now practically only the rich and the newly rich. A's are easy to come by, B's are the consolation prize; and unusual lack of attentiveness or failure to complete assignments results in a C. An F is an achievement, preferred by some to a C because it seems the result of an act of will on the part of its recipient rather than a sign of mediocrity. D had disappeared. With 40 to 60 percent of the students receiving honors, graduation ceremonies become something of an embarrassment for universities that regard themselves and are regarded as standard-bearers, for everyone knows that this is not a result of a breakthrough in pedagogy but of a cheapening of the product.

Allan Bloom is Professor in the Committee on Social Thought and at the College of the University of Chicago.

CONSEQUENCES OF GRADE INFLATION

But what is wrong with this, particularly since there is good reason to think that college students are working as hard as they ever did, certainly harder than they did in the late sixties? The old system of grading was after all only a convention, and we simply adapted over time to a new one. Well, in the first place, the devalued currency may still serve for domestic purposes; but external consumers, that is, the professional schools (the market to which our products are now largely seeking to appeal), no longer trust our seal of approval. The college record does not reveal real talents or achievements, certainly not true superiority. Hence they rely on letters of recommendation and standardized tests. And since letters have suffered the same kind of inflation (after all, they are written by the professors who give the grades and whose generosity is encouraged by governmental threats to confidentiality), the tests emerge triumphant, possessing at least a certain harsh objectivity. So students too begin to consider the tests as genuine measures of accomplishment, and the machines of the Educational Testing Service replace the universities as the source of evaluation and standards. The idea of a liberal education with its multiplicity in unity, the variety of learning and sensitivity that it promotes, begins to fade as its authority, never effective for more than a brief moment in any event, is supplanted. The student can hardly take the university very seriously as the source of education, rather than as a propaedeutic to vocational training, if it is not master in its own world, if what it uniquely gives is not understood to be what prepares him for the life he is going to lead. It is one thing for a student to want to be a doctor but know that a distinct university experience precedes medical training and that his admissibility to medical school will be determined by his undergraduate performance. It is quite another thing if he thinks that the university is preparing him for specialized examinations in the profession of his choice. In this latter case, the integrity and independence of this civilizing pause in life are undermined. It is somehow absurd that the four years of study and experience, which can reveal a student's virtues in a comprehensive and concrete way, are depreciated in favor of a one-shot test.

But there is much more. In spite of the meaninglessness of grades, the new dispensation has made grade-grubbers of the students. The grade-point average does count for something. The B is almost assured, thus the A becomes extremely desirable and apparently within the reach of almost anyone. So many A's are given that an A cannot be proof of real talent for or mastery of the discipline in question; it is merely useful for the larger purpose of keeping averages high. This heavy concentration on grades for their own sake is a direct consequence of the prejudice against grading of the sixties. Then it was argued that one should seek knowledge for its own sake, and ungraded or pass-fail course options were insisted on. Mindless reformism in its indifference to reality had its usual result, the exact opposite of what is intended.

Doubtless, the desire for distinction is not the same as concern for knowledge, but it is a powerful motive that can attract the young to studies they may later learn to love for themselves. If grades represent real achievement in a discipline, they act both as guardians of it and incentives for respecting it. Grades and honors are, if properly used, a means to education; disinterested love of knowledge is its proper result. The agitation against grades took this rare result of a good education to be the common possession of every beginning student. The success of that agitation suppressed both the motive for achievement and the awe for disciplines whose teachers do not respect them. But it did nothing to excise the natural love of honor from the souls of the young. This passion to be first, allied with the practical necessity for ranking students imposed by the outside world, preserved the importance of grades (which had inflated partly as a way of having grades while making them meaningless). The grade is thus both pursued and despised. Its significance in relation to the learning of a discipline has been effectively destroyed.

The consequences have been severe for the morale of students. There is now a certain self-irony, for they are aware that this sort of egalitarianism is fraudulent. Legitimate egalitarianism lets you be what you are; demagogic egalitarianism tells you that you are what you know you are not. If everyone is said to be beautiful, then the word loses its meaning without anyone's having benefited or even having been persuaded. It is ridiculous to say that half of all tailors or farmers or doctors are excellent and that practically all the rest are very good. Rather than leveling, our university egalitarianism has raised everyone into the aristocracy of the intellect. Of course, students don't believe any of this. They want real measures of their worth. They simply cease to respect the university as a place to be tested and formed for life and come to doubt the seriousness of their teachers.

And the whole cause of learning is done a grave disservice by the obvious arbitrariness of standards. Just as the college diploma no longer guarantees any definite learning, so the peaks, the honors diplomas in those universities recognized to be best, have been lowered. We face the danger that the real, uncompromising standard of truth will slip away from us while we are busy redistributing the distinction that by nature belongs to the pursuit of truth.

FACULTY RESPONSIBILITY

How did all this come to pass? The fault, of course, lies with the professors. They not only gave the grades but wanted to; and here lies the larger significance of this tale, for undergraduate grade inflation is only a symptom of a softening of the university's core. The fuzzing of the external standard applied to students is the reflection of decay in the internal standard in the professors' souls. They are no longer sure what they want to teach or even what they as scholars are doing or aiming at. But to be somewhat more precise, it is not professors in general whom I am characterizing, it is professors of humanities and social science. And, of course, from their part of the university came the grade inflation. The natural scientists have a clearer grasp of their objects and of what constitutes distinction in their disciplines; they keep their eyes much more surely on the inner necessity of their science, are concerned primarily with its advancement and view achievements of students with that end in mind.

It does not do to say, as some do, that it was always so, that as long ago as Aristotle political science was not expected to be as exact as mathematics. His standards for judging political science were as stringent as those he applied to mathematics; they were merely of a different kind. And once degrees with high honors in philosophy or English were as rare as those in physics. No, something new happened, and it goes to the heart of the problematic relation of the life of the mind to democratic society. For this reason mere exhortation or censure will not suffice, any more than calls to republican virtue rallied the Romans when Rome had become a great empire. I mean to suggest not that our situation is as hopeless as that of the Romans, rather that we have to face a fundamental change in our spiritual situation, not just an egregious slippage in our standards.

RADICAL EGALITARIANISM AND INTELLECTUAL INTEGRITY OF THE UNIVERSITY

This weakness or softness in the humanities and social sciences clearly revealed itself in the 1960s. America went through one of its periodic fits of radical egalitarianism.[1] This is a phenomenon intrinsically connected with our regime, which is founded explicitly on philosophic principles of equality. The institutions established to incarnate that equality were intended to control the most radical egalitarian impulses, those that rebel against the inequalities necessary to preserve equality and promote human excellence. But those impulses are always with us, fueled by the presence of unjust inequalities and by doctrines of equality that do not accept the restraints thought necessary by the Founding Fathers. There is always the temptation to rebel against nature, against the natural inequalities of body and soul as well as against those derived from convention.

In the sixties this humor for the first time in our history struck out against the universities and intellectual life in general.[2] Previously our universities were somehow not the target of American populistic passion,

1. I am limiting myself to the American experience, although the intellectual problem itself (and its underlying political source) is global, producing somewhat different effects as it is refracted in various national media.

2. An apparently moderate expression of such radicalism is John Rawls's *A Theory of Justice* (Cambridge, Mass.: Harvard University Press, 1971), which argues that all inequalities, and in particular superior talents, have a right to development and expression only so long as they benefit the most disadvantaged members of society. Talent is community property, to be cultivated or not according to the will of society. This book has become a standard text on rights and is accepted across a surprisingly broad spectrum of American opinion.

and the egalitarian response to the great East-Coast universities had been to build universities in their image across the country. The best American universities maintained a relatively serious intellectual posture, partly out of love of truth, partly out of snobbism, and partly because they had as models and censors the European universities, which had, up until World War II, the very highest standards and produced many truly great scholars. When the attack on the intellectual integrity of the university came, all three elements of this structure had already been undermined, and it collapsed at the first assault.

THE MORAL CLIMATE OF THE SIXTIES

One must try to reconstruct what professors were faced with in the sixties to understand their response. Students were in the vanguard of the onslaught, and professors found it hard to resist their strongly felt, or at least strongly expressed, sentiments. For professors, too, are American and find it difficult to resist public opinion. Moreover, in a country where utility is the dominant principle and the dignity of the theoretical life is correspondingly diminished, life flourishes only to the extent that those who live it and the community at large are of the comfortable persuasion that theoretical pursuits are useful. The quiet voice of reason hesitates before outbursts of moral indignation. And the first issue that came on the scene was the one best suited to touch American conscience: race. Slavery was America's greatest injustice, and it offended our leading, perhaps our only, principle of justice, equality. No thoughtful and decent citizen could shirk the responsibility of doing his utmost to stamp out its legacy. Citizenship and scholarship make different demands on us, and we generally lack a mediating principle. The university's purpose is to understand, not to change, the world. But that is not always the view of many of those who are part of it, and in the sixties many wanted to use the university to reform society.

It was one thing to make every effort to be sure that all those who could and wanted to participate in the special higher educational community did so. It was another thing to change its character in order to accommodate those who had been left out. But the latter happened in spite of, and partly because of, the best intentions. First, admissions standards were lowered. Then came a tacit, and sometimes explicit, easing of grading standards. There followed changes in curriculum and instant discovery of new fields of study to respond to demand. Next there was a fatal agreement to use race as a criterion in the search for faculty, which meant an abandonment of the university's hard-won transcendence of race, class, nation, and religion—a transcendence based only on the universality of truth. As a consequence, segregation in housing accommodations and even in the classroom began to be tolerated. And, finally, one witnessed repeated and ill-resisted attacks on freedom of speech and freedom of thought. These were joined to an even more ominous self-doubt as to the integrity of the disciplines—weren't they after all more or less subtly racist? All this was accompanied by a surge of Marxist thinking that interpreted the university—previously held to be the symbol and the reality of liberal democracy's devotion to the principle that the truth shall make men free—as the vehicle of "bourgeois ideology."

On the back of the moral sentiments given currency by the civil rights movement rode the antiwar movement that, although its appeal to legitimacy as a force within the university had no ground whatsoever, increased the passions of self-righteousness to such a degree that whatever was demanded by its proponents became instantly respectable. The essence of its appeal was hostility to all authority, not merely the authority of elected officials (elections, of course, are all fraudulent) who were sending the young men to war, but also the authority of tradition and that of teachers, and, even more, the authority of talent, virtue, science, and the quest for truth. The university's organization, the distinction between professors and students, and the primacy of learning over teaching, were understood to be part of a general system of domination, as was slavery. The result of these opinions was great suspicion of the faculty, an erosion of its autonomy and central position in the university, and a further transformation of the curriculum to meet demand, a sweeping away of much of traditional learning that could not justify itself in the eyes of the students.

The last of the three great waves of moralizing that broke on the university was feminism. It took advantage of the general mood of moral certainty, profited by the analogy to slavery, and claimed a stake in the ideology of liberation from domination. Feminism did not alter the tendencies set afloat by the other waves; it only reinforced them. In particular, it broadened the attack on the traditional curriculum, in that most works of literature and philosophy can be said to be sexist and thereby discredited, whereas charges of racism can be leveled at only a few. And insistence that the university take part in the fight against sexism, particularly against conventional male and female roles, required a much more difficult and questionable effort because, while almost everyone in universities was against racial distinctions and knew in some measure what it would mean to overcome them, at least in the universities, neither of these conditions prevailed in the case of the women's movement.

The three cardinal sins of the egalitarian creed—racism, sexism, and elitism—became dogma in the university. Since the scholar's eye is very easily diverted from his elusive goal, which has so little popular appeal, the whole apparatus set up to fulfill the new goals proved very distracting. Universities acquired new bureaucrats to oversee the policies, and the old ones pledged to dedicate themselves to their efficacy. The federal government, instructed and emboldened by the example the universities were themselves setting, had no hesitation about imposing affirmative action on them. Many universities assigned to the task an administrator with the wondrous title of "compliance officer." Now, no one who is thinking about such things can be thinking about education and scholarship. The spectacular lawsuits that hit the front pages do not tell the real story of the subtle poison that now permeates the atmosphere of the university. The special character and vocation of the university and its inner confidence are threatened. Among other things, hypocrisy runs rampant, the hypocrisy of those who insist the programs work and tamper with the facts or deceive themselves, and the hypocrisy of those who believe they don't work but who know the fatal consequences of being tagged a nonbeliever.

"ANTIELITISM" AND UNIVERSITY PURPOSE

So-called elitism is the vice most directly related to standards, because standards are what is meant by elitism. And antielitism provides the greatest challenge to the university. Antiracism and antisexism were only dangerous to the extent that they promote an egalitarianism inimical to the intellectual life. Properly understood, demands for genuine equality of blacks and women can be easily met without changing the essential character of the university. But the stupid, the tendentious, the self-seeking and the intellectually lazy cannot be so integrated. The various disciplines require talents of a sort that are hard to deny and which no teacher should fail to favor. There is a natural rank order—not necessarily always respected, but always there—that education must encourage, for the good of the community, for the good of learning, and for justice to individuals.

Elitism is nothing but a pseudoscientific term popularized by social science which makes something natural seem conventional and perverted. And, in some measure, the rhetoric of antielitism was resisted; it was resisted by the natural scientists. They passed the buck to the social scientists and the humanists, who proved more accommodating. Natural scientists too were Americans and were in general favorably disposed to the new mood. But they were also sure of what they were doing. The optimistic view that science is the necessary and sufficient condition of democracy— the ambience in which science slumbered with good conscience—was fading, partly under the influence of the radical critique; however, their objects, the way in which those objects should be studied, and what constitutes truth about them are all clear to scientists and agreed upon. The model science is mathematics. Perhaps contemporary science has purchased its authority by a narrowness that is in the long run deleterious to science itself; it has certainly done so by making itself incapable of speaking about anything human and the world of concern to us.

But for all that, the scientists cannot deceive themselves that they are teaching science when they are not. They have powerful operational measures of competence. And inwardly they believe, at least in my experience, that the only real knowledge is scientific knowledge. In the dilemma that faced them—mathematicians wanted, for example, to see more blacks and women hired but could not find nearly enough competent ones—they in effect said that the humanists and social scientists should hire them. Underlying this attitude was a profound contempt for the humanities and social sciences, although the natural scientist often paid lip service to them. Indeed, the sixties brought to the surface the submerged fact that the university no longer has any real unity of purpose, no community of subject matter or vision. The natural and the human sides of the university are now almost accidental traveling companions, as it were, sharing the same ship. Neither really has much need of the other. The split is papered over with clichés about culture for undergraduate consumption; but after the liberal education part of the curriculum is gotten through, the two worlds part company never again to meet.

Believing that there are no real standards on the other side, scientists assumed that adjustments there could easily be made. With profoundest irresponsibility, they went along with various aspects of affirmative action, assuming, for example, that any minority students admitted without proper qualifications would be taken care of by other departments if they did not do well in science. The scientists did not anticipate large-scale failure of such students with the really terrible consequences that would entail; they took it for granted that they would succeed somewhere else in the university.

COLLAPSE OF CONVICTION

The really crucial aspect of this whole story is that the humanists and social scientists gave in or, rather, gave cheerful assent; for I can only believe that had they anything like the conviction the scientists had as to the value and validity of their work, they would have fought and succeeded in their fight. But that conviction was lacking, and we must address ourselves to the reasons for that lack of conviction in order to diagnose our ills and prescribe for them.

In the first place, social science and the humanities deal with the human world on which the political movements of the sixties and seventies were trying to impose a new interpretation. For the activists these disciplines were, to the extent that they in any way promoted differing views, the enemy that had to be defeated. No radical group, so far as I know, thought relativity or evolution notions that had to be opposed.[3] Only certain applications of natural sciences—providing arms for imperialism or technology for capitalists in their efforts to pollute the environment—were condemned, and scientists could easily disavow such uses of their work and were eager to do so.

But American historians taught that equality is the fundamental principle of this regime and that this principle, subscribed to by all the Founding Fathers, in the long run doomed slavery. These professors were by their very teachings enemies of those whose interest was to show that this regime is

3. Earlier communists, of course, did. But the movements of the sixties were less theoretical and less concerned with self-contradiction.

root and branch racist and must be supplanted by another. In order to keep in the good graces of the wave of the future, so famous a historian as Edmund Morgan had a sudden conversion and found that equality was an ideological invention of the Virginia aristocrats to deceive poor whites into allying with rich ones to keep down the slaves rather than following their true class interests, which would have dictated solidarity of poor whites and blacks.[4] Thus history makes its autocritique and purges itself of racism. Only those who were willing to make such concessions could avoid the danger of frightful accusations and of losing their moral footing as equality moved forward.

But it is not only that the humanists and social scientists were alone in the front lines that caused their weakness. Rather, concurrently, they were experiencing an inner doubt about the reality of their disciplines. In the simplest terms, they too believe that knowledge is scientific knowledge and that to the extent they are not scientific, they have no foundations. Here the situations of the humanities and the social sciences diverge. They are united in that both must talk about human things and that *the* model of science or knowledge makes it very difficult to do so. But their responses to this difficulty differ. The social sciences try in one way or another to be scientific, to quantify the study of man and thus break away from the tainted embrace of the humanists and escape to join the naturalists in their white laboratory garb. The humanists, in contrast, seek another source of legitimacy, hoping the sciences will cede them a little piece of their empire, which they will promise not to explain away. *Imagination* and *creativity* are typical watchwords against the advance of science, but they prove increasingly empty to the extent that they cannot find a place in nature.

REACTION OF THE SOCIAL SCIENCES

This difference accounts for the difference between the humanities and social sciences in their reactions to the demands placed on them by students and the community. The social sciences, with the partial exception of economics, had long since abandoned the attempt to give a simply mechanical account of man and society in favor of Max Weber's method that distinguishes facts from values. Social facts, like natural facts, admit of scientific treatment. Social science, it was alleged, had not previously succeeded because it mixed value judgments with factual statements. A value-free social science could attain to the same kind of objectivity as natural science. But this assertion is at the same time an admission that something specifically human escapes the purview of science. And that something is what is most important from the point of view of life. Protestantism, democracy, and science are all equally values, themselves unsupported by reason, that form and transform the facts reason apprehends.

4. *American Slavery, American Freedom: The Ordeal of Colonial Virginia* (New York: Norton, 1975).

Thus when students accused social scientists of studying the wrong things, of being indifferent to values and marching to the drum of those who paid them, the latter had very little to say in response. They could not criticize the students' values on rational grounds; they were actually intimidated by those values, both in their content and by the students' commitment to them. They could not seriously defend academic freedom because it is merely one value, a preference no more valid than any other preference. Hot commitment at least evidences its holder's concern for values, a claim that cool reason cannot make. In the topsy-turvy perspective introduced by the fact-value distinction, irrational intensity becomes a means, the only means, of validating preferences. The students brought this home to their teachers. There was a premium on commitment, real or feigned (and there are no objective criteria for distinguishing between the two); and the social scientists began to wonder whether their preference for liberal democracy was not just conformism as opposed to the more unconventional preferences of the students.

David Easton, in a presidential address to the American Political Science Association, gave the response.[5] He said, in essence, that social scientists had been insensitive to value questions and that if the students, now called "post-behavioralists," would leave them be, in the future social science would be useful to their ends. He handed over the sword of sovereignty to them and surrendered the university to the only two forces that have much vitality in the contemporary world, science and public opinion. And, as scientists frequently see with anguish, public opinion is the senior partner. Science provides the power; public opinion decides how it will be used. Easton admitted that reason and hence the university have no standard with which to guide, instruct, or resist the preferences of public opinion. He called for more "engagement" on the part of the social sciences, an engagement responding to the demand for "relevance."

REACTION OF THE HUMANITIES

Professors of the humanities, in contrast, reacted with a kind of despair. They sensed themselves to be irrelevant, for what did Sophocles or Milton have to do with the urgent issues of the day? Many of them threw in their lot with the revolution almost as a form of penance for having idled in green pastures while there was suffering in the world. The humanities were in an uncomfortable position. They do not have the authority of science, and they are somehow connected with tradition, style, and form—all of which are contrary to the taste of democracy and anathema to the radical movements. The peculiar agony of their situation can be judged by the kind of arguments about proper writing style to which teachers of English have had to

5. "The New Revolution in Political Science," *American Political Science Review* 63, no. 4 (December 1969): 1051–1061.

stoop and by how many of them have joined the attack on grammar. The humanities curriculum was ravaged in the sixties. Respect for and knowledge of the classics have declined drastically.

The humanities had no response like that of Easton's to make. They could only stand idly by, watching their clientele leave and preparing to water down what they served. What happens to standards in the humanities when the old literature is not taken seriously is illustrated by an example the *Oxford English Dictionary* gives for *standard*: "We always return to the writings of the ancients as the standard of true taste." This is the polar star of the humanities as is mathematics for the natural sciences. When it does not shine, we are adrift; and the fact that it was clouded over is the cause of the easy capitulation, which in turn is the cause of its near extinction.

The humanities are the realm of deepest crisis. To begin with, nobody is quite sure what they are. The field has no rhyme or reason. If one looks at natural sciences one sees the sense of its divisions and also their interconnections. They can give an account of themselves. Although the status of the social sciences is much more problematic, something similar can be said of them. The humanistic part of the university in contrast is just a heap of departments without any discernible order or vision of a whole of which they are parts, no account of what kind of knowledge they are seeking or what they contribute to the education of the whole man. At best, with a sort of insecure snobbism, they say they stand for culture. The field looks like a pile of leftovers—the incomprehensible and humane residue—after the various sciences divided up the world. In the midst of the humanities sits the enfeebled giant philosophy, which once had the overview of the disciplines and assigned them their place in the coherent whole of human knowledge. It has become, mostly, either history of philosophy, that is, history of now refuted attempts to establish such an overview, or methods of science, the rules by which the disciplines must be played. Nobody really looks for the truth, or a significant portion of it, in the humanities. They seem to exist as the shrine of the unsatisfied longings for knowledge of the good life.

HUMANISTS AND SCIENTISTS

Illustrative of our present intellectual situation is a recent article in *The New York Times* describing the visit of a professor of music to Rockefeller University. The life scientists working there brought bag lunches and listened to the musicologist's lecture. The project was inspired by C. P. Snow's silly ideas about the two cultures, the rift between which will be healed if humanists learn the second law of thermodynamics and physicists read Shakespeare. This enterprise would, of course, be something other than an exercise in tolerance and spiritual uplift only if the physicists learned something important for his physics from Shakespeare and the humanist similarly profited from the second law of thermodynamics. The fact is that nothing of the sort ensues, that for the scientist the humanities are recreation (often deeply respected by him, for he sees that more is needed than what he offers but is puzzled about where to find it), and that for the humanist the natural sciences are at best indifferent, at worst the alien and the hostile.

The *Times* quoted Joshua Lederberg, the president of Rockefeller University, an institution from which philosophy was recently banished, as saying after the lecture that C. P. Snow was on the right track but "counted wrong," there are not two but many cultures, one example of which is that of the Beatles. This represents the ultimate trivialization of a trivial idea that was just a rest station on a downward slope. Lederberg did not see in the humanities the human knowledge that complements the study of nature but just another expression of what is going on in the world. In the end, it is all more or less sophisticated show business. *Culture* here has exactly the same debased meaning it has in sociology when youth or drug "cultures" are spoken of. What originally had high meaning becomes eviscerated and meaningless in a sea of democratic relativism. *Sous entendu* in Lederberg's statement and almost everyone's belief is that natural science has a special status. The rest is just a matter of opinion or taste. There is no human truth for the humanities to get at.

THE BANEFUL INFLUENCE OF NIETZSCHE

This crisis in the intellectual unity of the university and the concomitant lack of communication among its members have been brewing for a very long time, and the university disturbances only sharpened them and made them more obvious. From antiquity through the eighteenth century, science was an articulated whole, each of whose parts was necessary and coherent with the rest. Man was one part of nature, and the study of man was understood to be a rational natural science. The teachings of physics and biology were not such as to make man as we know him incomprehensible. The great philosophers were equally great natural scientists and great political scientists. But toward the end of the eighteenth century, physics had emancipated itself and attained what was believed to be metaphysical neutrality. Its results contributed little or nothing to the original question of philosophy, What is the good life? Nature as it appeared in mathematical atomism was too low to act as a standard for morality.

Under the aegis of philosophy a new organization of the sciences was established that seemed to save the human phenomena. The distinction between nature and freedom, or nature and history, was established. Natural science was to study nature, and human science man. The distinction was founded on what were argued to be two dimensions of the real. The human sciences, particularly history, philology, esthetics, and morality, were to provide the rational basis for the understanding of man and the answers to the questions of greatest concern to him. Under the influence of this inspiration the great nineteenth-century scholarship flourished: it had its purpose in the moral result that was expected of it. However, the results were not such as to justify the expectations of, for example, Kant, while the separation from nature had become permanent. The aimlessness and dispiritedness of the human sciences were powerfully diagnosed by Nietzsche among others as early as the 1870s. And he added a new element to the academic malaise by arguing powerfully that the human sciences could never be sciences, that reason about human things was but rationalization. He invented the term *value* in its modern sense and argued that values are products of the unconscious and works of art.

Nietzsche's teachings, which were profoundly antiacademic, became a powerful part of academic opinion and a major element in the lack of coherent purpose in the human studies. The impulse he gave did not establish new disciplines or revitalize the old ones. Rather, it contributed to their self-doubt and an eagerness to attach themselves to modernism in the nonacademic arts. The new social sciences invaded their domain and took away a large part of the belief that important truths were to be learned from them. They became otiose and largely antiquarian. While natural science went from success to success, the place of the humanities in the university was preserved by tradition, not by any living need for them. And their primary function came to be preservation of tradition.

DEMOCRACY AND THE VOCATION OF THE HUMANITIES

But this is just where modern regimes are most inimical to the intellectual life. As Tocqueville so brilliantly showed, men in democracies have confidence in their own judgments and above all accept no authorities. Tradition is just information. Moreover, the principle of utility dominates their lives. Natural science can be admired for its utility in the production of well-being. But the humanities cannot; and to the extent they try to justify themselves on utilitarian grounds to an audience motivated by utility, they corrupt themselves. They are of value precisely because they are reminders of something other than utility. Their highest vocation in a democracy is to present alternatives to the dominant views of man and the good life for the sake of freedom of the mind. But that vocation is most threatened and least appreciated in a democracy. When the humanists themselves doubt the value of tradition, the cause is hopeless. Only the most uncompromising awareness of and attention to the authentic seriousness of Plato or Shakespeare can keep the flame alive.

And I contend that that concern is now very weak. The latest trend (succeeding many others, all of which had as their purpose to find something useful in the classics without having to take them seriously as authorities) is criticism, particularly a new brand, a Nietzscheanism at third hand. One form of it is called deconstructionism, which is premised on the impossibility of understanding authors as they understood themselves. This means that we cannot look for objective wisdom in the writers of the past. We are, as it were, the creators of the texts. Whether intentionally or not, this conceit most successfully of all cuts us off from the influence of the past and is the final step in democratization. The teachers of this view are the Huey Longs of the intellectual world, every man a critic.

My argument is that the humanities above all should be the source of standards for the university as a whole, as opposed to the specialized criteria provided by natural science. The dedication to the great classics of philosophy and literature generates nonarbitrary standards, and the motive of that dedication is the relevance of those classics to our situation. For we can only recognize that there is an intellectual crisis in the light of the standards they provide. They may not have the answers, but they can show us both the questions and give us guidance about how to study them. The burning issue always and especially now is the place of man in nature. Contempt of that issue is the source of the disunity in the university. The disease is above all in the humanities, and the cure lies there, too.

13

Trends and Standards in British Higher Education

DAVID MARTIN

In the universities of the United Kingdom we confront a variety of problems. We experience increased direct government control, difficulties with respect to finance, and bottlenecks in recruitment of staff and in promotion. These are problems of internal organization. We also have other kinds of problems, such as the division of higher education into two sectors and the relatively high proportion of students coming from the higher social groups. Not all these problems are serious, and some people do not regard them as problems at all.

But before I turn to these and other issues, I must comment on the disappearance of a problem. We no longer have to deal with student unrest. Student "occupations," and mass meetings to back up student demands are largely a thing of the past. Such few echos of that time as remain are minor and largely concern foreign students. For example, there was a demonstration some four years ago when Richard Nixon addressed students at the Oxford Union; it was largely composed of Americans. There were also demonstrations about the same time at the London School of Economics (L.S.E.), and elsewhere, over the question of higher fees for students coming from abroad. Naturally, this agitation was largely led by non-British students. All such demonstrations were tiny and ineffective. In any case, so far as fees were concerned many overseas students still found it cheaper to be educated in Britain than in their own countries.

David Martin is Professor of Sociology at the London School of Economics and Political Science.

DECLINE OF UNREST

The major period of unrest lasted from 1967 to 1971 and rose to a climax in 1969 over the dismissal of a lecturer at L.S.E. on a charge of supporting student violence. In fact, violence was relatively rare and the response of the authorities always quite mild. The curve of concern followed the curve of events in America with disconcerting precision. We know that we often travel in the wake of the United States, but we do not care to think of ourselves as an epiphenomenon of a transatlantic reality. After all the Americans were involved in the Vietnam war and we were not, and the issues that students claimed to be fighting over, such as bureacracy, impersonality, lack of participation, remained unsolved when the Vietnam war came to a close.[1]

So we social scientists have a problem: we do not *really* know why the unrest ceased unless imitation of America was a very important element in the whole affair. The rebellious students themselves gave voice to reasons for unrest, but the quiet generations following 1971 did not bother to explain their lack of revolutionary fervor. True, there was more participation, but it was soon evident that the new generation of students found participation boring and time consuming. It fell to a small minority of politically minded students to bother themselves with participation, leaving the rest quite apathetic. Even the politically minded minority shifted somewhat to the right, or rather, came to include a significant right-wing element where previously there was nothing but different shades of red.

The problems remaining from the time of troubles turn around the fact that one cannot have *more* participation and *less* bureaucracy. The old, relaxed style of life among university teachers has been eaten into by endless committees and consultations. Mutual understanding has been partly replaced by machinery. A young academic can now dedicate a sizable proportion of his energies to minor administrative tasks that in no way advance his subject or serve the true objects of learning. Meanwhile, the students themselves are rather apathetic or else increasingly concerned with subjects that advance their careers and promise material rewards. Whereas during the revolutionary period sociology was all the rage, indeed *enragé*, the period following was marked by increased interest in subjects like business management and accounting. From 1978 to 1980, British candidates in these subjects increased by 2.6 and 4.2 percent, respectively.

DEMOGRAPHIC AND ECONOMIC TRENDS

In any case, during the mid-1970s fewer applicants knocked at the doors of our universities. We moved from a situation in which some students com-

1. Perhaps I should say that *no* disruptions in England were on the American or the continental scale. Events at L.S.E. were minor by comparison, and arose because it is an international institution, dedicated to social sciences, with a very high proportion of graduates, especially from the United States. It has also been the nursery of elites, especially in India and Africa.

peted desperately for university places to a situation where some universities sought out students. Now, as I shall show later, the situation is partly reversing itself again.

In this connection, the factors are rather complicated. There is, for example, a demographic factor: the postwar "baby boom" fell off in the 1950s, followed by a much smaller boom that ended in 1964. So far as the fall in the birth rate after the immediate postwar boom is concerned, the effects were masked because the universities were taking up a larger proportion of the college-age group. This was the period following the Robbins Report when it was generally believed that what was good for universities was good for the country, that expanding universities went hand-in-hand with expanding economies and general social well-being. Now, however, this confidence is partly eroded and universities take an almost static proportion of the age group, thus exposing themselves to downward fluctuations in birth rate. A downward fluctuation will reach us in the mid-1980s, though the decline is least marked in those social groups of which a large proportion attend university.

So far as the second decline in births after 1964 is concerned, it still directly affects only the elementary and secondary schools, but their need for fewer teachers indirectly touches the universities. We have suffered overproduction of teachers, which has fed into the general problem of graduate unemployment during the recent period of economic difficulty. Graduate unemployment is in part related to general unemployment, but it is worsened by the previous period of expansion whereby many of the current staff of universities were recruited fairly recently. (Hence plans to offer early retirement to senior academics.) Unemployment has a somewhat ambiguous effect on universities. Nobody wants to be an unemployed graduate, but most would prefer attending university on a grant to receiving unemployment benefits; study is preferable to boredom. Too, for graduates who are employed, the rate of economic return on a degree over the course of a lifetime is now less than it once was. Obviously, as the number of graduates expands the average gain from the prospect of relatively high remuneration at the age of sixteen becomes more enticing.

Thus many contrary influences are at work. One major consequence of university expansion in the sixties is that once facilities are created they do not easily contract. Moreover, expansion was accompanied by the formation of larger bureaucratic establishments with supporting personnel who became thoroughly entrenched. These supporting personnel, as Professor Neil Smelser of the University of California, Berkeley recently emphasized in a lecture at L.S.E., helped to erode the prime collegial operation of the universities. Learning suffered relative displacement in terms of resources if not of prestige. Bureaucracy defended itself against the rational need for some contraction. (All the same, reduction of nonacademic staff is easier than reduction of academic staff.) This is to put the matter in an impersonal, structural way. In more human terms, the bureaucrats dug themselves in, whether needed or not, and as the threat of contraction increased so did defensive unionization. Something similar happened, on a smaller scale, among university teachers. The Association of University Teachers became affiliated with the Trades Union Council, and it soon seemed virtually impossible to dismiss a university teacher.

EDUCATIONAL DIVERSIFICATION

Meanwhile, the universities supplemented their traditional academic function by expansion in the direction of vocational or nongraduate certification. They took on people who returned in mid-career and serviced subprofessional groups who sought credentials. Until recently, the lower professions expanded without seeking university diplomas, but now such groups as, for example, social workers, seek the accreditation of subacademic skills through the university and higher education generally. The Open University in Britain, which operates through radio and television, very nicely illustrates this movement. One may, perhaps, anticipate further expansion in facilities for those in middle life because of the return of women to education. In general, one may say that the educational system copes rather tardily with the expansion of numbers in the subprofessions and is reluctant to dilute its academic purpose in order to do so. The polytechnics have more readily accepted the task of subprofessional accreditation, and this gives credibility to a somewhat unreal distinction between the universities, with their academic traditions, and polytechnics with their more vocational orientation.

We encounter here a status distinction that obtains between the humanistic disciplines and *pure* science on the one hand, and technological and subacademic practicality on the other. Here Britain has traditions distinct from France, and even from the United States. We still pay respect to the gentlemanly ideal as expressed in the ethos of personal cultivation and diffuse civility. This was once exhibited in an education in classical literature, but it now includes all the humanistic disciplines and pure science. Students are aware of this, and many of them despise practicality and dislike the commercial attitude. Given that more seek the civilized ideal than can be placed and absorbed, this also can encourage a radicalization in the humanities. On the other side, the counterelite in engineering and associated disciplines presses for status and recognition commensurate with its high rewards. Polytechnics and engineering establishments are well paid but not equally well regarded. There is some tension within the upper educational strata. One further result is that from time to time there are too few candidates for scientific education, and this affects teaching in the schools. It does not undermine the quality of the elite institutions like Imperial College of London University and Cambridge, but it can do damage lower down in the system. The Finniston Report sought to remedy the lack of status accorded engineering, of which more later.

Since status differentials have been referred to, it is worth pointing out one paradoxical consequence of the shift toward vocational training and toward the certification of subprofessions. This is, if you like, a move in an egalitarian direction, which, however, only affects part of the university system. The distinguished institutions—notably Oxford, Cambridge and Imperial College, L.S.E., and King's College and University College of London University—are able to resist. This strengthens distinctions *within* the university system itself, as between the "pure" and the practical-*cum*-vocational.

All I have said so far is by way of background and was true prior to the advent of a Conservative government led by Mrs. Thatcher. She has made it clear that universities are no more popular with a section of the Conservative party than with Labour. Under the Conservative government finance has become yet more stringent, the influence of the state has become greater, even though the government is committed to laissez-faire, and rationalization has been speeded up. As regards the last, it need not necessarily affect academic standards; the aim of rationalization is simply to ensure that resources, say, for teaching Russian, are not too dispersed in a number of centers. Of course, some attempts at rationalization are ham-handed but the process helps rather than hinders maintenance of standards.

ACADEMIC STANDARDS

I now turn to consider the question of standards, first with regard to the qualifications of entrants and the standard of degrees, and second the quality of university teachers. I trust that everybody will recognize the almost impossible nature of the task: the statistics I cite refer to different kinds of things, discussed for convenience under a single rubric, or to things whose natures and aims are shifting. I also trust that everyone will recognize the caveats that have to be entered. I cannot possibly explain all that has to be taken for granted if what I suggest is really to follow by way of secure conclusion. As we all know, the imponderables are crucial, and we often have to guess at the objective truth, without ignoring or distorting such quasi-objective indicators as may be at hand.

Let me give an example as to what administrators call the "feedstock" of the university. The qualifications of students applying to universities are governed by the situation in the schools. Here the independent and the state schools differ in their approaches. The majority of the former, leaving aside progressive or experimental schools, have gone for measurable, examinable achievement, believing that parents want tangible value in return for good money. This policy has further disadvantaged the pupils of state schools, because the state schools, at least in theory, have tried to pursue aims of an intangible egalitarian-*cum*-expressive kind. In practice, the state schools have proved almost useless as vehicles for egalitarian reform, and their expressivist aims mostly disintegrate in boredom, lack of motivation, low teacher morale, and quite a lot of sheer anarchy in both behavior and curriculum.

I think it reasonable to say that this disintegration has been checked. Reports have documented mediocre standards of performance relative to resources available. The government has asked for attention to basic skills of numeracy and literacy. There has been some revival of the "Protestant ethic," and there has been a recovery of the concept of ethos. Thus the research of Michael Rutter rehabilitated the idea that the overall pattern and tone of a school are more important than the separate variables that compose it. Rutter's *Fifteen Thousand Hours* aroused fierce debate, not least because it was conducive to inferences that suggested a return to more settled, patterned forms of classroom management.[2] But certainly his book is just one element, part reflection, part cause, of a return to ideas about the embodiment of a particular spirit, tone, and style in the rituals and patterns of school organization.

This is *not* a return to draconian control and competitive emulation, but a restoration of patterns and overall aims that, to my mind, provide the basis for scholastic interest, motivation, and striving. I would like to distinguish rather carefully between schools based on external control and emulation, and schools based on settled patterning and a search for all the varied kinds of excellence. When I advocate standards, I am advocating an organic sense of what things are good and worth seeking, not an endless competition in which almost everybody feels a sense of inferiority or second-class citizenship in the academy. Whether in school or university the reproduction of potential academics, all others being seen as so much "feedstock" for the system, seems to me as inhumane and antieducational as obligatory sporty machismo or untended psyches jostling in existential anarchy.

I will give another example, also bearing on both school and university. It concerns the crucial element of formal structure, say, in language or in the skills required for basic computation or simply the capacity to write a decent sentence and spell a simple word. The disintegrations of the sixties, assisted by dominant fashions in the education departments, undermined the essential elements of rote and memory that provide the foundation of vision, flexibility, and creativity. The consequences of these developments seem to me evident in recruits to universities. For example, the sense of the temporal character of history, based on the structure of date and sequence, had dissolved in vaguely intuitive notions. In all these dimensions there is now partial recovery. Nevertheless, the Inspectorate and the University Grants Committee proceed on the assumption that basic capacities and skills are not being acquired and that for these there are no valid alternatives.

There is, of course, a genuine issue here, one related to the debate about specialization. The short three-year course in British universities requires a high degree of specialization, compared with American schools, of students at the ages of sixteen through eighteen. Such specialization does not neces-

2. Michael Rutter, *Fifteen Thousand Hours* (London: Open Books, 1979).

sarily subserve educational values; it can yield science students who are scientistic rather than scientific. This distortion generates dangerous narrowness: engineers who have neither an informed view of the ranges of material with which the intelligence may deal nor any sense of the styles and kinds of judgment. I assume that when we talk about standards, we are, on the one hand, concerned with ascertainable and reliable competences, but on the other with the command of every kind of rigorous judgment, especially in those areas least susceptible to mere numbers and metrics.

STUDENT ENROLLMENTS

What, however, do the measured attainments show, supposing that in a preliminary way they provide interesting indications? Well, competition for university admissions is increasing after a period of slackness, even allowing for the increase in the size of the age group. In the late 1960s and early 1970s, the supply of students in science and engineering, areas of national priority, showed signs of drying up. That is now rectified. The 1979 statistical supplement to the seventeenth report (1978–79) of the Universities Central Council on Admissions (UCCA) finds more candidates applying for physical sciences, for mathematics, and above all for computer science. The pressure on vocational subjects continues, though there has been some drop in the number of candidates for such heavily overcrowded subjects as medicine and business management studies. Standards for entrance to medical courses have become very exacting, by way of contrast to the easy entrance some ten years previous. The rapid increase in recruits to engineering is falling off somewhat. The UCCA reports rising overall numbers and a rise in the proportion of women applying and being accepted. Ten years ago female recruits were some three in ten and they are now four in ten. Overseas candidates, though increasing in numbers, have fared badly, in accordance with government policy. There are more foreign applicants, at least for elite institutions, but fewer are admitted.

The "feedstock," if I may persist in advertising this barbarous terminology, is also differentiated by social status. Little needs to be said about this, except to report the usual decline of the proportion of candidates with each shift downward in the scale of social status. Indeed, the differential between status groups has marginally widened. In 1979 the children of professional and technical workers came from a group representing 10.3 percent of the population, which provided 36.8 percent of the successful candidates. The comparable figures for clerical workers were 6.3 and 10.2 percent, and for laborers 6.5 and 0.9 percent. The upper status groups have somewhat better results in their preuniversity "A level" examinations.

The "A level" grades are the results of examinations students usually take at seventeen or eighteen years of age, and they reflect a fairly stable status ordering in the hierarchy of universities applied to. This order is Oxbridge, Older Civics, Newer Civics, New Universities, and former colleges of advanced technology. London is a scattered element in this hierarchy, since it rivals Oxford or Cambridge in particular subjects and in some of its major institutions such as University College, Imperial College, and L.S.E., but it also has a tail that brings it on the average between the older and the newer civic universities. One must add that the hierarchy of universities in the United Kingdom is a gentle one, and that roughly comparable standards of degree examination are maintained, assisted by the practice of external examining.

Within the sciences, the physical sciences have the highest standard of entry, followed by engineering and biology. There does not seem to be all that much difference of entry standard among subjects in the social sciences, foreign languages, and literature, though qualifications required for social sciences are marginally depressed, and somewhat more so in the least prestigious institutions. The biggest gulf lies between physics at Cambridge and business studies at the former colleges of advanced technology.[3]

DECLINE IN FACULTY QUALITY

If we consider the outward marks of standards among university teachers, we may well do so through the information gathered by Professor A. H. Halsey, which focuses on the difference between polytechnic and university teachers.[4] The British system of defining university and polytechnic sectors creates a somewhat deflated view of higher education since the polytechnics would be accorded university status in most other countries. In any case, the supposed distinctions between the sectors are not really conveyed by contrasts between ancient and modern, or theory and practice, or even education and training. Much clearer differences exist in the quality of students admitted and the degree to which polytechnics are less intimate and larger, less autonomous and more local. A further difference is that pure science is the dominant giant in the university, whereas in the polytechnic this role is played by social, administrative, and business studies.

Significant differences become evident if we compare the class of first degree obtained by teachers in the two sectors, remembering that in British universities, the principal accolade is the class obtained at the first degree, not the doctorate. Over two-fifths of university teachers, but less than one-fifth of polytechnic teachers, obtained first-class honors. This relative position has not altered during a period in which polytechnic pay has at least come to equal university pay. But the standard of recruits from 1970 onward has altered, so that in the most recent period about one-third of university

3. The more detailed breakdown by subject (as reported in the *Times*, March 13, 1981, and derived from UCCA) shows small relation between degree of competition for places in a given subject and the grades achieved at "A level" by the successful candidates. Classics, for example, gives places to 82 percent of applicants but these on the average have high grades.
4. A. H. Halsey, "Politics of Higher Education," *Times Higher Education Supplement*, 19 September 1980; "A Tale of Two Systems," *Times Higher Education Supplement*, 16 November 1979; "The Decline of Oxford and Cambridge," *Times Higher Education Supplement*, 27 June 1980.

teachers appointed had a first and only one-seventh of polytechnic teachers. The fall in standards dates from a point before the 1970s, so that in the period immediately prior to the expansion (1955–1962) the proportion of university teachers with firsts dropped to under half, and in the period of expansion in the 1960s to two-fifths. Agreement seems widespread that many relatively mediocre people were taken on in the 1960s as an inevitable concomitant of rapid expansion.

BLOCKAGE IN APPOINTMENTS

A little more may be said on this point because it is quite important. Assuming the decline to be genuine—and here sampled opinion of university teachers and the figures agree—we have a blockage consisting of staff tenured in the 1960s. Given the cessation of all expansion in 1975 and the recent contraction, this means that able people are discouraged from even trying to enter. I am not sure why the newer appointees are not of higher quality, but my impression is that just now a pool of very high ability is simply frozen out. I am also inclined to think that those few now entering are very good indeed; they certainly ought to be, given the numbers chasing each post. No doubt, also, there is considerable frustration over the relative lack of promotion available for those recruited in the sixties, despite some encouragement for early retirement, and this compounds the frustration of those unable to get in at all.

The situation is somewhat mitigated if we use the doctorate as an index of quality rather than the first degree. As the proportion of firsts among university teachers dropped, so the proportion of doctorates rose. On the criterion provided by the possession of a doctorate, the quality of university staff rose by 20 percent between 1962 and 1969.

DISPARITIES IN RESEARCH

That leads us to the question of research and back to consideration of the contrast between the university and polytechnic sectors. Says Professor Halsey, "Over half the university teachers supervised research students compared with less than a quarter of polytechnic teachers. Nearly all university teachers are currently engaged on scholarly research work which they expect to lead to publication, compared with 60 percent of the polytechnic teachers. A quarter of the former have published more than 20 articles, half the latter have published none."[5] These figures reflect the emphasis in the universities on research relative to teaching and administration, especially where promotion is concerned. Indeed, university teachers spend about 40 percent of their time on research, which is slightly more than they spend on teaching. One should, perhaps, add here that the polytechnics vary greatly from department to department, and also include a great deal of nondegree work so that the best department in a polytechnic

5. A. H. Halsey, "Politics."

may well be of university standard in general quality and orientation of its teachers.

With respect to research, a great deal of recent comment addresses the low completion rates of research done by graduates in the social sciences. Does this provide a further qualitative criterion, applying to either teachers or postgraduates? Probably not, since some of the most prestigious institutions, like the L.S.E., have among the worst completion rates. Why this is so is another question, but clearly a tightening up is in process, started by the present government and fueled by the search for economies. The low completion rates result from many causes, including a certain lonely contemplation among social science graduates who sometimes tackle projects either multifaceted or imprecisely focused and so cannot bring them to completion. In contrast, science graduates work on defined, delimited topics, and often as underlings to established researchers (though that can mean they receive scant credit for their contributions).

ATTITUDES TOWARD STUDENT PARTICIPATION

Certain questions relating to standards arise in connection with the attitudes university staff have toward student participation, above all in the matter of appointments. Neither polytechnic nor university staffs are happy to see student participation on appointing boards; in fact, this is very much a minority practice, and when adopted students do not play a major role. Both polytechnic and university teachers also rather firmly oppose any policy of basing promotion, even in part, on student evaluation. Similar attitudes, perhaps a little more relaxed, govern the opinions of teachers regarding student participation in defining student admission policy, type and content of courses, and examination procedures.

This firmness within the teaching body is generally reflected in actual practices, though obviously various consultative bodies measure student opinion on courses, and students have some representation on governing bodies. But nowhere is the determining or predominant voice given over to students. It is even my impression that teachers recruited in the heyday of the late sixties, with the usual zeal of poachers turned gamekeepers, are harsher than their elders in insisting on the subordinate nature of student status. Certainly the amount of work involved in operating a whole battery of diverse examination procedures exhausts both teachers and students, and the innovations of the previous decade lost favor as their practical disadvantages became clearer.

Of course, a major fear of most teachers, and a major hope of a few, has been the political leverage that student participation might create. The marginal role allotted students precludes this from being much exercised in any serious way, even in matters where they might tip the scales in otherwise balanced contests. But in any case, the divergence between the political attitudes of faculty and students has largely closed. The leftward and liberal bias, relative to what one might expect of a profession, remains, though attenuated at the time of the last election. Conservatives are most to be found among professors ("full professors" in American terms), heads of departments, engineers and technologists, and the medical faculties, whereas the reverse is true among social scientists.

Anyway, there is very widespread political apathy among students, and such mild radicalism as exists is now more often channeled through the official Labour party. Even the National Union of Students, once wildly unrepresentative and beginning at the point on the spectrum where traditional politics ends, has become more temperate. In other words, student politicking is now not a major threat either to the standards that faculty members maintain or to their autonomy, and any student activity tends to fasten on matters of direct concern to the student body, like the cost of living in hall or raising fees for foreign students. When university and polytechnic teachers think of threats to standards and to their autonomy, their minds turn to the effects of government cuts on facilities, staff-student ratios, and new initiatives.

THE ECONOMIC AND POLITICAL CLIMATE

This leads naturally to more general reflections on the present condition of universities. Expansion ended half a decade ago and actual contraction is occurring, with once inconceivable redundancies in the offing and maybe the closing of institutions. Thus the cuts envisaged in the polytechnic sector over the next four years entail redundancies of 17 percent. Rationalization hits famous institutions, including such excellent centers of learning as the former women's colleges of London University, Westfield and Bedford. Westfield is in the shadow of possible closure, and Bedford faces possible staff cuts of 20 percent. These are incidental but highly indicative examples.

Also major reorganization and realignments of power are under way. A new body is envisaged that will remove the polytechnics from local control and into a more centralized system. Also, bodies once celebrated for their ability to act as a buffer between government and universities are encountering pressures that make this role less easy to fulfill. Indeed, of recent years the University Grants Committee has in a major way spent its time coping with the vagaries in government financing.

A little bit more needs to be said by way of reiterating this coldness in the political atmosphere, which also reflects chilliness in much of the public at large. Freezing of attitudes and funds arises partly because correlation between expanding higher education and general social and economic benefit is no longer so widely believed. Insofar as it is still believed, faith is restricted to technology. This coolness also arises in part because the public was genuinely sickened by the troubles of the sixties, which in Britain at least were based on very flimsy grounds. People are now less certain that students are usefully engaged in socially beneficial study. In any case, students themselves shared in the blasted expectations, and did not come forward in the projected numbers. No doubt, they took into account what seemed to be reduced gains over a lifetime for those who had a degree and the prospect of graduate unemployment. However, this pessimism is probably quite mistaken in the present unhappy condition of the labor market, where each extra increment of education, at least up to a first degree, improves chances of employment.

That, at any rate, summarizes the trends of the seventies and these were tied in with Britain's responses to the economic malaise. On this I quote a succinct paragraph from Charles Carter's *Higher Education for the Future*; Carter cites "restrictions of government expenditure, more careful budgetary control, high interest rates and the like," and continues,

> In earlier years new forms of welfare expenditure had been loaded on to the budget in response to public demands and political pressures, with little consideration for the ability of the economy to bear them. Now the pendulum swung the other way, and people began to think, not only of the absolute need for a particular kind of expenditure, but also of the relative importance it should be given within the total social budget. Higher education did not actually do too badly in this era of questioning and control, but there has been a considerable disappointment of previous inflated expectations, and a shock to morale when plans have been cut or when reasonable proposals for development have been frustrated. . . .[6]

DEFENSIVE AND CONSERVATIVE ATTITUDES

Alongside this chill in public attitudes and freeze on public resources, we have the response of the academic world itself, which Charles Carter describes as defensive and which I must admit I rather share. As the conservative government grows more radical in its search for the roots of British ills, so academics become more conservative, at least in their desire to conserve the status quo. Most people on the Committee of Vice-Chancellors and Principals reacted to criticism by shrugging shoulders, and more of the conservative minded were appointed to higher administrative office.

This then is the background: left-liberal academics are supporting conservation, and some conservative politicians are in a mood for radical change and moreover seek that change within the context of a laissez faire economic policy that exalts the test of profit. Paradoxically, this laissez faire approach does not let the universities alone but rather imposes more direction than ever before. As for the test of profit, a second paradox is that the defense of certain activities based on usefulness is met with the argument that if they are *that* useful then surely they can move onto the open market outside the shelter of universities. Clearly, there is a sharp clash within political conservatism between the utilitarians, bent on the calculus of

6. Charles Carter, *Higher Education for the Future* (Oxford: Blackwell, 1980), pp. 37–38.

profit, and those who believe in an intellectual fabric that supports culture, the arts, and higher learning as goods in themselves.

NEW DEVELOPMENTS AND PORTENTS

To discuss ideas and developments that are in the wind, I lean on a recent discussion in the *New Universities Quarterly*.[7] The first question concerns the role of the Committee of Vice-Chancellors and Principals and is put by the chairman of that body, Sir Alec Merrison. He holds that the main aim of universities is not numbers but *quality of people and of research*. He notes that for a long time the universities have been protected by the University Grants Committee, and this encourages them in the present situation each to fight in his own corner. In fact, they need to work out an overall strategy: for example, perhaps the selectivity, elitism, and differentiation that govern the award of research grants and government contracts should be extended to the organization of universities. There is a whole nest of questions here. Will this give the victory to the strong, who are not necessarily the best? Will the amount of pushing and shoving necessary finally be more costly than the waste that admittedly exists in the system? How much further should we push the principle that each institution should look to its sectors of excellence and weed out the weaker growths? For although it is clear that wastefulness results from each university attempting everything, it is not so clear that savings result from all rationalizations, tidyings up, and the concentration on this or that level of service or center of excellence.

A particular issue of quality arises in connection with engineers. The Finniston Report showed concern at the lack of recruitment to engineering departments, the low social esteem in which the engineer is held in Britain (by comparison, say, with France), and the relation between the university and the engineering profession. The report proposed, for example, the creation of an engineering authority that would exert pressure by outside professionals on the university. It also proposed in-service training. The report's basic thrust, to relate the university to the world and to prac-ticalities, in turn shall affect the actual content of first-degree courses, as is already happening in medicine. Universities will not be free to determine the syllabus and structure of engineering courses nor to mount courses at will. Such considerations could also apply to the social sciences to some extent, though how they can apply to classicists, theologians, students of literature, and so on, is less clear. The proposals of Finniston will them-selves lead to more differentiation and selectivity. For example, not all universities and probably no polytechnics should be engaged in Master of Engineering work. As Sir Frederick Dainton comments, "It may well prove to be an odd by-product of proposed stratification of courses for formation of associate, registered and diplomate engineers that it should bring

7. "Universities as Evolving Institutions: A Discussion," *New Universities Quarterly* (Summer 1980).

into sharp focus the separate institutions in which these varied forms of
education should take place and thereby provoke the much needed re-
examination of the roles of Further Education colleges, polytechnics and
universities. . . ."[8]

Perhaps I may summarize the present debate about quality as bound up
in considerations of how to rationalize, to differentiate, and to be selective.
In a sense, of course, we are already highly selective in excluding 86 percent
of the age group and in having a very mild gradient of quality within
universities with a matching generosity of resources. It so happens that such
differentiation runs counter to the predominant value system of British
universities, which also exalts a very high degree of autonomy. More selectivity is bound to involve a shift of power toward the state, which seems to
be the unhappy result of having a high-quality education system in a no-
growth economy.

I would like to add a word on what has happened since I wrote the
preceding. In the words of Lord Annan, Vice-Chancellor of London University, my remarks were composed during "the first patter of rain before the
deluge." The newspaper headlines since then tell the story. An article by
Lord Annan in a Sunday paper had the headline "Universities: cuts, yes—
carnage, no." Diana Geddes, in *The Times* for 30 March, 1981, wrote under
the headline "Bankruptcy and closures: the grim future that is facing our
universities." *The Times's* account of the parliamentary debate on 18 March
was headlined "Fear that universities will slide into state of mediocrity."
"Universities under stress" said *The Times's* leader for 19 March. So the issue
of standards has been posed. However, there is so much confusion and
secrecy that it is in fact very difficult to know how standards will be affected
and what will in the end be done. An article in *The Times Higher Education
Supplement* for 24 April indicates this difficulty by referring to "the tangled
issues of rationalization and the cuts which the University Grants Committee must unravel."

The probable aim, according to Diana Geddes, is a single system of
higher education with, perhaps, a premier league of institutions, providing
a full range of undergraduate, postgraduate, and research facilities; a second
with more restricted range; and a third with undergraduate provision only.
If this is done, it is bound, in her words, to set colleague against colleague;
to result in blocked promotion; to prevent brilliant young graduates from
entering on a scholarly career, and to result in first-rate academics being
thrown out alongside second-rate ones.

CRITERIA OF CONTRACTION

The Vice-Chancellor's Committee in its response to the Report of the Select
Committee on Education, Science and the Arts with regard to funding,
argued that the relevant criteria do not consist solely of the size of the

8. *New Universities Quarterly* (Summer 1980), p. 301.

teaching department, but include the needs of scholarship, of research, of postgraduate training, of continuing education, and of national and regional requirements. All that, however, is very general. More specifically, there is a rejection of any policy of "equal misery all round." The broad object is to *reinforce success* and to *encourage differentiation*, and that means the closing of departments, maybe of faculties, even conceivably of institutions, and the concentration of postgraduate facilities. That implies redundancies, and the enormous cost associated with redundancies. Moreover, those redundancies will operate in a singularly unjust way, since at some institutions tenure refers to periods from six months to a year, with appropriately small compensation, whereas at others tenure arrangements imply redundancy costs of up to £200,000 for each academic. It also means the tacit abandonment of the Robbins principle, which affirms that all those suitably qualified by ability and attainment should have access to higher education.[9]

THE SCOPE OF CONTRACTION

A further chapter in the chronicle of gloom was published on 1 July. More than 12,000 university places disappeared, with the worst losses concentrated in a handful of universities. These maimed institutions comprised, in particular, the former colleges of advanced technology such as Salford, Bradford, and Aston. This appeared the more odd because these are largely technological universities, some of which had been encouraged to expand as recently as 1977 and—like Aston—had in any case often been conspicuously successful in placing their graduates. The net result is that one in seven of those who in the 1980s might have expected a university education will not have it, and that those who do attend will have available 90 percent of the resources of 1980, and 80 percent of what was available in 1970. Some 3,000 lecturers' jobs are likely to be lost over the next three years, together with another 4,000 nonacademic jobs, and this estimate does not take in account the uncertain impact of the greatly increased fees for foreign students.

The Guardian of 3 July 1981 summarizes the letter to the universities as follows:

> The U.G.C. [University Grants Committee] says it is recommending a substantial reduction in the numbers in social studies courses to improve staff-students ratios, a small increase in the numbers reading business studies, and discussions between the universities to preserve the teaching of minority foreign languages.
>
> In science, it wants better use of resources, with the implication that there is room for more students on many existing physics and chemistry courses. It wants new biological science developments, particularly

9. Cf. W. Roy Niblett, "Robbins Revisited," *Studies in Higher Education* 6, no. 1 (1981).

those which have high potential for the economy, to be encouraged at the
expense of traditional biology.

The plans assume a small increase in those reading mathematical
sciences, engineering and technology although there would be some
redistribution in the last two. Numbers reading agriculture should fall,
but those reading veterinary science should be maintained by slightly
smaller cuts. Pharmacy gets the worst deal because it is expected to take
the major share of a cut of one quarter in the number of places available to
subjects allied to medicine.

The committee also says it can no longer afford to protect clinical
medicine, but that schools should be able to preserve 1980 intakes
because of some advance funding. Dentistry is getting a smaller than
average cut.

The response to these cuts, which are larger than those imposed any-
where else in the economy, has been very critical. *The Guardian* leader
headline ran "Universities: First, bash the real priorities," referring to the
way the U.G.C. had depleted the resources of engineering centers. The
leader criticized the U.G.C. as "a clique," mysteriously appointed, accoun-
table to nobody, and proclaimed that "the autonomy of the universities
vanishes into the maw of the U.G.C.'s independence." The Committee of
Vice-Chancellors and Principals was unusually outspoken in a statement
reacting to the U.G.C.'s interpretation of government cuts. The statement
declared that the short-term savings fall far short of the compensations for
dismissal, and added that this was "an attempt to run down the British
university system" which would operate in "an invidious and divisive way,"
and would destroy opportunities for teaching and research for a whole
generation. As to *why* all this was so, nobody could be quite certain.
According to one view, the civil servants at the Department of Education
and Science have long wanted to curtail university independence; according
to another the "arts establishment" on the U.G.C. interpreted the government directives by clobbering the technologists; according to yet another,
those universities that had lowest entry requirements or were not represented on the U.G.C. suffered worst. Whatever the reasons, the effect is
clear: a massive shrinkage in the size and an erosion of the autonomy of the
British university system.

TOWARD PROVINCIAL MEDIOCRITY?

I permit myself a concluding personal view. First, it is pretty well impossible to tell how it will affect standards in the universities. The hassle and cost
may outweigh possible gains. Second, the politics accompanying the processes of contraction and rationalization are not likely to favor the survival
of the fittest, but of the most vociferous. For example, such a criterion as the
amount a department spends of research council money favors expensive

research to the detriment of research based on books. All kinds of criteria are adduced, such as "A levels" of students admitted, cost per student educated, the proximity of similar facilities, staff-student ratios, peer judgments, and so on. It seems clear that such criteria can be switched around at need to achieve whatever is the desired result. Third, it seems clear that the international character of many famous British institutions could be undermined. In terms of cultural influence and of a worldwide community of personal links and intellectual commerce, we could witness a drastic decline, and British universities could become purely provincial. Fourth, the degree of emphasis on practicality and applied virtue may well damage the effort to provide theoretical underpinnings. Admittedly some theorizing is mere navel gazing, but the new policy of the Social Science Research Council is ominously atheoretical.

In short, while British universities resisted the assaults of antinomian students and seditious dons in the sixties, and the damaging nonsense of student participation in areas properly academic, now under a Conservative government they may sink into a mean and provincial mediocrity, controlled by centralizing state power in the name of ideological laissez faire. Those of us who opposed student anarchy in the sixties find our critique has been taken up in a philistine and narrowly utilitarian way.[10]

10. Immediately prior to going to press, it is worth noting that a massive lobby during a Commons debate on 18 November 1981 achieved almost nothing. It was at least hoped that the period of contraction would be extended from three to five years. Instead the government announced that £50 million would be made available to "assist" with the cost of redundancies. The government also intends to work on the assumption that costs over 1982–83 would rise by no more than 5.5 percent (comprising pay rises of 4 percent and price increases of 9 percent), which is less than half the current inflation rate. Mr. Geoffrey Gaston, secretary general of the Committee of Vice-Chancellors and Principals, said that these decisions revealed "the Government's dismal persistence in its policy of running down the higher education system" (*"The Times Reports,"* 22 December 1981).

14

Government
and the University
in the United States

ROBIN W. WINKS

The puzzled American finds the European university debate too ideological. Issues of Right versus Left are at the very core of the European argument, while for the time they are on the periphery in the United States and (outside Quebec) in Canada. The moderate, more responsible European Left quite rightly sees recent university reforms as desirable means, even at the cost of temporary destabilization of university governance, of bringing essentially medieval institutions—intended to educate leaders—into line with democracy. The ghost of Burke hovers over every dispute in Britain between advocates of the new versus the old universities, and the ghost takes center stage when the Open University or the University College of Buckinghamshire, as it was once styled (that is, the Independent University), are appraised. The political Left feels that European universities still lag well behind even American universities, those products of capitalism, in providing students with critical means of inquiry and access to faculty. Making the university responsible to society in some sense is at the top of their agenda.

In Europe the Right argues, with greater or lesser subtlety, that the university itself—the institution that stands for the universe of knowl-

Robin W. Winks is Professor of History at Yale University.

edge—is a value, and that preserving and passing on the great traditions of the West to future generations is the aim or purpose of education. These scholars are often labeled *elitist*, a term of disrepute. As some American academicians have said, *"King Lear* is in, *Tarzan* is out." This group feels that the university owes allegiance to mankind, that it is or should be without country, a citadel of knowledge without walls, and that mankind should be placed ahead of any government or any sector of society, however neglected or needy that sector may think itself. One best judges a people by what they choose to preserve, by what they take pride in, and by the way in which they hold the high standards of yesterday in readiness for tomorrow. The Right believes that *reform* is a code word for destruction of the university, for its capture by the politically committed (usually Marxist) who would use it to serve dubious and dangerous purposes.

AMERICAN AND EUROPEAN UNIVERSITIES

This is a contest in which Americans are at a loss. From the outset American universities were far more democratic than the European. Emphasis was more on practical than on historical knowledge. With the advent of the land-grant colleges, American universities turned to agriculture, engineering, librarianship, journalism, even business, subjects offered only recently at the university level in Europe; by the mid-nineteenth century, American universities were service oriented. Even the great private universities, while preserving Latin and Greek, saw they owed Americans an opportunity to learn French or Portuguese, to study German or British history, decades before European universities felt any responsibility for the study of American history or literature. The United States benefited enormously from preparing its citizens for the world, and for a future that would be transformed, in part through the influence of those very Americans. European universities were more parochial. There was a chair of African studies at Northwestern University before there was such a chair at the University of London, the seat of imperial power. History remains the most studied subject at Yale; its students do not consider the skills learned in interrogating evidence to be useless for future careers in law or medicine. Again, reform in the United States meant tinkering modestly with the university, since it was already service oriented. Europeans of the Left, however, accused Americans of precisely that, tinkering, and of not undertaking fundamental reforms, in part because they did not fully understand that the reforms they sought in their own institutions were less urgent or even unnecessary in America. In the United States the push, in education as in politics, has been leftward, and some bewail loss of standards, but here the argument is over degree of democratization, not (as in Europe) over the issue of democratization itself.

As one seeks to preserve cosmopolitan research universities and strives to relate what the public deems arcane to the needs of the public, one cries out for more research, not into teaching methods or core curriculums, the staples of the colleges of education, but rather for more comparative research into systems of, and expectations relating to, higher education.

ISSUES AND COMPLAINTS

As a research agenda, let us look at the specific issues, or complaints, about which Americans speak when they refer to government interference with the university. Aside from the global complaint that any interference is out of the question because it presumes an authority some feel does not exist, or ought not to, six issues stand out. These issues find their focus in the sciences, and most particularly in scientific research, though they arise in the social sciences and humanities as well. Each issue has special urgency in the sciences, since the money involved is usually substantially greater. Each issue can be parodied with particular cases of what lawyers refer to as "the horrible example." Those examples tend to be drawn from legislation intended largely for the governance of the sciences when it is applied inflexibly to other fields, in which less money is involved (and we all know that academic politics become most bitter when least is at stake) and in which any kind of accounting—which by its nature involves quantification—is exceptionally difficult if not misleading.

I do not mean to sound cynical, for the issue is real. Indeed precisely because little is at stake financially in several of the complaints, the tension is all the greater, for one may always compromise on matters of money but not on matters of principle. Academicians in the less well-paying fields—philosophy, history, foreign languages, and English literature—are especially sensitive to matters of pride and prestige just because their status derives from intangibles. Any suggestion that one may "prove" by some form of accounting the cost effectiveness of education is quite properly rejected. For all such efforts are doomed, and even to play at them is to cater to the philistines among us who, as is the case in most government agencies, must provide an annual report on "proof of effectiveness." The scientist is most burdened by the mountains of paperwork involved in meeting government regulations, but the humanists are most vocal, and in the end most effective, in combating subordination of education to the computer.

RESENTMENTS AND DISAFFECTION

The first major issue is the substantial increase in administration necessary to comply with government regulations. Affirmative action, compliance reports on the handicapped, accounting for federally administered student loans, and ever-growing student and faculty litigation have forced universities to double and triple legal offices and staff for management of grants and contracts. Every department or school of any size needs a business manager. The faculty observe this growth in administration and believe, in part correctly, that the new people have been hired at the cost of increased class size, reduced operating budgets, and frozen tenure possibilities for younger faculty. Thus the academic staff often becomes demoralized and rages at the administration.

If an administration is successful in turning faculty anger against the government, the effect may be divisive for the university, which has generally unified itself after the disruptive days of the late 1960s. For almost always it will be revealed that certain disciplines (economics and law, for example) command far greater return in the market and thereby attract to the university more surveillance; and that science departments, particularly those in medical schools, command by far the largest grants, and hence are responsible (it will be argued) for bringing the machinery of compliance. From these attitudes flow other debilitating results: a faculty that once chose not to inquire into the considerable differences between salary scales in law, say, and modern Chinese literature, now may do so; faculty become aware that a university is not and never has been run on a principle of equity. In consequence the university, by hiring staff to protect its principal mission of research and teaching, is seen by faculty as having abandoned rather than helped them.

Attention then turns to pay differentials, fringe benefits, and teaching loads, all matters once beyond notice among gentlemen. Soon the specter of faculty unionization arises, and the administrator is not to be blamed if he concludes that had he hired two more sociologists rather than two more accountants, this menace might have been postponed. Since second-rate faculty turn to collective bargaining and since unionized faculties rapidly become third rate (because the more independent refuse to cooperate as a matter of principle), some universities enter a further downward spiral. Obviously the connection between growth in staff and shrinkage of faculty is far more complex. Obviously, too, other resentments arise, especially when people unused to university climates, who do not understand that courtesy is the highest form of efficiency in a society that communicates by nuance, appear to take over. Disaffection of faculty moves rapidly and inevitably toward loss of faith in the institution once those who cannot speak the language think of themselves as "in charge."

Every faculty in the nation has tales of horror to tell about new administrators from the world of business who think a university may be run like a corporation, who refer to proud and independent scholars as "employees," or even "labor," and who cannot distinguish between a civil servant in the statehouse and a professor in his study. Truth to tell, in a public institution there is little legal difference, but academicians—invariably convinced that they could have made far larger incomes in the outside world—deeply resent their depreciation. In some institutions, staff even forget they work solely for the benefit of the students and faculty. Something like class warfare invades what was once a monastery.

THE TENSIONS OF ADMINISTRATIVE OVERSIGHT

In so poisoned an atmosphere, even the smallest governmental intrusion may touch off a furor, our second issue here. In the United States federal regulations require all universities that accept federal grants and contracts to collect "effort reports" on their faculties conducting sponsored research. Compliance with the Office of Management and Budget is not a matter of discretion, though universities complained about both the principle of reporting and the nature of the reports. Most recalcitrant universities were granted a year's grace during which they sought, first, to persuade the government to change the requirements in order to recognize the shared purposes of faculty activities; and second, to persuade departments that viewed such reporting as both unwarranted and, in the case of those that felt they had nothing to report, ridiculous, that they must comply for the good of the university.

One can easily satirize this invasion of the life of the university, and many have. Some departments have declared that they will not comply, and let the devil take the university down with them. Professionals already accustomed to other forms of effort reporting become impatient with their colleagues, who appear ready to open a Pandora's box, best left closed for the good of the community. Again, the sense of community, continuity, and tradition is threatened.

Why does such a seemingly small matter bother some academics so much? In part because it is a lie to say that 50 percent of one's time is devoted to instruction, another 30 percent to research, and 20 percent to administration, since academics do not work a forty-hour week. It also bothers professors that the reporting assumes forty-hour weeks, the very life most have sought to escape. Furthermore, the reporting implies that the government, from which they may also have sought escape, has the right to ask how they spend the day, an invasion of privacy.

But perhaps this matter bothers faculty particularly because it arises from the common practice in American universities of applying an indirect-cost figure, known as overhead, to all federally supported research projects. This figure represents financial recovery by the university from the grant for services provided indirectly to the grantee—for his office space, heat, and light; for the books that must be in the library for countless searchers so that the project may go on, books that will nonetheless help many others. Quite properly the university passes on to the government part of the cost of general operations on the premise that university expenditures are swollen by the workload generated by the project supported by the grant. Quite properly the government wants some formula for calculating these costs and wants proof that they were incurred. The result may be an overhead figure as high as 67 percent of the total grant. Because the university counts on this additional sum, it finds itself both dependent on the government and angry about that dependence.

To be sure, the best-led universities have diversified their support port-folios with care, to guard against permanent commitment on the basis of soft money; to be certain that grants and tenure issues are separable; to use grant moneys to remodel buildings to serve a grantor's purposes and the university's other needs. The grantor, entitled to know that his money is spent on the intended project, obtrudes increasingly into the university, unconvinced that a research chemist may be better for having a medievalist nearby, his office warmed by the same pipes that bring heat to the labora-tory. The result is steady bickering and frequent quasi litigation over the various standard-deduction formulas by which such matters may be com-puted. The spiral turns upward yet again, with more legal counsel and more contract officers needed to adjudicate and administer the problems. Since the amount of money the university receives from the federal government to reimburse indirect costs is determined by the formula, which is adjusted periodically, all faculty play a role in determining the future overhead recovery rates, even though many see no benefit arising from the grants.

The universities do exactly what the government fears: they strengthen the institution through reallocation of unencumbered funds to activities less capable of attracting outside assistance. The outcome, yet again, is hostility between disciplines, as some departments begin to think they are virtually self-supporting and the others are on the dole. Since the calcula-tions on effort reporting are, by any reasonable academic standard, quite ridiculous, humanists feel once again that philistines are at hand—the administration, the medical school, the department of physics. They bring ridicule on the institution. The anger generated is distressingly out of proportion to the actual paperwork.

TEACHING, RESEARCH, AND ACCOUNTABILITY

Soon the university becomes aware of a third irritation: special interest groups within government have seized power to promote their particular desires. Given lack of coordination among government agencies, account-ing procedures differ; as a result, universities cannot efficiently coordinate their reporting. One private university, Stanford, estimates that accounting costs alone will amount to $300,000 this year (which represents the salary of several full professors). Research and teaching are very much interdepen-dent in some disciplines—in lecturing the researcher at last discovers what he truly has concluded, just as the historian may rightly say he does not know what he believes until he writes it down—but various government departments differently calculate percentages of workloads as well as define these allegedly separate activities. This is tantamount to a fundamental attack on the nature of knowledge in the American university. To teach well is to exemplify research, but this is not credible to an accountant who is, indeed must be, wholly disjunctive in his thinking. Financial practice distorts cognitive process.

Science is at the core of the university; it is also at the core of private industry and of many national government objectives. Acrimony should not continue to impair their mutual understanding. Wild declarations that the universities have, through governmental regulation, been nationalized serve only to confuse and frighten the general public. Good intentions, good will, and intelligent action are eroded by the apparent inability of universities and the government to agree on how to achieve what both (generally) want: a productive relation based on mutual appreciation and cooperation.

University research is often said to be pure; but the taxpayer expects results, and as with recombinant DNA, these may seem impure. As the government increases funding for basic research in universities, public demands for acceptable results become increasingly strident. In 1960 the federal government spent just $1 billion in grants and contracts to universities for research; in 1978 the sum neared $3 billion. In 1958 the federal government financed 32 percent of basic research conducted at universities; by 1978 the figure was 72 percent.

Yet who is to blame for the adversarial relations that have developed? Federal auditors may reasonably want proof that federal money was spent as intended. Enough examples of bad judgment, even dishonesty, have occurred in American universities to make auditors wary. They turn to what they know: methods of accountability that relate to business and government itself, methods that are not compatible with the long-cherished assumptions of faculty or with the old, grotesque, mysterious, ever-untidy product that we call education.

I argue that faculty have allowed the conceptual terms of reference to be imposed from outside and have then walked away from the fight, leaving others to fight on their behalf. Since costing practices appear to be the issue, accountants and financial managers speak for the government in the negotiations, and rightly so; but the universities have allowed other accountants and financial managers to negotiate for them. The result has been rather akin to a major court case in which well-trained lawyers have at each other, each bargaining for and against the admissibility of evidence. Rather, faculty members who understand the mission of the university must inform themselves about the question of accountability, and ought to play a major role in all negotiations. Accountants may analyze the process by which money is accounted for; they cannot measure the results. Faculty have abdicated their responsibility to maintain control over the appraisal of results by resigning to financial officers the earlier, tedious chore of negotiating the framework of purpose.

AFFIRMATIVE ACTION

Our fourth issue is affirmative action, which much offends some faculty. I include here, though many would not, all those government regulations that relate to increasing the number of tenured minority and women, to making universities more accessible to the handicapped, and to according students the right to examine test papers. I find unconvincing most arguments accusing undue government interference in these areas. It is undeniable that few women receive tenure, that minorities are underrepresented in student populations, that universities thoughtlessly build new libraries or dining halls that those in wheelchairs cannot reach. It is undeniable that women are entitled to engage in sport at a level equivalent to that of men and are generally denied the facilities for doing so because the public will not pay (or at least not pay in large numbers) to see them play—yet.

I recognize that there are real risks and high probabilities of reverse discrimination, and that tokenism, and new and subtle forms of racial bias and insult may result. Yet as to affirmative action I cannot feel angry at a government that reminds institutions which pride themselves on their sense of humanity and morality that they have, as often as not, failed to live up to their own principles. I am only sorry that government should have to insist that mankind might find its own ways to fundamental justice.

CONFIDENTIALITY AND PRIVACY

The impact of privacy legislation intended to protect Americans against their government is yet a fifth irritant. No group should be more supportive of this legislation than educators, since by their very nature they are critics. Yet privacy law has worked in divisive ways in universities. Students may now have access to letters of recommendation, unless they waive that right. But all employers and graduate schools reasonably discount letters about which there is a presumption that the student has, even by the merest thought of access to them, shaped their content. Parents may not receive grade reports of their sons and daughters who, being over eighteen, are entitled to privacy with respect to their performance, even though those parents may be paying over $10,000 a year for their education and feel entitled to know how well they are doing. Faculty committees, deliberating and voting on tenure, must make available their correspondence, notes of telephone calls, and—according to a recent Georgia judicial decision—the nature of their vote in closed meeting, to assure the goals of affirmative action have been served. Hearsay, inadmissible evidence, improper standards relating to lifestyle, or other irrelevant considerations must not play a part in the decision.

An even more complex problem arises from an aspect of the Privacy Act of 1974, which was intended to protect individuals who supply information about themselves to government officials for the purpose of engaging in government-sponsored research; this information cannot be used for purposes other than those for which it is given. The act requires that those who provide information about themselves and their research must be consulted before the information is released for a different use at another time. Contractors, including universities, are bound by the act, so that innocuous data often have to be kept in locked files with access logs for recording who examined what.

Subsequently, an attorney ruled that the act's provisions applied to all data on individuals collected under contracts, not only to the data collected for the specific purpose of the agency involved. This ruling would have prevented a university from using a subsequent, and unanticipated, analysis of medical data (collected under an earlier grant) for fresh purposes, to the general hindrance of knowledge. Put differently, the act could have led to the restriction of ideas, a notion universities have always found unacceptable. Since the data might have been submitted a decade earlier when the new uses arose, the costs of finding the person to seek permission to use the data and the attendant deceleration in research momentum might well put an end to the new project. In this case university representatives were able to persuade the government to overrule its own attorney's opinion, but the instance is instructive to all who are concerned with unexpected consequences of apparently desirable, or at the least benign, regulations.

Again, I do not feel inclined to exaggerate the difficulties of privacy legislation. Privacy is a desirable end in itself; universities ought not to think themselves exempt from the normal courtesies; if a person does not want known his or her age, residence, place of birth, or taste in reading matter, unless such information can be proven as related to employment, surely academics, those most private of individuals, ought not to object to paying the price of putting their principles into practice for others.

CENSORSHIP AND ADVANCE APPROVAL

Finally, there is the question of censorship. The wise university does not engage in classified research for the Department of Defense. But then the wise university did not accept large sums from the Shah of Iran or accept financial aid packages from so-called booster clubs so that better football coaches might be purchased. Though the university is not for sale, some proved to be, making the task of resisting sales harder for the rest, as funds became ever scarcer and heating costs ever higher. One might argue that the university that created a chair in Libyan studies was doing nothing more than meeting the needs of its students by finding an indirect way of reducing heating bills and thus, one hopes, tuition costs.

But the general problem of prior approval of publications remains. No educator is unacquainted with the problem, though it usually takes simple forms. One may not destroy the income of a writer by photocopying his or her work and distributing it in quantities to one's students. One may not submit a manuscript to more than one publisher at a time. One ought not to expect the respect of one's colleagues if one publishes in an unjuried journal, or in a journal on whose board of editors one is serving. One ought not to expect to escape lawsuits if one writes libelously. Such matters have long been understood, and though at times problems have arisen with respect to them, the problems have seldom been couched in terms defined specifically for the university by the federal government.

Again, the prudent university declines support from any source that demands the right of review and approval in advance over publication of research. The university is, after all, committed to free and open access to knowledge. A donor might grant a professor sole access to a collection of literary or historical papers—common enough in England, uncommon in the United States—and he might or might not accept the condition of sole access, though at the cost of much abuse by others who wish to examine the papers. But no donor may dictate the results that are to arise from his gift.

Still, governments often do not abide by this principle. The situation may be more serious in Europe than in North America; nonetheless, granting agencies of the United States federal government have increasingly sought to require that publications arising from research they have funded must be submitted for approval in advance. (The Central Intelligence Agency may place this condition on its own employees, of course; indeed, any employer may place such a condition on any employee who knowingly enters into such an agreement. But the agency is not the employer of the faculty member to whom a grant is given; that member is defined as a principal investigator for the grantor and remains an employee of the university, whose regulations must override any expectations on the part of the grantor). The government may argue any of several reasons why it must approve publication: because the public safety is at stake if medical research is released prematurely; because the research may not meet customary agency standards and thus prove embarrassing if examined by congressional funding committees; because the agency's mission is to achieve a certain social goal, and the research may be harmful to that goal if released prematurely or in a form not couched in the conventional language relating to the goal; or simply to avoid offending the taxpayer.

These are not necessarily improper objections, though all may be rendered improper, and all may be smoke screens for goals that are truly improper. So the university researcher rightly opposes any such conditions. In 1979 the government nonetheless ruled that information or data "which might adversely affect the public and the Government's formulation of public policy with respect thereto," could not be released by grantees. The example given, publication by a cancer researcher of early findings that might lead the public to believe that a cure had been found, reflected a sense of 1984—that is, of a "Big Brother" ready to protect the innocent from being misled—which many faculty found insulting. Here again two goals were in conflict: the government not unreasonably wished to protect its citizens from lung cancer, or laetrile, or public demand for the application of research findings that were merely indicative. But the university, committed to education, knows that each individual researcher must be permitted to make mistakes for himself.

FEARS FOR AUTONOMY

I have, of course, left uncovered many areas of concern. Universities fear that changes in the federal tax system will hurt, or help, some particular sector of higher education. They fear that the government will—as it has attempted—seek to dictate admissions standards to medical schools. They fear that monitoring or restructuring of student loans and grants will erode the freedom of the university to choose its own students. They fear that academic freedom may come once again under attack. They know that the government will seek to pressure universities toward more intensive study of troublesome areas as defined by foreign affairs and to lesser study of somnolent areas; they know that government will seek to define what constitutes an education through its own employment criteria; they know that the government will pursue the chimera of standardized tests. These fears and this knowledge keep the university community united, despite the first of my set of major concerns. So long as the government continues to seek to intervene so clumsily in university affairs, universities will retain their independence. But the day may come, and soon, when by charm and intelligence, and above all by the power of the purse, which exerts an intelligence of its own, the government will enter the fold.

In a democratic society a university must be independent. Its faculty must not be the creatures of other bodies, consultants who draw the greater part of their income from outside the university, members of legislative bodies who calculate their teaching to the electorate's mood, purveyors of popular fiction and mass textbooks who seek course adoptions in states that will not admit of a multiplicity of views. Too often academicians use the government as a metaphor for a larger fear: that they are not as independent as they must be if they are truly to serve the highest of educational goals, the life of man thinking. If the university is not free and democratic, then society is not free or democratic. For the university is, in free lands, a reflection of the highest aspirations of its people.

THE ILLUSION OF POLITICAL NEUTRALITY

One of the most cherished illusions of American academics is that their universities may stand aside from the political process and that their universities therefore provide special protection against partisanship, against involvement in the daily routine of government, and against the moral compromises of politics. The American public, which by and large pays for these universities, probably never shared this illusion and tends to regard the so-called nonpartisan actions and policies of the universities as political acts. As a result, public confidence in universities has declined seriously, and in the end tragically, over the last decade.

American universities always have been a reflection of the culture that produced them. State universities usually are an upward extension of the state's secondary school system; universities of quality seldom grow upon public school systems that are inferior. The public school systems always have been closely related to certain social and political goals: they have been the principal road to assimilation of immigrants, they have helped preserve the healthy diversity one finds from state to state by reflecting the needs of the state rather than reflecting one another; and they have made possible a greater variety of types and qualities of higher education for young Americans than any other nation provides or could provide. Of the 2,600 universities and colleges in the United States, few dispassionate educators would claim that more than 200 provide anything approaching a quality education. Many are "second-chance" institutions, or community colleges that serve local social and political purposes. Others offer skills, or training for a particular job—business management, textile design, or journalism, as examples—and may provide education as well as training, but only incidentally so and only for those students who consciously seek both.

Americans rightly cherish this diversity. Much of America's vitality has come from competition among its regions, and many Americans still think of themselves in regional (or even state) rather than national terms. Southerners are not alone in having an identity that sets them apart, at least in their own minds. The tension between the regions in the late nineteenth century and in the twentieth has been a healthy one, and the sense of regional as opposed to national primacy has been a source of great pride to many universities. This regional pride—Coloradoans' notion that their state university is the "Columbia of the West," or Emory University's sense of itself as a displaced Ivy League institution—helps preserve genuine regional identity. These identities are as much political as they are social.

DIVERSITY AND RESPONSIVENESS

One benefit, and an enormous one, arising from this regional diversity has been that American education is not homogeneous in content and purpose. Americans have not become the uniform, conformist society that foreigners expect. All the forty-five or so universities of Great Britain are, at their upper levels, conventionally said to be of approximately the same quality, the prestige gap between "Oxbridge" and "Red Brick" notwithstanding. An honors degree from Lancaster may be taken to mean approximately the same thing as one from Sussex, and a first from Oxford theoretically is not superior to one from Swansea (although it may be awarded with greater frequency at Oxford). In a compact country such uniformity may be wholesome, but in the United States it would not be. One of the glories of American higher education has been that most Americans who sought a university could find one suited to their abilities and talents. If they performed toward the top in their league, they could expect to go on to compete in a bigger league. The universities rewarded those who could thrive in competition. A few universities—a very few—became national centers by drawing upon the nation; most strove only to be best in their region or state.

The basic orientation of American higher education has been to the needs of a mass public. When American agriculture required rationalization and massive input of systematic knowledge, agriculture and mechanical colleges were created. When the nation felt threatened by the Soviet Union,

Russian studies programs were launched. When attention turned to Southeast Asia, Southeast Asian studies boomed; when Southeast Asia became a source of pain and embarrassment, universities were happy to accept federal money to provide instruction in subjects that were, in the final analysis, not matters of abstract or theoretical scholarship but of public policy. In short, universities have shown a commendable responsiveness to the needs of the nation as well as to regional needs, often undertaking instruction in a given subject before the society as a whole recognized the need, and equally often accepting from the government and the foundations a mandate that was essentially political in its ends.

By the late 1960s the universities became a kind of intellectual Supreme Court for the land. Just as the Warren Court used sociological jurisprudence to lead public opinion in a certain direction, so too were the universities expected to be a long stride ahead of public attitudes—but no more than a long stride. Universities could not venture so far ahead as to appear socially irresponsible for they could not afford to forget the people who financed them: the taxpayers, the alumni, and the government.

Universities proved to be abysmally ignorant about public relations. Academics who could expain why Socrates took the hemlock could not explain to a skeptical public why they wanted to offer black studies, or to remove military training (ROTC) units from the campus, or to let students sit on faculty committees. Some universities capitulated to student demands; others did not while managing to appear to do so; some demands were legitimate and others were not; some administrators and faculty lacked courage and others had it—but virtually none was able to guide a confused public.

Thus many of the changes in American universities that appeared to be most radical reflected in part a long-standing responsiveness to social and educational needs. Some universities, such as Columbia, fully deserved the fate that befell them, for faculty allowed control to slip into the hands of administrators who reasonably enough chose to run the universities as they saw fit. Though the notion of the multiversity was not compatible with most scholarly pursuits, most scholars were too busy tending their own gardens to be aware of the encroaching jungle. Clark Kerr of Berkeley and those who followed him were the Robert McNamaras of the computerized future. The universities neglected to point out a new direction for public opinion and fell out of touch with the public. Losing touch was a political act and reestablishing contact will be political as well.

FREEDOM, AUTONOMY, AND RESPONSIBILITY

By 1975 or so many universities in the United States were eager to rectify their relationship with the government. Recognizing the dangers of accepting government money, they phased out those programs, like Southeast Asian studies, that had no constituencies. They also benefited from a general liberalization in society: the public no longer demanded that black studies, or the presence of students on disciplinary committees, be justified. In the meantime, the national and state governments were now filled with the very products of the period of change in American universities, with young and ambitious bureaucrats who could recognize cooptation when they encountered it. They began to insist that universities explain how they used their money; why they were entitled to tax-free status; and by what means they justified their admission, hiring, and tenure policies. These are questions that government is entitled to ask, just as universities are entitled to fear the possibilities for conflict and invasion that such questions might entail. As usual, confronted with a problem in public relations the universities fell back upon their accustomed plea—they pled academic freedom, a term they perfectly well understood, or professed to, without recognizing that a decade of ferment about the purpose of the university in a democratic society had led Americans of all political persuasions to suspect *academic freedom* to be a euphemism for academic license, or job security, or even featherbedding and its upper-class equivalent, protecting the old school tie. As a result, the government mounted the kinds of invasions of privacy I earlier described, invasions to which academics rightly responded with indignation and wrongly with obtuseness and arrogance.

In the United States the relation of government and the university is not a matter of the Right versus the Left, as it is in much of Europe. Many universities opposed creation of a federal Department of Education, resisted affirmative action (more, I think, as it related to women than to minorities), and made a parody of effort reporting. The presidents of many universities spoke against their own personal principles in championing Ronald Reagan, who promised to take the government out of the business of education, to constrict or eliminate the Department of Education, and to reduce the burdensome paperwork of compliance reporting. Faculties, though still inclined to vote Democratic, leaned ever more toward the Republican line. Yet, both political positions pose dangers to the independence of the university. Indeed, *there* is the delicate balance the university must achieve: the university must be of the world yet not in it, must serve society without accepting its dictates and without arrogantly presuming to know what is best for others. This search for balance between freedom and public responsibility will be ever with us, and eternal vigilance will continue to be the price of autonomy.

15

Higher Education
in Portugal

VEIGA SIMAO
JOSE MANUEL TOSCANO RICO
EDUARDO CARREGA MARCAL GRILO

Until the early 1970s the history of higher education in Portugal is the history of its universities: the University of Coimbra was organized in the thirteenth century, the Universities of Lisbon and Porto in 1911, and the Technical University of Lisbon in 1930. During the forty-four years of Salazar's one-party corporate state, higher education did not change substantially. But in 1973, under Caetano, Salazar's successor, a complete reform of the educational system was promulgated in association with a national development plan. Reform measures included diversification of the system through the establishment of polytechnic institutes, higher normal schools, and four new universities. This network of institutions first was designed to decentralize academic authority, to promote competition among the institutions, and to decrease the influence of the professorial chairs. Second, the educational system was expanded to serve twice as many students, 12 percent of the university-age group rather than 6 percent. Third, pedagogical, administrative, and financial autonomy was accorded to all higher education institutions. Fourth, political considerations were to be eliminated from all teaching appointments. Finally, new forms of participation

Veiga Simao is Director of the National Laboratory for Energy and Technology in Lisbon, Jose Manuel Toscano Rico is Vice-Rector of the University of Lisbon, and Eduardo Carrega Marcal Grilo is Professor of Applied Mechanics at the Lisbon Technical High Institute.

in academic councils were to be established for students, instructors, and research staff.

With the revolution of April 1974 Portugal became a political laboratory in which power oscillated between proponents of a left dictatorship and supporters of democratic ideals. The country underwent a profound economic transformation; the banks, insurance companies, and other large corporations were nationalized; many companies began "autogestation." Agrarian reform in the south led to expropriation, redistribution, and nationalization of a large part of the land. Workers' wages were substantially increased, especially in industry. The rate of inflation accelerated, and the so-called middle class was on the verge of disintegration.

During this period of anarchy, the 1973 reform program was halted: the new higher normal schools were closed and planned implementation of polytechnics ceased. Politicians attempted to assume control of the universities, which became fully politicized. A profound convulsion swept through the universities, and a mixture of revolt, naive spontaneity, and mass manipulation generated an impulse to do away with all hierarchy. Power shifted abruptly from the chaired professors to the students. The governing body of each university, the plenarium, was reconstituted to include all students, teaching and research staff, and nonacademic employees. Thus all these constituencies participated in the plenarium's determination of general policy, including the appointment and dismissal of professors, the structure of courses, the creation and elimination of disciplines and subjects, the types of examinations, the evaluation system, and the like.

Between 1974 and 1976 this anarchical system prevailed. Many professors were expelled, accused of having cooperated in one way or another with the deposed government or with the police. Many accusations were never proven, and some firings were based on anonymous denunciations. Academic standards, teaching, and working conditions all declined rapidly; practically all research ceased.

In August 1976 the first democratic government since 1926 came to power. The first step taken by the minister of education was to reorganize his chaotic department. He defined stricter rules for the nomination of professors, for the curriculum, for the procedures of election of academic councils and the exercise of their authority, and for student evaluation. These measures were protested by the extreme Left, which accused the minister of being in the service of the bourgeoisie. The power struggle resulted in the conservatives' regaining power. As a result, the modernization of the universities slowed, and access to higher education is still restricted by economic barriers. But two large subsystems of higher education have been formed, the university and the polytechnic systems. The latter, also called short-cycle higher education, offers two- and three-year training courses, and it includes institutions for technical and professional training as well as those for the training of schoolteachers.

Fully to appreciate the role that Portuguese higher education must now play in the nation's formation of human capital, one need consider several basic features of the country. Portugal is highly dependent on other nations for its raw materials. The average annual per capita income is $1,900, and vast regional disparities exist. Compared with the rest of western Europe, Portugal is still a developing country whose economy is essentially agricultural. Our low productivity is caused by insufficient mechanization, especially in agriculture. Thus the role of education, particularly higher education, in the formation of human capital is of the utmost importance. The Portuguese university must help the nation overcome its backwardness; yet, at the same time, the university must support and advance those areas in which development is taking place and in which the competence of research already meets international standards. Moreover, the university has to reconcile and promote both humanistic education and specialized professional training.

RECENT REFORMS

Generally speaking, the measures promulgated in the past two years seem intended to transform the structure of the university, a hierarchy originally constructed on Humboldtian and Napoleonic models, into something more open and flexible along Anglo-American lines. A council of rectors now serves as a consultative agency to the government, and it represents the highest organ of interuniversity cooperation.

The faculties may now organize on the basis of departments. To ensure adherence to high standards, a department is required to have a minimum of fifteen teachers, at least five of whom must hold the doctorate and a full-time appointment. These departments have an autonomous life and administration. They are responsible for courses in their disciplines, although in practice they are much more oriented toward graduate work and rendering service to the community. It is still too early to assess the real capacity and operation of the departments. In principle, however, they should enhance the scientific activity of the universities, facilitate acquisition of new financial resources, and make available knowledge valuable to the economy and society.

Another innovation in the scope of higher education is the new law concerning teaching and research careers. Up to now the universities' hierarchies were pyramidal, with one single place as the peak of the academic career, to be filled by public examination. A new law abolished the pyramidal structure and should facilitate the promotion and professional development of present instructors. It increases their opportunities to advance in rank, raises their income, and guarantees state jobs to all assistants who fail to obtain the doctorate. This statute has won acceptance from many professors and lecturers but remains controversial nevertheless. The main controversy concerns the promotion—automatic in some cases, and by means of an examination of curriculum vitae in others—of professors who already hold the *aggrégation* to the highest rank.

Other innovations point toward limiting the role of present faculties to undergraduate studies. Both graduate studies and research are being transferred to structures connected with the university but not directly subject to its management. These new bodies thus have great autonomy and flexibility in shaping their work. How well this system will operate remains to be seen.

UNIVERSITY AUTONOMY AND ACADEMIC FREEDOM

While proclaiming the unquestionable principle of university autonomy, the government has quietly taken over the real substance of authority. The government has attained and consolidated its power by creating a greater separation between research and teaching, by retaining degree certification, by organizing new types of institutions, by dividing the traditional universities into smaller units, and by developing more subtle financial controls. Meanwhile the university proclaims its own authority and evades the real problems of its autonomy.

In practice the university has diluted its freedom in a number of ways. It has permitted to develop an extreme politicization of its members who are subject to external influences. It has failed to establish objective criteria for the making of its budget. It has shown preference to personal and political interests. It has not been open to new fields of knowledge and inquiry, and has demonstrated weak capacity for innovation in its traditional courses. Finally, it has shown little concern for the needs of society and for the development of genuine regionalization.

As a result of these attitudes and practices, one of the principal tasks today is to establish a clearer and more stable balance of power between the state and the university. Both institutions represent and serve the public interest. In truth, a modern university is no longer an institution that transmits abstract knowledge to a clientele of upper-class students who have slight connection with the professions. The modern university is rather increasingly involved in professional training and is the cornerstone of the nation's occupational structure. Because of this fundamental relation, the government's political and economic branches have become more interested in controlling the system of higher education. Yet although the university might seek to avoid such control, it cannot repudiate its responsibility for professional training. Upon the discharge of this responsibility depend its strength and importance, and its opportunity to participate in the reorganization of society.

Of course, all governments have a fundamental urge to control the system of higher education since they rightly think that implementation of their programs can be achieved only through use of the advanced training provided by institutes of higher learning. Both Western and Eastern socialist societies seek to plan their development, and planning depends on the existence of groups of intellectuals, scientists, and technocrats whose job is to create and administer organizations and resources under public and private sponsorship. Moreover, the radical Left believes in the necessity of a so-called democratic-centralist party capable of addressing the problems of "working-class consciousness." They hold that Lenin's old idea about the creation of a vanguard is even more feasible in this era of mass higher education. Indeed, all the contemporary ideological movements subscribe to the concept of the professionalization of higher education despite their disagreement on the nature of the economy, whether it is to be command or market.

Our situation gives rise to an important question: can any society afford to have the university at the service of transient political movements? The only answer is that, in the first place, the university must *work well* insofar as it both participates in the economy and engages in the discovery of new knowledge. And it must also *act well* by training lawyers, doctors, administrators, politicians, and so on. Fulfillment of these tasks makes it possible for the university to *move well* toward its ultimate end, which is the independent pursuit of truth. From an equilibrium among these objectives the university derives the strength that comes from serving society with wisdom and cultivating its own roots in the very essence of man. To foster man's spiritual and intellectual virtues the university requires a proper measure of autonomy and freedom.

MASSIFICATION AND QUALITY OF EDUCATION

Another major problem today is the continuously increasing number of students. Democratization has lowered the quality of higher education, and we must reverse this trend by finding ways to combine democratization with maintenance of academic standards. Diversification of higher education offers a solution. We need to prepare people for practical jobs. The danger, of course, is that diversification could lead to a first-class education for an elite and a second-class education for the masses. To avoid this, students should be able to transfer from one institution to another as their interests and abilities warrant. Moreover, dignity must be conferred on nonuniversity higher education.

Second, the university must engage in more scientific research. Only through a great research effort can we attain the quality of education that we desire. Legislation granting teachers freedom in their research is essential for progress. University research should, wherever possible, be related to the problems of the country. In our nonuniversity institutions, research should always have primarily a practical character. For economic development is the task that faces Portugal, and our higher education system must be designed with this task in mind. The nation's development requires the expansion and diversification of higher education, the maintenance of standards, and greater expenditure for research, both basic and applied.

THE ORGANIZATION OF RESEARCH

The organization and conduct of research are now undergoing changes as a result of two independent actions. The first is reform of the National Institution for Scientific Research, with the objective of providing it with greater operating flexibility and efficiency. The complete plan involves the formation of research centers, located at and staffed by the universities but administered by the National Institution. The institution will also finance research projects and programs, award scholarships and subsidies, sponsor publications and conferences, and the like. The second innovation is the creation of the career of research worker. Five categories of research worker are defined, each with specific rights, obligations, and criteria for promotion. The structure of this career, to a certain extent, is similar to that of the academic or teaching career. Researchers may also do some teaching in higher education institutions.

Too, a large number of cultural agreements have been signed with various countries. These serve as a framework for future conventions between universities, which would prompt beneficial cooperation with particular respect to graduate work and research. These international relations have already proved to be very helpful, and much more is expected from them as our universities and faculties continue to reap their potential benefits.

THE FUTURE

In the past seven years Portugal has undergone drastic and fundamental social and political changes. Although university reform has begun to rectify the excesses of the postrevolutionary anarchy, much remains to be done. We have already mentioned the problems of university autonomy, massification, and research. The university must continue to fulfill its obligations to society, but the government must extend to the university the autonomy it needs to carry out its missions. The crucial problem of access to higher education must also be addressed. Entry into a professional school directly upon completion of a secondary education cannot solve the problems of mass education and will only compound the tensions of access. The *numerus clausus* in Portugal should be established after the first educational cycle or the first academic degree in order to combine open and limited access defined by merit. This action would weaken the influence of social and economic advantage in access to higher education.

More generally, we must replace the passive university with a new concept, the university as a center for development. Research and development should be encouraged through contracts with public and private enterprises, social institutions, and national research and development laboratories. Creation of new courses and degrees should take account of prospective professional openings and should be accompanied by a legal definition of the administrative system.

In Portugal large questions remain to be answered. Can the university enter the world of Western culture and contribute to scientific and technological development? Can it help to create the conditions necessary for social and economic development? The integration of Portugal into the European Economic Community presents a new and decisive challenge to Portuguese education. Will she become a colonized territory or, as we all must hope, a full partner?

16

The University
and the Economy
in Sweden

FOLKE HALDEN

In the affluent 1960s, even in democratic Sweden, a social-democratic minister of education who is a doctor of social sciences, could say in the parliament: "The time has passed when it might seem natural that the universities could function as, if the expression be permitted, the San Marino of the learned." The postwar period has been marked by rapid growth of university entrants. Both the total and per capita costs of universities have increased. Even more important, perhaps, is that the share of national income allocated to the universities has increased significantly. These trends are carefully watched by ministers of finance and raise conflicts of interest. Given the economic stringency that today afflicts all industrialized countries, the universities inevitably attract attention.

Both the employment and the financial condition of the Western democracies call for very cautious action on the part of universities. Unless they analyze the implications of the changed situation for themselves, and find ways and means to cope with it, someone else will most certainly do it for them. In the long run that could be disastrous for academic freedom and university autonomy. Thus the universities have a moral obligation to face reality and to cooperate with society for the benefit of the economy.

The university must also take account of the development of democracy. The idea of codetermination has reached the universities, or will very shortly do so. Ironically, however, corporative tendencies have also inten-

Folke Halden is a member of the Swedish National Board of Universities.

sified. Since World War I, trade unions have become much stronger. But
instead of strengthening the influence of the general public, in many cases
this development has concentrated power in a few elected leaders.

THE SWEDISH SYSTEM OF HIGHER EDUCATION

All Swedish universities and postsecondary schools are—with one exception—state institutions. A national board that reports to the minister of
education has overall responsibility for the system. It gives advice on the
annual budget and long-term development, after consultation with schools
and faculties. This board is chaired by a full-time chancellor, appointed by
the government. Members of the board are also appointed by the government, but they are nominated by associations, the most important of which
are the national trade unions and the employers' confederation. In consequence, outsiders wield considerable influence over the system. Further,
board members also chair the five planning commissions; they prepare their
respective sector issues for board decision and action. These five sectors are
science and technology; social sciences, including economics and law; medical services; education; and arts and letters. On these commissions are
representatives from the trade unions, from industry and commerce, student organizations, and the universities. Too, each university has a local
board with very much the same composition, chaired by the rector. A
regional structure has also been instituted in the form of six boards with
roughly the same composition as the others.

Clearly, very close cooperation has been established by law between the
universities and society, with emphasis on labor and the economy. The ideal
is that knowledge acquired at the universities and new knowledge gained
through research should be placed at the disposal of all relevant sectors of
society, and that those sectors should inform the universities of their needs,
both qualitative and quantitative.

THE SWEDISH ECONOMY

Economic realities in Sweden, as observed from the standpoint of the
university, probably typify the situation that obtains in other countries
belonging to the Organization for Economic Cooperation and Development.

For a number of decades Sweden was considered advanced. Its rate of
education was high; it became an exemplary welfare state; and its economy
flourished. Sweden had an ample supply of raw materials (mainly iron and
timber) and electric energy, an intelligent workforce of high morale, and a
few inventions of international significance. Very few saw an end to progress; everyone was good at extrapolation. But suddenly the situation
changed. Home-produced energy was no longer sufficient and had to be
supplemented by imported oil and coal. So, too, our hydroelectric power,
the cleanest possible form of electricity, had to be supplemented by pollut-
ing methods of production, which later aroused serious environmental
concern.

People had become accustomed to affluence and could not imagine a limit to what could be afforded, either individually or collectively as a nation. So wages became the highest in the world, and the social security system grew increasingly elaborate and consequently expensive. The public sector and private service superseded industry as the leading sector of the economy, an imbalance that proved almost disastrous during recession.

Moreover, the Swedish economy became dependent on decisions made elsewhere. Sweden has no influence on the price of oil but depends heavily on its import. The home market is far too small for its industrial capacity, so foreign trade is of vital importance. But as competition in world markets has increased, Sweden has been forced to reconsider its total cost position and to reduce public expenditure to free resources for industry. Quite simply, the public service sector of the economy now accounts for about 30 percent of output. There is general agreement that this sector must not further enlarge. The biggest subdivisions of the public sector are health services, social welfare, and education. Can education's cost be reduced?

HIGHER EDUCATION: COSTS AND PRIORITIES

One way to reduce the cost of higher education would be to decrease the number of new entrants for a few years. But this policy has its difficulties for the generation born eighteen-to-twenty years ago is comparatively large. It will be hard to keep them out of the university, especially since the market for labor is weak, but we must somehow reduce entry, even though this decreases our national investment in knowledge and skills.

Sweden must also decide on its educational priorities. In terms of per-student cost, the humanities and the social sciences are comparatively cheap, for they do not require expensive equipment. Expensive fields include medicine, the natural sciences, and engineering; but it is unthinkable to decrease enrollments in the very fields that defend our standard of living. Consequently the government, as well as the public, recognizes that the natural sciences and technological studies must be treated more generously. But this policy does not altogether settle the problem of priorities.

Our very concern for culture dictates a minimum level of support for the humanities and social sciences. Also, the internationalization of Sweden's markets requires proficiency in foreign languages. Our situation imposes also a need to understand social and political conditions around the world. These are good reasons for industry and commerce not to emphasize immediate scientific and technical needs at the expense of the humanities and social sciences. In the modern world the latter are necessary, not decorative.

INDUSTRY AND DEMOCRACY

In the open society of modern liberal democracies, human attitudes and behavior are of decisive importance. Authoritarian styles of industrial management are simply impractical and impossible given a workforce composed of individuated and expressive personalities. And workers' behavior and morale mean the difference between profit and loss in business and industrial enterprise. Moreover, concentrated industrial authority is on a collision course with our very strong trade unions.

The Swedish trade unions organize and mobilize almost 100 percent of the labor force, both blue and white collar. Their bargaining strength is very impressive. They are equally strong in the public sector. By legislation the unions have become involved in management. Even the government has to negotiate with the unions on political issues such as the budget. Representatives of the unions sit on the boards of directors of the larger companies, and elected union officials have far-reaching rights. Thus national economic decisions must reflect not only economic and legal considerations but also public opinion and attitudes.

In this new institutional and psychological environment, the principles of industrial and economic management are changing. The ideology behind the new management is of international origin and significance, and the new management will no doubt, therefore, spread all over the democratic world. It requires that the understanding of microeconomic analysis be improved and broadened, a task imposed on the schools and the universities in the interest of economic rationality and efficiency. Indeed, economics is one of the fastest growing fields of study at the Swedish universities. A call for reduction of university entrants must take these facts into account.

ENVIRONMENTAL PROBLEMS

Interest in environmental problems is rising. Alarming reports about the pollution of air, water, and soil have led the universities to attend to these matters in both teaching and research. Technology is involved as well as chemistry and biology, and interdisciplinary programs have been developed.

Legislation and public opinion force industry to address environmental aspects of productive activity, sometimes at high cost. Environmentalism is a sphere in which universities, as impartial and neutral institutions, probably have to expand. Reductions of effort and expenditure cannot be recommended. For the trade unions will use their influence on the university boards, as well as in the parliament, to maintain present budget levels, at the very least. They will insist also on maintaining expenditure on the ergonomic aspect of work, on which serious research is just getting under way.

LEADING PRINCIPLES OF UNIVERSITY ADJUSTMENT

Clearly, a mechanical method of cutting costs across the board is not advisable. Therefore, we need a more analytic and a more discriminating approach that will enable us to use our resources in the most effective manner. Here the universities should take the lead; the alternative is political and administrative fiat. To preserve academic freedom and university autonomy, higher education will have to make voluntary and calculated sacrifices of some activities for the sake of others. I now propose to set forth the principles by which our adjustment to present and future circumstances should be managed.

First, the tendency to simultaneously expand in various directions must be checked. The universities should do only what no one else can do better: research and the education of students for research; the education of graduates should be based on and oriented to research.

Other institutions could undertake at least part of the training that is based on established knowledge and experience. Even business enterprises can do that themselves or by way of their associations and federations. The government can take a hand with schools that require less expensive equipment than universities. Above all, voluntary organizations could offer adult courses that are of a consumptive nature, as distinguished from investments in future skill and competence. The university should concentrate on the pursuit of new knowledge and leave the vocational dimension of life to others.

Second, the principle of concentration has a structural and geographical application. There has been a tendency to make higher education available all over the country by opening small local university branches or small independent colleges, often without appropriate connections to a research-based institution. As long as the economy was expanding, this probably did not do much harm; but it is a wasteful expenditure of our educational resources and should not be continued in the present economic situation. To attempt to strengthen these small schools by allocating research capacity to them would require a large investment that would weaken the universities and benefit neither society nor the economy.

Only large universities can offer all disciplines and specialities. Even small countries cannot embrace the full academic spectrum of study and research. Hence national concentration is necessary to do well those things that are decided upon. Moreover, the big universities should do what they are best at, that is, act on the principle of comparative advantage according to a national plan for education.

Third, we must apply the principle of collaboration. In addition to the research the university has decided to conduct and has been equipped for, it must scan the international horizon for news, information, and early warnings of novelty and innovation. This demanding job should be undertaken by academies and similar institutions. Similarly, collaboration with consumers of research and technology, for example, industry, will also strengthen the university. Exchange of ideas is a form of collaborative education beneficial to both parties. Equally important can be cooperative research. Industry puts about as much money into research and development as the authorities give to the universities. Their research efforts differ, but synergistic effects can flow from cooperation.

Above all we require a long-term program, focused on the basic social needs as they appear today. And right now the problem is economic through and through. How are we to survive as a highly developed welfare state, when there is no clear and present danger to individual security, no immediate risk of material destitution or cultural privation?

CENTRAL AREAS OF RESEARCH

As identified by several responsible groups, the central areas of research seem to be the following: first, basic research in the natural sciences, mathematics, and data processing; next, applied research on the work environment, in social planning, energy technology, and materials technology. All these require cooperation among several disciplines and faculties. Also important are cooperative research projects that involve the universities, industry, political authorities, trade unions, and the public. And lastly, information gathering about international research must continue.

For these programs the universities can count on financial support from the government and from industry. These projects offer the universities a central role in the reconstruction of the national economy. This would redound directly to the benefit of Swedish citizens and indirectly to the benefit of the developing countries, who can view the economic plight of the West only with anxiety.

THE GOAL: DYNAMIC ADJUSTMENT

The market for labor depends on both the structure and the state of the economy. Demand for highly qualified personnel varies with circumstance, in particular, available resources and the occupational structure, to which individual ambitions must be adjusted. Account must be taken also of population fluctuations, the birth rate, and age differentials. If population growth is zero, numbers of certain specialists must be fixed accordingly, as is the case with new physicians and teachers. One cannot extrapolate into the future on the assumption of continuous growth in our time.

So far as the university is concerned, rational adjustment requires intersector transfers of human and material resources without expansion of the whole. Resources must be diverted from some scientific and technological specialities in order to expand others. Thus even if the higher education budget remains constant or decreases, there is still scope for change and reform. Such dynamic adjustment is crucial in a period of economic constraint.

EDUCATION AND SOCIETY IN HISTORICAL PERSPECTIVE

The ancient universities were designed to meet the needs of the church and of the kings and princes who were engaged in building their administrations. The task of higher education was normative, namely, to strengthen the faith and the realm. Several hundred years ago the Enlightenment brought a new attitude toward education, but even as recently as forty or fifty years ago the universities were for the happy few, perhaps 1 or 2 percent of each age group. Demand was not intense for such professionals as teachers, doctors, lawyers, clergymen, and others.

Society today is not like that of the Middle Ages or even the society that existed before World War II. Consider the case of Sweden. In 1959 the public sector of the economy accounted for 31 percent of the gross national product; in 1979, 60 percent. As far as education is concerned, only a little more than a decade ago did nine years of compulsory schooling become available for everybody. There are still a few million adults who have had only seven years of primary school, and this at a time when 90 percent of Swedish children go to school for at least eleven years, and about 80 percent of them go on to postsecondary education of some kind.

The structure of society is rapidly changing. Social mobility is high. After 1945 industry expanded enormously; agriculture and forestry shrank and industrialized. Society's needs for intellectual services changed radically: research and development, advanced education and research, highly trained experts and specialists—all came into demand. We are now entering the postindustrial era, and the public service sector enlarges as society assumes responsibility for individuals from conception to the grave. Thus a shrinking industrial sector must provide the necessary financial resources for the entire community. Accordingly, industry and business think they are entitled to service in return, and they expect something from our educational institutions. Business and industry do not wish to infringe on academic freedom and university autonomy; rather they want the academics to step out of their ivory towers and help. Needless to say, management should not appropriate the tasks of the universities, nor should the academics assume the responsibilities of management.

A DANGER AND ITS EVASION

There is an obvious danger that if research concentrates too much on the problems at hand it can become shortsighted and even shallow. The universities must not be turned into consulting firms. It is the duty of all involved to see that a proper balance is maintained between basic and short-term or applied research.

The growing volume of higher studies and research has led to an enlarged academic bureaucracy. Bureaucracy is, of course, necessary up to a point, beyond which it hinders the activities it is intended to organize. Industry experiences identical phenomena, and in both the academic and the business sectors we need to think more about freedom of action. We must discover how the delegation of decision and responsibility can raise morale and call forth innovation and creativity in an effective and responsible manner.

Many of us are persuaded that the solution to the economic plight of the university is not to be found in more administration and regulation. Rather, we need both more stimulation and more confidence in our universities. Thus will we elicit their indispensable contributions to the revitalization of our battered economy.

17

University "Democracy" in the Netherlands

AREND LIJPHART

The Dutch student "revolution" of 1969 was a minor incident. The real revolution came in 1970 when government and parliament overreacted to the events of the preceding year by passing the University Governance Reorganization Act, which imposed an unprecedented and, in comparison with similar laws in other countries, extreme "democratization" on the Dutch universities. Hans Daalder aptly characterizes this as a "revolution from above," and Henry L. Mason does not exaggerate when he calls the act a "truly astounding" one.[1]

THE UNIVERSITY GOVERNANCE REORGANIZATION ACT OF 1970

Before 1970 the Dutch universities were governed by two parallel authorities: the professoriat was in charge of teaching and research, and a board of regents ran the administration. The highest professorial organ was

Arend Lijphart is Professor of Political Science at the University of California, San Diego.

I am very grateful for the assistance that I received from Hans Daalder and Hans Daudt in the preparation of this chapter.

1. Hans Daalder, "The Netherlands: Universities between the 'New Democracy' and the 'New Management,'" in *Universities, Politicians and Bureaucrats*, ed. Hans Daalder and Edward Shils (Cambridge: Cambridge University Press, 1981), p. 174; Henry L. Mason, "Reflections on the Politicized University: II. Triparity and Tripolarity in the Netherlands," *AAUP Bulletin* 60, no. 4 (December 1974): 384. See also F. J. M. Feldbrugge, "Lekken dichten in een wrak schip: Kanttekening bij wijziging van de W.U.B.," *Universiteit en Hogeschool* 23, no. 1 (September 1976): 24–25.

the senate, to which belonged all the full professors and only full professors. This principle of exclusive professorial authority was repeated in the various faculties and subfaculties into which the university was, and is, divided: the faculties of letters, social sciences, law, mathematics and natural sciences, medicine, and so forth; and the subfaculties within these faculties, such as political science and sociology in the social sciences, and the subfaculty of history in the faculty of letters. At the bottom level, that of the chair, the full professor had almost absolute authority. This system of university government resembled a feudal structure of authority: great decentralization and diffusion of power in the system as a whole, combined with virtually unlimited power of the professorial "lords" in limited realms.

The Reorganization Act of 1970 retained the division of the university into faculties and subfaculties but encouraged amalgamation of closely related chairs into *vakgroepen*, or discipline groups; these may be compared with departments in American universities, although they are usually smaller and more specialized than their American counterparts. The much more important changes introduced by the act were to abolish the board of regents, to cancel the sovereign authority of the professoriat over teaching and research, and to create elected governing organs at the university, faculty, subfaculty, and *vakgroep* levels. At each level, representatives are elected by and from three constituencies: members of the academic staff, among whom the full professors constitute only a small minority; students; and nonacademic staff. A fourth group is represented on the highest organ of the university: representatives of the general public are nominated by the elected members and appointed by the minister of education.

Representation of the three or four constituencies is defined in terms of maximum and minimum shares of seats. As Table 1 shows, the share allocated to the academic staff decreases at ascending levels of authority. In the university council, academics may occupy only about a fourth of the seats, but in the faculty and subfaculty councils they must have at least half and in the *vakgroep*-boards the majority of seats. In the executive committees at the different levels, the academic staff is more strongly represented, and the deans of faculties and subfaculties as well as the chairmen of *vakgroepen* have to be elected from the professors and readers (*lectoren*, a rank immediately below full professors—but merged into the professional rank in 1980).

In practice, the university "democracy" created in 1970 has led to the weakening of academic control of teaching and research, to politicization of the university, and to a gradual decline of academic standards. I shall analyze the three principal causes of this lamentable deterioration of the Dutch universities: indifference of government and parliament; firm and probably irreversible institutionalization of "student power" at all levels of university government; and strong opposition by only a small minority of academic staff to the democratized university.

The erosion of academic quality is sufficiently pervasive to permit gener-

TABLE I

Composition of the university, faculty, and subfaculty councils
and the *vakgroep*-boards according to
the University Governance Reorganization Act of 1970

	University council	*Faculty and subfaculty councils*	*Vakgroep-boards*
Academic staff	Min. of 27.5%[a]	Min. of 50.0%	More than 50%[b]
Students	Max. of 27.5%	Max. of 50.0%	Less than 50%
Nonacademic staff	Max. of 27.5%		
Representatives of society	Min. of 17.5%		

[a] This minimum percentage is based on the assumption that the "representatives of society" will not be given more than the minimum of seven seats to which they are entitled in a forty-member university council.

[b] The act (prior to the 1977 amendments) prescribed that the *tenured* academic staff be allocated at least 50 percent of the seats; hence the tenured and nontenured staff together should have the majority of the seats.

alizations, although there are many important differences among universities, faculties, subfaculties, and *vakgroepen*. For instance, comparison of the faculties reveals that the most serious damage is suffered by the faculties of social sciences and letters, whereas medicine, mathematics, and natural sciences are relatively intact.

THE GOVERNMENT'S MALIGNANT NEGLECT

The University Governance Reorganization Act, in the form in which it was adopted in 1970, was labeled "experimental." This is a misnomer because a true experiment, in which a careful comparison would be made between the effects of the existing system of university government and one or more reformed systems, was never considered. The law was intended to apply to all institutions of higher learning and to their organizational subdivisions without significant differentiation. However, the act's provisions were limited to a trial period of six years unless parliament explicitly approved an extension. A one-year extension to 1977 was passed without meaningful debate. The government then proposed to extend the act for another five years, until 1982. This proposal was considered by the Second and First Chambers of parliament in the 1976–77 session.

During the Second Chamber debate in November 1976, two apparently favorable developments occurred. First, the pattern of support for the act changed. When the Second Chamber had dealt with the government's proposals in 1970, all the parties on the left, including the large Labor party, cast negative votes; they argued that the proposals were too conservative, and they advocated even more democratization. By 1976, this opposition had disappeared almost completely. The Labor party was now in favor, and some of the smaller leftist parties opposed only certain features of the act.

It would be quite mistaken, however, to interpret this turnabout as a sign of a more fundamentally critical attitude of government and parliament toward the idea of the democratized university. The change in support for the act had very little to do with the parties' views of its merits and can be explained to a large extent by the exigencies of coalition politics. In 1970 there was a coalition cabinet of the center parties (the Catholic and the two Protestant parties) and the Liberals, the principal party on the right. The latter had grave doubts about the bill, but they could not aford to vote against it because it was the main achievement of G. H. Veringa, the minister of education who had just been chosen as the Catholic party leader in the Second Chamber elections scheduled for early 1971. Liberal opposition to his bill would have led either to its defeat in the Chamber or to its passage with the aid of the Laborites—most of whom were really not dissatisfied with the main provisions. Because the Liberals were anxious not to endanger renewal of the center-right coalition by antagonizing Veringa, they had no choice but to vote for the bill. With Liberal support it was sure to pass, and the Labor party could, therefore, safely play its oppositional role and vote no without risking the bill's defeat.[2]

Six years later, a center-left had replaced the old center-right coalition. The Labor party had not only entered the government but had also assumed special responsibility for educational policy: both J. A. van Kemenade, the minister of education, and G. Klein, his undersecretary in charge of higher education, belonged to the Labor party. Thus it came as no surprise that Labor backed extension of the 1970 act, and that the Liberals, now the main opposition party, criticized several of its provisions. But the Liberals, who usually put up vigorous opposition on other issues, did not bother to vote against the proposal as a whole—another clear sign that the pattern of governmental and parliamentary attitudes toward university government had not undergone any basic change.

Encouraging also was that the government proposed and the Second Chamber accepted a number of amendments intended to alleviate some of the worst aspects of democratization. The most significant amendments limit the role of students in both the governing boards of the *vakgroepen*, the smallest organizational units, where the most important decisions on teaching and research are made, and appointment committees for professors and readers.[3] The 1970 act was silent on the composition of the *vakgroep*-boards,

2. H. F. Cohen, *De strijd om de Academie: De Leidse Universiteit op zoek naar en bestuursstructuur (1967–1971)* (Meppel: Boom, 1975), pp. 163–164.

3. The other changes that are worth mentioning briefly improve opportunities for

but the amendment specifies that the majority should be professors, readers, and other tenured staff of the *vakgroep*. The rest may be representatives of the nontenured academic staff, nonacademic staff, and students. According to this rule, the tenured and nontenured academic staff controls at least a clear majority and possibly as much as two-thirds of the votes. As to the appointment committees (which prepare nominations of professors and readers), the 1970 act stated that they should consist mainly of professors and readers, but "other experts" could also be members. In practice, "expert" was quickly wrenched to include students and, sometimes, nonacademic personnel. A new provision now prescribes that the faculty council's decisions on the composition of appointment committees specify not only the names of the members but also the reasons they were selected— presumably to curb the practice of routinely placing one or more students on the committees.

However, these changes have not substantially ameliorated the situation. The new provisions do not deviate from the spirit of the 1970 act but rather make explicit what was carelessly left implicit. For instance, the government's explanatory memorandum on the 1970 act asserted that the tenured academic staff should have at least half the seats on the *vakgroep*-boards, but naively argued that this was "self-evident" and hence need not be prescribed by law. The memorandum also made clear that the term *expert* should be taken seriously and was not meant to be a mere euphemism for "student."

Second, the one real, albeit very minor, improvement proposed by the government was rejected by the Second Chamber. The government's proposal on the composition of *vakgroep*-boards was, as described above, to give a majority to the tenured teachers but, in addition, to give at least a two-thirds majority to all permanently appointed staff, both academic and nonacademic. In the faculties of social sciences, letters, and law, which have relatively small nonacademic staffs, this rule would have raised the tenured teachers' minimum share of seats from a bare majority to close to a two-thirds majority. During the Second Chamber debates, the Labor party introduced an amendment to eliminate this provision, and the Chamber overwhelmingly approved it.

Third, it has turned out to be very difficult to make illegally constituted *vakgroep*-boards conform to the rule guaranteeing a majority of the seats to the tenured academic staff. In February 1977, a few months before the amendments were formally enacted, 22 percent of the *vakgroep*-boards did not even conform to the old rule requiring that the tenured academic staff hold at least half of the seats. A year later, 35 percent of the *vakgroep*-boards

---

instituting appeals against decisions of *vakgroep*-boards, subfaculty councils, and faculty councils, but the procedures that must be followed are extremely cumbersome and do not offer effective protection against decisions that are detrimental to the quality of teaching and research.

failed to have majorities of the tenured staff in accordance with the new rule.[4]

Fourth, it is impossible to alter the practice of placing students and nonacademic staff on appointive committees because the required reasons can easily be invented. Even before adoption of the new rule, academic staff occasionally demanded explanation of why students or nonacademic personnel were sufficiently expert to serve on the committees. The answers exemplify the kind of arguments that are used. Three students served on the committee for a chair in German literature at the University of Amsterdam. One student was selected on the grounds of being a native of East Germany, older than the average student, intelligent, and capable of positive contribution to discussion; another was deemed an expert because she was talented, bright, and articulate, would probably soon attempt her candidate's examination (usually scheduled after about three years of study), was already attending several more advanced lectures, and had also studied some sociology.[5] For the appointment committee in international relations at the same university, a secretary was appointed because a secretary could "certainly be regarded as a person with the required expertise in administrative matters."[6]

Fifth, the changes in the 1970 act do not affect the composition of the representative councils at organizational levels above the *vakgroep*. In practice, representatives of the academic staff have usually had either exactly half or a bare majority of the seats in faculty and subfaculty councils—and sometimes, in violation of the law, a minority of the seats—and only slightly more than one-fourth of the seats in university councils.[7] Nothing was done to strengthen the academic staff at these levels.

Finally, and most seriously if the slightness of improvements are considered, the government and parliament deliberately decided to extend the act until at least 1982. An amendment to limit the extension to 1980 was unsuccessful, supported only by the right-wing opposition. Because the deleterious consequences of the law had become unmistakably clear by the mid-1970s, this deliberate endorsement reveals the profound indifference of the Dutch political elite to academic quality.

In a few cases, the government went beyond malignant neglect of the university, adopting actively malignant policies; the so-called Daudt affair provides the best example of such behavior. The basic issue was who should be responsible for the content of courses and study programs in the subfaculty of political science at the University of Amsterdam: the political

4. H. Daudt, "Laatste inventarisatierapport Commissie-Polak," *Wetenschap en Democratie* 4, no. 4 (1978): 215–216.

5. Letter by A. H. Touber to the editor of *NRC Handelsblad*, 3 December 1976.

6. Quoted by H. L. Houweling, "De vervulling van een vakature," *Wetenschap en Democratie* 3, no. 2 (December 1976): 104.

7. See D. J. Kraan and H. Schijf, "Besluitvorming in faculteitsraden," *Acta Politica* 12, no. 3 (July 1977): 397–398.

science teaching staff or coalitions of radical students and a few teachers, mainly not from political science.[8] Professor Hans Daudt and a small group of loyal supporters in the academic staff were overruled in the subfaculty and were opposed also at higher levels of the university. Valiantly and indefatigably, they then appealed to various bodies outside the university. Their position was consistently upheld: by the administrative court, whose verdict was confirmed by the central administrative tribunal; by decisions of the interuniversity coordinating committee for political science; by the advice of the Polak Commission on University Reorganization; in hearings by the education committee of the Second Chamber; and in the conclusions of a special advisory committee appointed by Undersecretary Klein himself.[9] Just as consistently, however, Klein sided with Daudt's opponents.

The universities fared somewhat better under the center-right cabinet in power from 1977 to 1981. In particular, A. Pais, the new Liberal minister of education, tried to curb some of the serious violations of the law that were occurring in Dutch universities. But he did not attempt any fundamental changes in the University Governance Reorganization Act. Pais was ousted after the 1981 parliamentary elections. In the new center-left cabinet, he was succeeded by van Kemenade, whose indifference to academic quality had become unmistakably clear when he was minister of education from 1973 to 1977.

During the period of university decline since 1970, one ray of hope was the advisory commission—the Commission on University Reorganization, chaired by J. M. Polak, a professor of law—established to study the operation of the act and to formulate a comprehensive set of recommendations on university government. The commission conducted a series of excellent studies of the implementation and functioning of the act. Over the years it has offered advice, usually of a narrowly legalistic and unduly cautious nature, on a variety of minor points. Its final report, published in March 1979, was equally circumspect, but it did explicitly recommend a limited rollback of university "democracy."[10]

THE INSTITUTIONALIZATION OF STUDENT POWER

In the early 1970s it was not yet clear how potent the new student power would be and how it would be used. The 1970 act legislated a great deal of *potential* power to student representatives, but it was not certain that the full potential would be attained. Their share of seats was defined in terms of maximum proportions without guaranteed minimums, and their seats could be reduced if turnout in the elections fell below a certain threshold. In

8. H. Daudt, "Politiek in plaats van wetenschap: Een voorbeeld uit de praktijk," *Civis Mundi* 14, no. 4 (July 1975): 147–150, especially p. 149.

9. H. Daalder, "De Commissie-de Roos en de FSW-A van de Universiteit van Amsterdam: Een beschouwing," *Wetenschap en Democratie* 3, no. 4 (June 1977): 231–254.

10. J. M. Polak et al., *Gewubd en gewogen: Rapport van de Commissie voor de Bestuurshervorming ex Art. 56 WUB* (The Hague: Staatsuitgeverij, 1979).

practice, students were generally given the maximum or close to the maximum number of seats. And although the turnout by students is generally very low—rarely more than 50 percent—it is usually sufficient to clear the 35 percent hurdle specified by the law. Moreover, in the early years a number of student boycotts of university elections resulted in empty student seats in representative councils, but the activists soon discovered that operating within the new permissive system was a more effective strategy.

In the six university councils analyzed by the Polak Commission, the academic staff representation was the legal minimum in three cases and slightly more than this minimum in the other three cases, but never exceeding 37.5 percent of the total number of seats. Students were given the maximum number allowed by the 1970 act in five of the six university councils.[11] Moreover, the position of the academic staff has generally not been strengthened by the representatives of society in the councils. As Mason writes, these "representatives from off-campus have decidedly not been old-style notables but, typically, social workers, civil servants, high school teachers, housewives, journalists and faculty members from other universities with 'progressive' reputations."[12]

At the faculty, subfaculty, and *vakgroep* levels, the tendency to reduce academic staff representation to the legal minimum is repeated. In 1977, only 39 percent of the faculty and subfaculty councils and 54 percent of the *vakgroep*-boards gave the academic staff more than the bare minimum of seats. And the usual pattern in these governing organs with relatively strong academic staff representation has been to allocate only one or a few seats above the legal minimum. However, there has been cosiderable variation among the universities in this respect. Table 2 presents the figures for the faculty and subfaculty councils, classified by university. Of the larger universities (the first six listed in the table), the University of Leiden, the Free University, and the Catholic University of Nijmegen have been relatively generous to the academic staff. In contrast, the Universities of Amsterdam and Groningen have strongly limited the academic staff's representation in the faculty and subfaculty councils.

Even more striking has been the movement to minimize the special role of professors and readers in the appointment committees for professors and readers, in clear violation of the law. According to the 1970 act, these committees should normally consist exclusively of professors and readers, although occasionally other experts with demonstrable special competence in the field in question could be added. In practice, most faculty councils have ignored the clear intent of the act. As Table 3 shows, 61 percent of the appointment committees in 1975–76 included one or more students. And in almost one-fourth of the committees, professors and readers were reduced

11. *Het bestuur van universiteiten en hogescholen onder de WUB* (Tilburg: Instituut voor Sociaal-Wetenschappelijk Onderzoek van de Katholieke Hogeschool Tilburg, 1978), p. 82.
12. Mason, "Reflections," p. 386.

TABLE 2
Representation of academic staff
on faculty and subfaculty councils,
classified by university, 1977

| | Percentage of councils having: | |
	More than legal minimum	Legal minimum or less
Leiden (20)[a]	70	30
Groningen (18)	17	83
Utrecht (18)	44	56
Amsterdam (27)	11	89
Free University (28)	75	25
Nijmegen (15)	67	33
Tilburg (6)	0	100
Rotterdam (4)	0	100
Wageningen (1)	0	100
Delft (15)	13	87
Twente (7)	29	71
Eindhoven (9)	33	67
Total (168)	39	61

Source: Adapted from Commissie voor de Bestuurshervorming ex Artikel 56 Wet Universitaire Bestuurshervorming 1970, *Een planmatige aanpak van de verdere invoering van de WUB* (The Hague: Staatsuitgeverij, 1977), p. 65.
[a]Number of councils at each university given in parentheses.

to a minority. These figures did not obtain in all faculties: the worst abuses occurred in the social sciences and letters where 52 and 44 percent, respectively, of the appointment committees had only minorities of professors and readers, and 82 and 100 percent, respectively, included students. Table 3 also shows the University of Leiden to be the only large university that was not in continual violation of the law.

This student power has led to the lowering of academic standards in two, often interrelated, ways. Students have behaved as politicians and agitators. They have attempted to give as much of an ideological (usually Marxist) slant as possible to courses and examination requirements. Especially in the social sciences, and especially when coalitions could be made with radical members of the academic staff, these efforts have frequently been successful. In other faculties, the student representatives have often behaved like trade

TABLE 3

Composition of professorial and readers' appointment committees,
classified by faculty and by university, 1975–76

	Percentage of committees having:	
	Minority of professors and readers	*Student members*
Faculty		
Medicine (62)[a]	3	22
Mathematics and natural sciences (43)	28	53
Letters (38)	44	100
Social sciences (33)	52	82
Engineering (72)	7	44
Other (83)	28	92
Total (331)	23	61
University		
Leiden (48)	19	35
Groningen (27)	37	81
Utrecht (39)	33	74
Amsterdam (31)	45	87
Free University (47)	45	74
Nijmegen (36)	3	67
Tilburg (2)	0	0
Rotterdam (17)	12	47
Wageningen (14)	14	64
Delft (48)	6	46
Twente (15)	13	60
Eindhoven (9)	0	11
Total (331)	23	61

Source: Adapted from Commissie voor de Bestuurshervorming ex Artikel 56 Wet Universitaire Bestuurshervorming 1970, *Een planmatige aanpak van de verdere invoering van de WUB* (The Hague: Staatsuitgeverij, 1977), pp. 54 and 76.
[a]Number of committees in parentheses.

union leaders, fighting for less work, fewer hours, and easier advancement. Sometimes the two roles are combined, for instance, when academic credit is claimed for political activities or reading requirements reduced to create time for ideological effusion.

Foreign professors teaching in the Netherlands have been particularly struck by these results of student power. Alvin W. Gouldner, the well-known sociologist and no foe of the radical left, comments: "The old, upper-class concept of the university as a four-year drinking bout is given a new ideological packaging. Students claim they are being 'exploited' when asked to read more than 1,000 pages for a yearly seminar." Maurice Punch, a British sociologist, reports that at the University of Utrecht, "to end authoritarian exploitation of students by senior academics, all courses are specified in hours and all reading is regulated by number of pages." Furthermore, "to remove the power of the teacher, group assessment has been introduced. In my group, for instance, three students produce a paper of patent weakness. The others say it was a reasonable effort in the short time available, and the majority pass it." In a letter explaining his resignation from a chair at the Free University of Amsterdam in 1980, Martin Rudwick writes: "I am only the latest in a series of foreign professors of various nationalities . . . who have resigned from their chairs at various Dutch universities in the past few years for broadly similar reasons. Our common experience is that of finding the present academic environment in the Netherlands incompatible with effective teaching and research at internationally acceptable standards." He adds that the gravity of the situation is not only recognized by the foreign professors but is also "freely admitted by some of the better (and generally older) Dutch scholars and scientists, who are aware how far the universities have slipped from their earlier academic eminence."[13]

The most dangerous long-term aspect of student power is its effect on appointments. The student–trade unionists demand easy graders and "good"—that is, entertaining—teachers. The student-politicians want to appoint ideologues, frequently using the argument that there should be a balance between bourgeois and Marxist approaches. In order to avoid trouble, the teaching staff has often given in to these demands or neglected candidates whose appointments would be opposed by the radical activists. As Daalder points out, "the presence of politically committed student members in appointment committees reinforces this readiness to engage in a delicate calculation based on other than scientific and scholarly criteria."[14]

In the final analysis, however, it is unfair to blame the students for

13. Alvin W. Gouldner, "A Last Letter from Amsterdam," *Wetenschap en Democratie* 2, no. 4 (June 1976): 271; Maurice Punch, "Don's Diary," *Wetenschap en Democratie* 3, no. 1 (September 1976): 66, 67; Martin Rudwick, "Widespread Intellectual Apathy in Dutch Universities," *Times Higher Education Supplement*, 22 August 1980.

14. Daalder, "The Dutch Universities between the 'New Democracy' and the 'New Management,'" *Minerva* 12, no. 2 (April 1974): 253.

corrupting academic standards. The real culprits are the Dutch politicians who precipitately created student power and then stood indifferent to its pernicious consequences. But a major share of the blame must also be placed on the academic staff who have either failed or not even tried to resist the students.

THE ACADEMIC STAFF: DIVIDED AND DEMORALIZED

The academic staffs at the universities, if fully united, might have been able to prod the government out of its indifference, but they have been very far from unified. Mason contrasts the bipolar situation at German universities with the tripolarity of the Netherlands: between the Marxists and non-Marxist radical democratizers on the left, and the opponents of the 1970 act on the right, there is a rather amorphous middle group of those who may not be enthusiastic about the act but believe that it should be given a chance to prove itself.[15] The proportion of academic staff belonging to the Left is still relatively small, but the middle group is large, and they cannot be mobilized against the act. The act's opponents are only a minority, and they comprise three subgroups: the "appeasers," who believe that disruptions can be avoided and that a tolerable level of academic quality can be maintained by clever manipulation and opportunistic compromises; the "escapists," who withdraw into their specialized teaching and research or even leave the university altogether; and the "fighters," who are willing to take a public stand against politicization and excessive democratization. Thus committed opponents of the act are simply a minority of a minority.

The deep divisions among the academic staff are thoroughly demonstrated by the large-scale opinion survey ordered by the Polak Commission in 1978. Polled were a representative sample of 1,465 academics and samples of nonacademic staff and students at all Dutch institutions of higher education.[16] Of the academics expressing an opinion, 54 percent agreed with the statement: "The present system of university governance does not give sufficient weight to the views of the professional academics." But a very large minority of 46 percent disagreed. Of those stating a general opinion of the University Governance Reorganization Act, only 34 percent disapproved and 66 percent went along with it.

Opposition was strongest among professors and readers and decreased at each of the three lower ranks. The professors and readers were more than twice as likely as the academics in the lowest rank to disapprove of the act and its denigration of professional expertise. The junior staff (*wetenschappelijke medewerkers*) consists mainly of teaching and research assistants who have not yet earned a doctorate. One of the reasons for temporizing by the

15. Mason, "Reflections," pp. 385, 388–398; see also Mason, "Shared Authority, Triparity, Tripolarity: Cross National Patterns of University Government," *Polity* 10, no. 3 (Spring 1978): 312–324.

16. *De universitaire bestuursstructuur: Nu en straks* (Tilburg: Instituut voor Sociaal-Wetenschappelijk Onderzoek van de Katholieke Hogeschool Tilburg, 1979), pp. 20–23.

academic staff is that this category includes the junior academics, who in most countries are usually classified as students, not faculty.

It is especially interesting to examine the views of the academic staff about their representation in the different councils and boards and their membership on appointment committees. Table 4 presents the results of the 1978 survey. At the level of the *vakgroep*, only 23 percent of the academic staff felt that the tenured staff should have the majority of the seats, although this is mandated by the law. A large majority of the junior staff, most of whom are not tenured, and clear majorities of the generally tenured middle-level and senior staff and even the professors and readers favored less influence for the tenured than the law prescribes. Compared with the 23 percent overall support for the legal norm, the percentages obtained in the letters and social science faculties were lower still—15 and 18 percent, respectively—and they reached the highest level in the medical faculties—28 percent.[17] Table 4 also shows a clear monotonic relation between rank and opinion on *vakgroep*-board and council representation.

As far as academic staff representation on faculty and subfaculty councils is concerned, 90 percent of the respondents desired to be represented at no less than the minimum permitted by law, and 66 percent preferred a majority position. Here again, as Table 4 shows, the differences between the ranks is striking: 85 percent of the professors and readers, but only 52 percent of the juniors, opted for a majority position. Sentiment was weaker for a majority or at least 50 percent academic staff representation on the university council. Nevertheless, at this level of university government the greatest academic staff dissatisfaction appeared; only 28 percent of the respondents preferred the current practice of limiting the academic staff to a minority role in the university councils. Finally, only among the professors and readers did a majority, 51 percent, favor appointment committees whose membership is restricted to academic staff. Most of the respondents favored a majority role for the academic staff and, by implication, participation of one or more students. Differences among the faculties in this respect were striking; among the faculties of letters only 19 percent wanted only academic staff to serve on appointment committes, but in the medical faculties 52 percent preferred this composition.[18]

The most interesting questions in the survey elicited the perceptions and preferences of the academic staff concerning the strength of student power in ten areas (see Table 5). For each issue, respondents were asked whether they thought decision making was, and whether it should be, exclusively by the academic staff (represented in Table 5 as a score of 0), mainly by the academic staff but also partly by students (25), equally by academic staff and

17. J. Schoot, *Ervaringen en wensen rond universitair bestuur* (Tilburg: Instituut voor Sociaal-Wetenschappelijk Onderzoek van de Katholieke Hogeschool Tilburg, 1979), Table W 10.3.2.
18. Ibid., Table W 10.4.8.

TABLE 4
Opinions of the academic staff
concerning their representation, 1978
(in percentages of those expressing opinion)

	Professors and readers	Senior academic staff	Middle-level academic staff	Junior academic staff	All
On Vakgroep-boards					
Tenured academic staff should have:					
majority of seats	41	25	18	6	23
half of seats	19	15	12	10	14
Academic staff should have:					
majority of seats	29	37	35	43	36
half of seats	7	18	25	26	19
minority of seats	3	5	10	15	7
On Faculty and Subfaculty Councils					
Academic staff should have:					
majority of seats	85	72	53	52	66
half of seats	11	22	34	31	24
minority of seats	4	6	13	17	10
On the University Council					
Academic staff should have:					
majority of seats	63	56	41	35	50
half of seats	17	22	24	25	22
minority of seats	19	23	35	40	28
On Professorial and Readers' Appointment Committees					
Academic staff should have:					
all seats	51	41	33	28	39
majority of seats	38	44	49	49	45
half of seats	1	3	2	6	3
minority of seats	10	13	16	17	14

Source: Adapted from J. Schoot, *Ervaringen en wensen rond universitair bestuur* (Tilburg: Instituut voor Sociaal-Wetenschappelijk Onderzoek van de Katholieke Hogeschool Tilburg, 1979), tables W 10.3.1, 10.4.1, 10.4.7, and 10.5.1.

TABLE 5
Perceptions and preferences of the academic staff
concerning the degree of student power
in ten issue areas, 1978

	Perceived	Preferred	Preferred change
Contents of the precandidates' educational program	20	24	+ 4
Teaching methods of the precandidates' program	21	31	+10
Contents of the postcandidates' educational program	22	29	+ 7
Teaching methods of the postcandidates' program	23	34	+11
Determination of the research agenda	12	20	+ 8
Appointments of academic personnel	16	18	+ 2
Overall educational program	29	30	+ 1
Overall research program	16	19	+ 3
Rules concerning course examinations	25	30	+ 5
Questions concerning comprehensive examinations	21	25	+ 4
Average of ten issues	21	26	+ 5

Source: Adapted from J. Schoot, *Ervaringen en wensen rond universitair bestuur* (Tilburg: Instituut voor Sociaal-Wetenschappelijk Onderzoek van de Katholieke Hogeschool Tilburg, 1979), Table W 10.2.1.

Note: Responses expressed numerically on the following scale: 0 = no student power; 25 = student power subordinate to academic staff power; 50 = equal student and academic staff power; 75 = academic staff power subordinate to student power.

students (50), or mainly by students with limited academic staff influence (75). The first six issues concern decisions at the *vakgroep* level, and the remaining four at the faculty or subfaculty level.

The average strength of student power received a score of 21, and the academic staff wanted to increase this to 26. It is striking that strengthening of student power was regarded as desirable in all ten areas, including academic appointments and decisions concerning the overall research program of the faculty or subfaculty and the research agenda of the *vakgroep*. As Table 6 shows, only the professors and readers wanted to reduce student

TABLE 6

Perceptions and preferences of the academic staff
concerning the average degree of student power,
classified by rank and by faculty, 1978

	Perceived	Preferred	Preferred change
Rank			
Professors and readers	23	22	− 1
Senior academic staff	21	25	+ 4
Middle-level academic staff	20	28	+ 8
Junior academic staff	18	29	+11
All	21	26	+ 5
Faculty			
Social sciences	25	28	+ 3
Economics and law	18	26	+ 8
Letters	25	30	+ 5
Mathematics and natural sciences	17	25	+ 8
Engineering	20	24	+ 4
Medicine	18	23	+ 5
Other	25	28	+ 3
All	21	26	+ 5

Source: Adapted from J. Schoot, *Ervaringen en wensen rond universitair bestuur* (Tilburg: Instituut voor Sociaal-Wetenschappelijk Onderzoek van de Katholieke Hogeschool Tilburg, 1979), tables W 10.2.2. and 10.2.3.
Note: Responses expressed on the same scale as that in Table 5.

power, but only slightly, and the other ranks all preferred increases. There is again a clear monotonic relation: the perceived degree of student power gradually decreases through lower ranks, and both the preferred degree and the preferred increase of student power vary inversely with rank. This desire to increase student power is present in all faculties: the preferred increase ranges from 3 to 8 points.

The weakness of the determined opponents of the 1970 act is also demonstrated by the pattern of support for the two national organizations that were established in response to the university crisis. In 1973, a brochure of proposals to strengthen the position of the academic staff in university decision making was sent to all academic staff by M. J. Broekmeijer, who took the initiative, and about 200 like-minded academics. The brochure invited expression of support for its proposals, but positive responses came from only 1,700 of some 15,000 staff members (11 percent). A telephone poll conducted about the same time found a higher level of support for the brochure's proposals, probably because this anonymous method made many "appeasers" and "escapists," and perhaps a few of the middle group, willing to indicate their approval: 26 percent of the total sample and 34 percent of those who had read or were generally familiar with the contents of the brochure.[19]

Broekmeijer and his colleagues began publishing a quarterly journal, *Wetenschap en Democratie (Science and Democracy)*, in September 1974. It undoubtedly stimulated awareness of the university crisis, but the number of subscribers evidences the group's weak support: in 1975, 728 subscribers (5 percent of all academic staff at Dutch universities); 996 in 1976 (7 percent); 1015 subscribers in 1977; and about 980 in 1978, when the journal ceased publication.[20] A second smaller organization, the Foundation for Unbiased Research and Teaching, had as its principal aim to counteract the politicization of the universities. Its only major activity was the organization of a sparsely attended one-day conference in Amsterdam in early 1976. It had approximately 400 adherents in 1975.[21]

The weak backing received by these two groups was not the result of the extremist or reactionary nature of their aims. If anything, they were overly sensible and moderate. For instance, Broekmeijer and his colleagues did not formulate any proposals to enhance the academic staff's representation in university, faculty, and subfaculty councils. Moreover, their recommendations presupposed that "the basic purpose and system of the University Governance Reorganization Act remain unaffected."[22] The Foundation for Unbiased Research and Teaching, although generally regarded as more conservative, similarly declared in its official statement of purpose that, while it condemned violations of the spirit of the 1970 act, it accepted the main principles.[23]

No large-scale strike or boycott has ever been conducted by academic staff groups against their minimal representation on various university boards and councils, even in cases in which their share of the seats was below the legal threshold. Because of the academic staff's internal divisions, such actions would have had little chance of success. Individual professors and

19. Otto Schmidt, "Een telefonische enquête naar de meningen van het wetenschappelijk corps over de brochure 'Wetenschap en Democratie'," *Wetenschap en Democratie* 1, no. 1 (September 1974): 3–5.

20. See *Wetenschap en Democratie* 2, no. 4 (June 1976): 286; 3, no. 4 (June 1977): 260; 4, no. 4 (1978): 263.

21. "Verslag van de tweede vergadering van de Afd. Leiden van de OWO," mimeographed, 29 May 1975.

22. *Wetenschap en democratie: De uitvoering van de Wet Universitaire Bestuurshervorming 1970* (Amsterdam, 1973), p. 6.

23. "Doelstelling," mimeographed (Amsterdam, 1974), p. 2.

readers have sometimes refused to serve on appointment committees on which, in violation of the law, students were serving. These protests have had little effect because even at the professorial rank solidarity has been lacking, and the protesters have been readily replaced by more pliable colleagues. Moreover, protesters have occasionally been subjected to bitter attacks by their fellows.

There are signs that the embattled minority is weakening in its resolve. Getting little help from their colleagues and virtually none from the government, the most they can hope for is a slowing down of the decline of the universities. This requires constant vigilance and enormous investment in time and energy—destructive of the satisfaction usually associated with teaching and research. It is profoundly demoralizing to realize that though many battles may be won, the war is a war of attrition that is virtually certain to be lost. Deep demoralization is evident in that 25 percent of the academic staff respondents in the survey stated that they frequently consider leaving the university.[24]

PROSPECTS: THE ADVICE OF THE POLAK COMMISSION

The comprehensive recommendations of the Polak Commission on the future government of the Dutch universities were published in March 1979. Although the report is couched in cautious language, it offers a devastating indictment of the 1970 law as having had an entirely negative influence on the quality of teaching and research and on administrative efficiency. Its central aim, the democratization of the university, has not been achieved either. Students, in particular, show little interest in participating in the various governing bodies or even in casting ballots in university elections. As a result, the student representatives are mainly self-appointed and represent small groups of politicized students. For example, only 28 percent of the students in the 1978 survey regarded the student members of their subfaculty councils as truly representative of the students in the subfaculty.[25]

The reforms recommended by the Polak Commission include strengthening the executive committees vis-à-vis the representative councils at all levels, and strengthening the influence of the tenured academic staff in university, faculty, and subfaculty councils. The basic rule advocated by the commission is that tenured academics should occupy the majority of the seats not only in the *vakgroep*-boards, as prescribed by the 1977 amendment to the act, but also in the higher councils. In the faculty and subfaculty councils, this means a change from a minimum of 50 percent academic staff representation to a majority for the *tenured* staff. In the university councils, the tenured academics would get a majority of the elected members (not counting the representatives of society) instead of a minimum of only one-

24. Schoot, *Ervaringen en wensen*, p. 31.
25. Ibid., Table S 14.2.3.

third of the seats for the tenured and nontenured academic staff together. The appointment committees for professor and reader should consist of professors, readers, and other genuine experts. However, the commission advises that one student and possibly one person from the nonacademic staff may be added. This recommendation would strengthen student influence as compared with the provisions of the 1970 act, but would reduce their influence in practice.[26]

It is highly unlikely that the Polak Commission's advice will halt, let alone reverse, the trend of academic deterioration. First, its recommendations entail merely marginal improvements and do not challenge the principle of the democratized university. Second, although Pais generally followed the commission's advice in the new higher education bill submitted to parliament in May 1981, the minister retreated in one basic respect: the academic staff's minimum one-third share of elected representatives on the university councils will not be raised. The one minor change is that more than half of this share must consist of tenured people.[27] Thus the tenured academic staff's representation could amount to only about one-sixth of the elected members—instead of the majority proposed by the Polak Comission. Third, Pais's bill was submitted to parliament shortly before a new cabinet was formed without the Liberals. His successor, Laborite J. A. van Kemenade, can be counted upon to retreat even further from the Polak Commission's feeble recommendations. An ominous sign is van Kemenade's announcement that he will ask parliament to extend the University Governance Reorganization Act without further changes until 1984. Finally, even if all the reforms proposed by the Polak Commission were miraculously introduced at once, they would already come too late for many faculties, especially in the social sciences. Here large numbers of student activists of the late 1960s and early 1970s have received academic appointments and have achieved tenure, while many serious scholars have left.

The unhappy conclusion is that it is no longer possible to undo the damage caused by the 1970 act. It is especially ironic that the democratized university, originally called an experiment, has been made permanent despite the fact that the experiment has failed dismally.

26. Polak et al., *Gewubd en gewogen*, pp. 145–146, 148, 152.
27. *Wet op het Wetenschappelijk Onderwijs: Ontwerp van wet*, Tweede Kamer der Staten-Generaal, Zitting 1980–1981, 16802, nos. 1–2, pp. 25–26; nos. 3–4, pp. 36–37.

CONTRIBUTORS

JOSEPH BEN-DAVID is George Wise Professor of Sociology at the Hebrew University in Jerusalem and professor of education and sociology at the University of Chicago. Among his publications are: *Fundamental Research and the Universities* (1968), *The Scientist's Role in Society* (1971), *American Higher Education* (1972), *Centers of Learning: Britain, France, Germany and the United States* (1977).

ALLAN BLOOM has been a professor on the Committee of Social Thought and at the College of the University of Chicago since 1979. From 1970 to 1979 he was professor of political science at the University of Toronto. In addition to numerous articles in the field of political philosophy, he co-authored *Shakespeare's Politics* (with Harry V. Jaffa, 1964) and has published translations of Plato's *Republic* (with notes and an interpretive essay, 1968) and Rousseau's *Émile* (with an introduction and notes, 1979).

SJOERD L. BONTING has been chairman of the Department of Biochemistry, College of Medicine at the University of Nijmegen, the Netherlands, since 1968. His major research interests include relations between enzymes and cell function, the biochemistry of the visual mechanism, and quantitative histochemistry.

MARTIN BULMER has been a lecturer in Social Administration at the London School of Economics and Political Science since 1975. His main research and teaching interests include the methodology of social research, the use of social research in policy making, and the history of American sociology between 1918 and 1930. He has edited a number of collections, including: *Working Class Images of Society* (1978), *Mining and Social Change* (1977), *Social Policy Research* (1978), and *Social Research and Royal Commissions* (1980).

JOHN W. CHAPMAN is professor of political science at the University of Pittsburgh, and associate editor of NOMOS, the yearbook of the American Society for Political and Legal Philosophy. He is the author of *Rousseau: Totalitarian or Liberal?* (1956) and numerous essays on political philosophy.

EDUARDO CARREGA MARCAL GRILO, a member of the engineering faculty at Lisbon Technical High Institute, now serves in the Portuguese Ministry of Education.

FOLKE HALDEN is a member of the National Board of Universities and Chairman of the Commission of Science and Technology. He was director of the Swedish Employer's Confederation from 1952 to 1980 and has been a member of various commissions on school and university reforms. Among his publications are *Industry and Education* and *Competence and Democracy*.

PETER GRAF KIELMANSEGG has been a professor of political science at the University of Cologne since 1971. Among his published works are: *Deutschland und der erste Weltkrieg* (1968, reprinted in 1980), *Volkssouveränität* (1977), *Nachdenken über die Demokratie* (1980), as well as essays in various journals.

AREND LIJPHART is professor of political science at the University of California, San Diego. He was, until 1978, professor of international relations at the University of Leiden, the Netherlands. His books include: *The Trauma of Decolonization: The Dutch and West New Guinea* (1966), *The Politics of Accommodation: Pluralism and Democracy in the Netherlands* (1968), and *Democracy in Plural Society: A Comparative Exploration* (1977).

NIKOLAUS LOBKOWICZ is currently president of the University of Munich. His major research interests are the history of Marxist thought, the philosophy of social science, and political ethics. Among his publications are: *Theory and Practice* (1967), *Marx and the Western World* (1967), *Marxismus und Machtergreifung* (1978), and *Wortmeldung zu Kirche, Staat, Universität* (1980).

DAVID MARTIN has been a professor of sociology at the London School of Economics and Political Science since 1971. His publications include: *Pacifism: A Historical and Sociological Study* (1965), *A Sociology of English Religion* (1967), *The Religious and the Secular* (1969), and *Tract against the Times* (1973).

JOHN ARTHUR PASSMORE is professor of philosophy at the Research School of Social Sciences, Australian National University. He is president of the Australian Academy of Social Science. Among his publications are: *Hume's Intentions* (1952), *One Hundred Years of Philosophy* (1957), *Philosophical Reasoning* (1961), *The Perfectibility of Man* (1970), and *Man's Responsibility for Nature* (1974).

RAYMOND POLIN has been a professor of philosophy in the Faculty of Letters of the University of Paris since 1961. He was president of the University of Paris, the Sorbonne (Paris IV) until 1980. He is a member of the Sciences Morales et Politiques of the Institut de France.

JOSE M. G. TOSCANO RICO has been vice-rector of the University of Lisbon since 1978. He has been president of the Scientific Council of the Faculty of Medicine and is currently president of the Scientific Council of the Institute of Hydrology.

GERD ROELLECKE has been professor of public law and philosophy of law at the University of Mannheim since 1969. He was pro-rector/vice-president of the University of Mannheim from 1970 to 1973, and vice-president of the German Research Society from 1974 to 1977.

WALTER RÜEGG has been professor and director of the Institute of Sociology at the University of Berne since 1973 and dean of the Faculty of Law and Economics since 1976. Among his publications are: *Cicero und der Humanismus* (1956), *Antike Geisteswelt* (1955), and two volumes of collected essays.

JOHN A. SCOTT is head of the Department of Italian, University of Western Australia (at Perth). Formerly he was director of the Graduate Center of Medieval Studies at the University of Reading, England. He is co-author of *The Continental Renaissance 1500–1600* (ed. A. J. Krailsheimer) and the author of *Dante Magnanimo: studi sulla "Comedia,"* along with other publications.

VEIGA SIMAO is director of the National Laboratory for Energy and Technology in Lisbon, Portugal. He was minister of education for Portugal from 1969 to 1974.

JULIO R. VILLANUEVA is director of the Department of Microbiology in the Faculty of Sciences at the University of Salamanca. He was rector of the University of Salamanca from 1972 to 1974. He has published, edited, or contributed to more than twenty-five books, including a compilation of his own writings entitled *Universidad, Investigación y Sociedad.*

ROBIN WINKS is professor of history at Yale University. He has been master of Berkeley College, Yale University, since 1977. Among his publications are: *The Age of Imperialism* (1969), *The Historian as Detective* (1969), *Failed Federations: Decolonization and the British Empire* (1971), and *Slavery, A Comparative Perspective* (1962).

INDEX

Designer:	Lisa Mirski
Compositor:	G&S Typesetters, Inc.
Printer:	Vail-Ballou Press
Binder:	Vail-Ballou Press
Text:	10/12 Garamond
Display:	Garamond